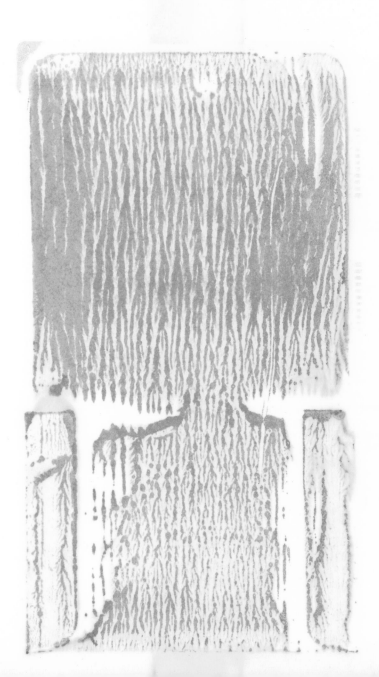

THE SEED OF WISDOM

Essays in Honour of T. J. Meek

THE SEED OF WISDOM

Essays in Honour of T. J. Meek

"With them the Seed of Wisdom did I sow"

RUBAIYAT XXVIII (FITZGERALD)

Edited by

W. S. McCULLOUGH

UNIVERSITY OF TORONTO PRESS

This Volume is dedicated to

PROFESSOR EMERITUS T. J. MEEK

B.A., B.D., PH.D., D.D., F.R.S.A., F.R.S.C.

of

University College

UNIVERSITY OF TORONTO

The papers contained herein were, with two exceptions, prepared originally for the Oriental Club of Toronto of which Professor Meek was the first President (*1952–1953*)

Introduction

THE ORIENTAL CLUB OF TORONTO was founded in 1952 by a group of Orientalists, classicists, and mediaevalists from the University of Toronto, who for professional or personal reasons had an interest in the languages, history, and culture of the Near, Middle, and Far East. Since its inception, four meetings of the Club have been held every year, and at each meeting a paper has been read and discussed. While these papers have been directed initially to a relatively small group comprising specialists from several disciplines, they have represented a substantial scholastic effort and some of them have been duly published. It is hoped that the present volume will give a selection of the hitherto unpublished papers the wider circulation which they deserve. The basic considerations in choosing the contents of the present volume were the intrinsic merit of the papers themselves, as well as the desire to represent the diversified academic interests of the Club. It is particularly appropriate that the majority of the papers should be related to the ancient Near East, the bailiwick of Professor T. J. Meek whose name this *Festschrift* is designed to honour. In two cases, those of W. G. Lambert and D. K. Andrews, the essays were written especially for this publication.

Professor T. J. Meek concluded his teaching career at the University of Toronto in 1952, just before the Oriental Club of Toronto was founded, but he was one of those actively concerned with the Club's establishment, and it was unanimously felt that he should be its first president. Practically all of the charter members of the Club knew him either as a teacher or as a colleague and they fully recognized the part he had played in strengthening and publicizing Near Eastern Studies at the University of Toronto. In the ensuing years Dr. Meek has not only attended the Club's meetings faithfully and participated in his incisive way in its discussions, but he has been active also both in research and in writing. His whole life, in truth, has been a vigorous effort both to sow "the Seed of Wisdom" and to cultivate it with all the resources of modern scholarship, to the enrichment of our understanding of the ancient Near East.

The editor wishes to record his indebtedness to the other members of the Oriental Club's editorial committee, Professors G. M. Wickens and F. V. Winnett, and also to Miss Francess Halpenny, editor of the University of Toronto Press.

The sponsors of this volume wish to acknowledge that the work has been published with the help of a grant from the Humanities Research Council, using funds provided by the Canada Council, a grant from the Publications Fund of the University of Toronto Press, and a grant from the University College Alumnae and Alumni Giving Fund.

W. S. McCullough

Theophile James Meek

THEOPHILE JAMES MEEK was born in Port Stanley, Ontario, on November 17, 1881. After graduating from the University of Toronto in 1903, he proceeded to McCormick Theological Seminary in Chicago from which he graduated in 1906. The next two years were spent in Germany at the Universities of Marburg (under Budde) and Berlin (under Delitzsch, Gunkel, Ungnad, *et al.*). In 1909 he began his teaching career at Millikin University, Decatur, Illinois, where he remained until 1918. Here, in 1915, he completed the work for a Ph.D. from the University of Chicago. After short periods at Meadville Theological School, Meadville, Pa. (1918–22) and at Bryn Mawr College, Bryn Mawr, Pa. (1922–3), he was invited to the University of Toronto in 1923 to the Department of Oriental Languages in University College, where he continued as professor until his retirement in 1952. For the last year and a half of this time he was head of the department in succession to Dr. W. R. Taylor. It was during his first year as Professor Emeritus that the Oriental Club of Toronto was founded, and Dr. Meek was chosen as its first president (1952–3).

Dr. Meek's professional interests lay in Biblical Hebrew, Akkadian, and related subjects, and in these areas he became recognized as one of the leading figures on this continent. In 1930–1 he was Annual Professor at the American School of Oriental Research in Baghdad. He served twice as Haskell Lecturer at Oberlin College, Ohio (1934, 1950). He was elected president of the American Oriental Society for 1942–3, and of the Society of Biblical Literature and Exegesis for 1943–4. He was made a Fellow of the Royal Society of Canada in 1946.

As a language teacher Dr. Meek will always be remembered by his students for his insistence upon precision, especially when translating from one language into another. Correct syntax became for him the pearl of great price. The fruits of this emphasis can be seen in *The Bible: An American Translation* (University of Chicago Press, 1927), of which he was one of the four Old Testament translators. This volume (revised in 1935) is a notable achievement in twentieth-century translations of the Bible. The same meticulous care is evidenced in Dr. Meek's renditions of various Mesopotamian texts in Pritchard's *Ancient Near Eastern Texts* (Princeton University Press, 1950).

Apart from a long-sustained interest in tennis during the summer vacations, Dr. Meek's one consuming passion was his work. Indeed it would be difficult to imagine anyone who devoted himself more wholeheartedly to study and research. His presence on the campus was a constant reminder to his colleagues and his students of the meaning of complete dedication to scholarship. This devotion did not prevent him from being a faithful teacher, but it did enable him, especially in his Toronto days, to produce a stream of publications, the chief of which are noted in his bibliography (pages 191–7). It was largely through these books and articles and through his papers read at meetings of the learned societies that the University of Toronto became known in North America as a centre of Oriental Studies.

The Oriental Club of Toronto is honoured to have had Professor Meek on its roll since 1952, and as a mark of its esteem it dedicates this volume of papers to him on his eighty-second birthday.

W. S. M.
F. V. W.

Contents

THE SEED OF WISDOM

Essays in Honour of T. J. Meek

1. The Reign of Nebuchadnezzar I: *A Turning Point in the History of Ancient Mesopotamian Religion*

W. G. LAMBERT

A HISTORY OF ancient Mesopotamian religion has not yet been written. All who concern themselves with this subject know that many changes took place within it between 3,000 and 300 B.C., but the time is not yet ripe for attempting an historical description of its development. The difficulties are a lack of material for many crucial periods and a conservatism which obscures and mitigates the effect of change. For example, Sumerians were succeeded by Babylonians, but although the one language superseded the other in everyday use at the beginning of the second millennium B.C., Sumerian was dominant in religion for about a thousand years longer, as Latin was to be in the Middle Ages. Such slow development frustrates the research worker who would like to pinpoint the moment of the introduction of new ideas and practices. This paper, in honour of T. J. Meek, one of whose permanent contributions to Assyriology was the publication of numerous bilingual fragments including many of religious content, is devoted to advancing the theory that one of the greatest changes in the course of Babylonian religion can be fixed in the reign of Nebuchadnezzar I.

The rise of Marduk to headship of the pantheon was certainly a remarkable change in Babylonian religion. It is well known that the city of which he was the god was utterly obscure until Hammurabi made it the capital of Southern Mesopotamia. Marduk himself had no prestige of purely religious origin and was as obscure as his town until its First Dynasty achieved an unexpected glory. By the time of Nebuchadnezzar II Marduk and his son Nabû were the supreme gods of Mesopotamia; and not only in that country were the greatest honours heaped on them, but outside its borders, among the Hebrews for example, Bel, "the Lord" *par excellence,* and Nebo symbolized the power of Babylon.

In this ascent to power Marduk did not simply replace an earlier god. Enlil, it is true, was once considered the highest power in the

Sumerian pantheon. However, his city, Nippur, had only religious and never political influence. Perhaps for this reason among others the preserved accounts of councils of Sumerian gods do not show Enlil as an out and out autocrat. On the contrary a quite democratic procedure was followed.[1] But Marduk's supremacy was absolute. The *Epic of Creation* shows how, in the framework of a council like that of the Sumerian gods, he demanded that if he were to rescue the gods from Tiamat's threat, he should assume absolute power. This has sometimes been obscured by a mistranslation of one line (II 127 = III 62, 120):

May I like/instead of you decree fates.

The "fates" were rules under which the universe—the gods included—functioned, so power to change them was supreme authority. The translation "like" would make Marduk only one among equals, but Heidel[2] has convincingly argued that "instead of" is correct. The rest of the story confirms that Marduk was proposing to take over all power from his elders. When he was victorious and surveyed the scene, he at once proceeded to reorganize the universe to his own specification without consulting any other god. He gave the Tablet of Fates to Anu (V 69),[3] and assigned functions to all the gods (Tablet VI). He held all might and all right.

In another sense, too, Marduk was thought of in terms which exceeded the attributes of Enlil. A small god-list published in 1896 identified Marduk with a selection of the major members of the pantheon. Despite the controversy which it aroused at the time,[4] and even more recently,[5] there is no escape from its plain meaning. It belongs to the well-known triple-column type of god-list, in which the ordinary name of the god in the central subcolumn is identified with a special name on the left, the particular emphasis of which is explained on the right. Thus, to take one line only,

^{d}*nin-urta* = ^{d}*marduk* = *šá al-li*
(*CT* 24 50, BM 47406, obv. 3)

[1]See T. Jacobsen, in *Zeitschrift für Assyriologie*(ZA), LII, 99–109.
[2]A. Heidel, *The Babylonian Genesis* (2nd edition, Chicago, 1951), p. 29[60].
[3]B. Landsberger and J. V. Kinnier Wilson, "The Fifth Tablet of Enuma Eliš," *JNES*, XX, 160, ll. 69–70.
[4]See R. W. Rogers, *Cuneiform Parallels to the Old Testament* (2nd edition), p. 191.
[5]J. J. Finkelstein, "Bible and Babel," *Commentary*, XXVI (Nov., 1958), 442–4.

can be paraphrased: Ninurta (is the name of) Marduk (as god) of the pick. This list then does manifest a syncretism of sundry gods with Marduk. Nor is this the only case. A prayer to Marduk begins by explaining various major members of the pantheon as aspects of him: Sin is his divinity, etc.[6] The most elaborate example–two fragments of a tablet containing a hymn to Marduk–has hitherto escaped notice. On one side of the tablet is a series of sections each of which identifies a particular aspect of Marduk (unfortunately in each case the word is broken off) with another deity, who is qualified with his usual epithets. An edition of the relevant lines is given in the appendix to this article. Thus Marduk did not simply replace another god. His supremacy was verging on monotheism, though some prefer to call it pantheism. This was a distinction not afforded to Enlil.

This case promises to be rewarding to chronological investigation. As the god of the royal city, and so in a special sense the king's god, one could expect frequent mention of Marduk, and since there was a long tradition of not mentioning a deity without some description, one should be able, with the help of the abundant royal dedicatory inscriptions, to fix the period in which Marduk assumed royal power over the gods.

An orthodox opinion has been current for some time. It is that Marduk was exalted to his supremacy when Hammurabi made Babylon the political capital of Southern Mesopotamia. The phrase "microcosm–macrocosm" has been evoked in support of this view. However, it is well to remember that neither of these words is Babylonian, and that a case rests not on appeals to general principles of doubtful validity, but on precise evidence. The evidence quoted in favour of this idea is usually the Prologue to Hammurabi's code of laws, which begins by stating that Anu and Enlil decreed for Marduk "supreme rule over all the peoples" (*illilūt kiššat niši*), and "made him great among the Igigi-gods" (*in Igigī ušarbi'ūšu*). The conclusion commonly drawn from these phrases is not sound exegesis. It was over the peoples, not over the gods, that Marduk was given authority. No Babylonian would have confused peoples and gods. Marduk did not, as in *Enuma eliš*, present his terms and get the previous rulers in heaven to abdicate in his favour. On the contrary, he was appointed by Anu and Enlil, and they appointed him only over the peoples. This was a limited promotion by superiors, not a take-over. The second

[6] *KAR* 25 II 3–24 E. Ebeling, *Handerhebung*, p. 14; dup. K 8978.

phrase supports this interpretation. Marduk was made great "among" (*in*), not "over" (*eli*) the Igigi-gods. His greatness was that of one among a number. Once this distinction has been grasped, everything falls into place. The military success of Babylon at once made the city the political capital of Southern Mesopotamia. Thereby the city god Marduk ruled the peoples, but not necessarily the gods. Ravn[7] and Schmökel,[8] without going into an exposition of the Prologue to the laws, have demonstrated that throughout the First Dynasty of Babylon Marduk was an insignificant god, the former from date formulae, the latter from personal names including the name of a deity. These scholars could have extended their researches into all the royal inscriptions and literary works from the same period: Marduk is never the supreme god. Enlil, or Anu and Enlil, remain heads of the pantheon. Although the beginning of the following Cassite dynasty is undocumented, there is no shortage of inscriptions, dedicatory and on boundary stones, from the last two centuries of Cassite rule. A careful study of these indicates no change in the position. Enlil, or Anu and Enlil, are still supreme in the pantheon, and Marduk still occupies a subordinate position. The first evidence of a change to be found in any official source comes from the reign of Nebuchadnezzar I, the fourth king of the following Second Dynasty of Isin, *c.* 1100 B.C. In a boundary stone from this reign Marduk is called "king of the gods" (*šar ilāni*). After this time Marduk's kingship over the gods is commonly attested.[9] In the light of the evidence presented below it is claimed that every reason exists for believing that Marduk's exaltation took place precisely in this reign.

A change of this kind could have come about as the result of the insight of one man, or one group of men, who pressed the case with such vigour that conviction and effort alone won the day. Yet such a case would hardly succeed unless current sentiment was in some measure prepared for the change. Revolutionary ideas, like plants, need watered soil in which to grow. Alternatively, the change could have come almost spontaneously. Trends over the previous centuries could have so moulded the climate of thought that only the slightest suggestion was needed for the idea to be accepted. Nebuchadnezzar the First's reign is so little known that all knowledge of persons likely

[7]In *Acta Orientalia*, VII, 81–90.

[8]In *Revue d'Assyriologie* (*RA*), LIII, 183–204.

[9]A full examination of the inscriptional evidence for the assertions made in this paragraph is being given in the writer's forthcoming edition of the *Epic of Creation.*

to have been involved has perished. The most we can do is to show that the circumstances of this reign were so exceptionally propitious to such a change that the evidence already presented can be accepted as giving the correct picture.

The ground for such a change had been prepared in the first place by Hammurabi. Whereas Marduk had been the least important of the gods before, he then had assumed a position among the great gods. The political situation in Southern Mesopotamia changed, due to Hammurabi, much more completely than he could ever have anticipated. The land had been made up of city-states, united if at all only for short periods under the suzerainty of a particular city. Henceforth Babylon remained politically supreme. As the centuries passed the mutual respect and tolerance of the various cities diminished in the face of Babylon's continuing imperial power. The idea of one city being by divine right the capital surrounded Babylon with myth and legend. Whereas Eridu had been considered the first city in Sumerian tradition,[10] and Sippar was called "the eternal city" in the time of Hammurabi's son,[11] in neither case was this done in any exclusive spirit; however, all such marks of distinction were attributed to Babylon in the late Cassite period. An inscription of one of the Kurigalzus calls Babylon "the eternal city,"[12] and the Weidner Chronicle,[13] which is certainly no earlier than the Cassite dynasty, considers Babylon the first city, as did *Enuma eliš*. An inscription of Nebuchadnezzar I refers to Babylon by the title "the holy city."[14] Such an elevation of the city, which had certainly taken root in the Cassite period, must have provoked the question why, if Babylon was the first city, should its god be inferior to those of Nippur and Uruk. The position of the city in cosmology must have been one factor in Marduk's rise to preeminence.

Probably the second factor was that the Cassite period had witnessed an example of religious imperialism quite foreign to the tolerance of the Sumerian city states. The fact that Enlil, the Sumerian god who wielded most power, resided in a city of no political consequence is a patent example of the respect in which the Sumerians held the established religious order. There was, then, no precedent for Mar-

[10]T. Jacobsen, *The Sumerian King List* (*AS* 11) (Chicago, 1939), p. 70.
[11]F. Thureau-Dangin, in *RA*, XXXIX, 6, l. 9.
[12]A. Boissier, in *RA*, XXIX, 98, l. 4.
[13]H. G. Güterbock, in *ZA*, XL II, 47 ff.
[14]IV R^2 20, no. 1, 9 and 11.

duk's elevation. But this was provided by the Cassite kings. They came into the country as foreigners, but settled down and adopted the culture of their conquered land. Their religion is little known, but they did bring with them gods of their own, in particular the pair Šuqamuna and Šimaliya, from whom they professed descent. The kings made no attempt, apparently, to alter the established religion, but they did persist in worshipping their own gods while accepting whatever blessings the local deities might afford them. Only one text shows anything of the way in which the royal household integrated the Cassite with the Mesopotamian pantheon. It is a clay tablet with an inscription of the last Kurigalzu, damaged and badly edited so that its importance has escaped notice.[15] It begins with a mention of "the creator gods," a reference to Šuqamuna and Šimaliya as the creators or begetters (the Akkadian *banû* covers both senses) of the dynasty. Then it describes how the great gods all assembled in the shrine of this Cassite pair to invest Kurigalzu with the trappings of royal office. The implication of this is not in doubt. The inferior assemble in the house of the superior. In Sumerian times such an assembly would have taken place in Ekur in Nippur. There is no doubt that Mesopotamian gods took part in this ceremony, for the term Igigi occurs, and the mention of several such gods later in the inscription shows that Kurigalzu was not exclusive in religion. Still clearer is the statement that the king hearkens to Šamaš (probably identified with the Cassite sun god), and Anu, Enlil, and Enki also hearken to him (i.e., Šamaš). The leading trinity of the old pantheon is now subject to other gods.

Such a situation, even if its influence was not felt outside the narrow court circle, could well have sown ideas in the minds of the priests of Marduk, who lived close to the scene of these innovations. Their own god could with much better claim head the pantheon. So long as the Cassites ruled, such an idea would never gain official support. The tolerance of the Cassites for the native gods would not extend to such a length. But privately the idea could flourish, and evidence for such a development is not lacking. The personal name *Marduk-šar-ilāni*, "Marduk-is-king-of-the-gods," occurs on a document from the reign of Kudur-Enlil.[16] Names of this type had flourished since early in the Old Babylonian period when, curiously, Sin is the god most commonly so described. Only in the late Cassite period is Marduk used in this type

[15] A. Boissier, in *RA*, XXIX, 93 ff.

[16] A. T. Clay, in *The Babylonian Expedition of the University of Pennsylvania* (*BE*), Series A: Cuneiform Texts, XIV, 121, 3.

of name, which soon afterwards dropped out of use altogether. Thus the first assertion of Marduk's supremacy comes from an unofficial source.

When the Cassites and their gods were finally driven out, the priests of Marduk could not set in motion any plan to elevate their patron within the pantheon. He was no longer in Babylon, his statue having been carried off by plunderers to Elam. Such a transportation of the divine statue indicated the god's displeasure with his city in that he had chosen to reside elsewhere. Only in the reign of Nebuchadnezzar I did the fortunes of Babylon recover enough for an attempt to retrieve the statue. This king undertook a successful campaign in Elam and returned with the precious statue.

The impact of this return on the period cannot be overestimated. Three accounts of it are preserved. The first is on a contemporary stone tablet recording a gift of land to a certain Šamua and his son,[17] priests who had fled from the attacking Elamite king. According to this document it was primarily to avenge these two people that Nebuchadnezzar undertook his campaign, which happened also to result in the recovery of Marduk. We may doubt if this document is really balanced in its statements. It is simply stressing those items relevant to the donation of land. No doubt it was more than two refugees that made Nebuchadnezzar set out on a serious campaign. The other two texts are literary. The one, of which only the beginning is preserved, is written in Akkadian poetry.[18] It begins with Nebuchadnezzar and his men praying to Marduk in Babylon. The king asks how long the god will reside in a foreign land, and in reply he receives a revelation from heaven. The text becomes broken at this point but part of the message is that Elam is to be given over to him. With only ten complete and ten damaged lines it is difficult to say much about this text, but it reads like a short historical epic. The other literary text is bilingual, and one fragment was published by Professor Meek himself.[19] It is one of those bilingual texts written in very long lines on

[17]L. W. King, *Babylonian Boundary Stones* (London, 1912), pp. 96–8.

[18]*CT* 13 48; H. Winckler, *AOF*, I, 542 f.

[19]Ki 1904-10-9, 96=BM 99067 was published by Meek in *American Journal of Semitic Languages and Literatures*, XXXV (1918/19), 139. He noted that it restored the text IV R^2 20, no. 1, and in fact it has now been joined to K 3444. K 3317 + 3319 was also used in the text of IV R^2 20, no. 1. Two additional pieces belonging to this work have been identified by the present writer: K 5191, a piece not belonging to either of the other copies and Sp. II. 524=BM 35000. A translation of IV R^2 20, no. 1 is given by Hehn in *Beiträge zur Assyriologie*, V, 339–44.

unusually wide and short tablets that are characteristic of texts from the Second Dynasty of Isin. The Sumerian is late, influenced strongly by the Akkadian. Although four incomplete copies are known, three from Ashurbanipal's library and one from Seleucid Babylon, only the ends of the lines are preserved. The narrative, if one may so speak of highly poetic imagery, begins with a description of victory in battle. So abruptly does it read that one is tempted to ask if this can really be the opening of the work. Perhaps there was a set of tablets and this is not the first. The story continues with a description of the piety of a certain god's slave, who gives himself no rest until he has seen his master's lofty form. His prayers were heeded, for the divine master (who is later named as Marduk) consented to return from "wicked Elam" to Babylon, where he was received amid universal acclaim and the bestowing of bountiful gifts. Although Nebuchadnezzar's name does not occur in the preserved portions of the text, there is no other king to whom it could refer. There is an account of a campaign of Nebuchadnezzar I in Elam on a boundary stone,[20] but this does not mention the recovery of Marduk's statue and may refer to another occasion.

As a hypothesis we suggest a direct relationship between this return of Marduk's statue to Babylon during the reign of Nebuchadnezzar I and the first occurrence of a statement of Marduk's supremacy in an official document of the same king. In the nature of the case the evidence can only be circumstantial. The ground was prepared during the Cassite period. Indeed, a personal name already asserts the doctrine during the latter half of the Cassite dynasty. There is good reason for doubting if the doctrine could have been proclaimed officially under Cassite rule. The immediately following years were inauspicious, since Marduk was manifesting his displeasure with his city. His return from Elam must then have been the first opportunity. Public attention was directed to him on this occasion, and amid the rejoicing and abundance of praise and presents what could have been more appropriate than the ascription to him of supreme authority in heaven and underworld? The bilingual text calls him "Lord of Lords."

If this hypothesis is correct, we may surmise that the priests of Enlil in Nippur would have given no willing assent to the new arrangement of the divine hierarchy. There is one more document from Nebuchadnezzar the First's reign that seems to betray a certain

[20]King, *Boundary Stones*, pp. 29–36.

resentment at the change. It is a boundary stone from the vicinity of Nippur.[21] It begins with a paean of praise to Enlil, a unique feature, for no other boundary stone begins with praise of any god. Right at the opening Enlil's supremacy over the other gods is asserted in terms perhaps stronger than in any other text:

Enlil, the lofty lord, the aristocrat of heaven and underworld, the noble, the lord of all, king of the great gods, who has no god who can rival him in heaven or underworld, at the giving of whose command the Igigi show submission and reverently heed . . .

It has long been acknowledged that Nebuchadnezzar I marks a revival of Babylonian power and culture after the Cassite decadence. It now appears that for religious reform also he deserves something of the esteem more usually accorded to his better known namesake of the sixth century.

APPENDIX

Ebeling published *KAR* 304 and 337 as "mythologischer Text" and "Hymnus an Marduk," respectively. A connection was suspected by the present writer, who observed that the reverse of each piece contained sections with epithets of different gods. An examination of the originals in Berlin, thanks to the courtesy of Dr. G. R. Meyer, Director General of the Staatliche Museen, Berlin, confirmed that they are parts of the same tablet, though they do not quite join. A small gap has to be put between them. The juxtaposition of the reverses is quite simple, thanks to the rulings which separate the sections. Ebeling omitted one in his copy, between lines 16 and 17 of *KAR* 304. The juxtaposition of the obverses is not so simple. After much patient endeavour the present writer concluded that in all probability line 9 of *KAR* 337 is continued by line 5 of *KAR* 304. But it seemed just possible that lines 10 and 5 respectively should be the matching ones. The discovery of the connection of the pieces has not, unfortunately, solved all problems. The two pieces are badly damaged and the uncertainty as to just how wide the gap between them should be prevents any major attempt to restore the lines. Certainly this is a most important text about Marduk, but only the discovery of more pieces will permit substantial progress. Thus we only offer a tentative edition of the sections of particular interest for our immediate purpose. Some improved readings were obtained by collation, and these are marked with exclamation marks.

[21] W. J. Hinke, in *BE*, series D, IV, 142.

---

8 . . .] x-*šu ig-mu-u*[*r* . . .

9 . . . *t*]*i-rit gi-mir ka-l*[*a* . . .

10 . . .] *šá-pal-šu kam*!-[*s*]*u x* [. . .

11 . . .] x *rapašti*^{ti} [. . .

---

12 . . .] x *ul-la-nu-uš-šu nap-ḫ*[*ar* . . .

13 . . . *ba-nu*]-*ú nik-la-a-ti* [. . .

14 . . . ^{d}*e*]*n-líl e*-x x x [. . .

15 . . .] x kiš x [. . . . . . *rapa*]*šta*^{ta} *šum-du-lu*? x [. . .

---

2 16 [x x-*k*]*a* ^{d}*adad e-rim si-ḫi-i*[*p ma-t*]*a-a-ti ur-ru*!-[*up* . . .

3 17 [*šá ina šá-g*]*i-mi-šu šamê*^{e} *u ersetim*^{ti}[^{m} . .]-*ú i-tar-ru-ru* [. . .

4 18 [. .] x a.ab.ba x x x x x [. .] ri? ḫu!? x x x x [. . .

5 19 [*gú-g*]*al*! *šamê*^{e} *u erṣetim*^{tim} *sēra*? x [. .] x x x x-*ku-ú* [. . .

---

6 20 [x x]-*ka* ^{d}*nanna*!-*r*[*u*] x x x [. .] x *u*$_{4}$-*mi u mūši mu*-[. . .

7 21 [*a-na*] *ta-mar-ti-šú purussâ i-nam-di*[*n-ma*] *ṣa-ad-da i-na-á*[*š-ši* . . .

8 22 [*šá i*]*t-ta-šu la i*!-*lam*!-*ma-du mam*?-*m*[*a*?-*na*?] x x-*ú na- áš qarnē*^{meš}

9 23 [*šá ina*] *šamê*^{e} *man-za-as-su ra-áš-bu* [*ina b*]*a*?-*li-šu š*[*i-ma*]*t nišī*^{meš} *la iš-ši*[*m-mu* . . .

---

10 24 [x x]-*ka* ^{d}*šamaš nu-úr šá-ma-mi ù*? [. .] me ri x ri *ilāni*^{meš} *rabûti*^{meš} x [. . .

11 25 [x x] *nap-ḫar ka-la mu-ta-*ʾ*-ir* [*ṣal-ma*]*t qaqqadi mu-nam-mir ik-let nišī*[^{meš} . . .

12 26 [x] x *ka-la-ma saḫ-pu šá-lum-m*[*a-tú* . .] x x-*ri-ru* šu x x [. . .

---

13 27 [x x]-*ka* ^{d}ut. u$_{x}$.lu *bēlu gaš-ru* x [. . *a-bu*]-*bi ra-kib me-ḫ*[*e-e* . . .

14 28 [*šá ina t*]*a-ḫa-zi-šu dan-nu* zaq mu? [. . .] x-*a-ti la ut*-x [. . .

15 29 [x x] x-*ru* ^{d}bil.gi *ez-za*! x [. . .] ḫar x [. . .

---

8 . . .] . . he took firm control [. . .
9 . . .] authority over everything that is [. . .
10 . . .] bow beneath him . [. . .
11 . . .] wide [. . .

---

12 . . .] . apart from him all [. . .
13 . . .] who [does] clever things [. . .
14 . . .] Enlil . . . . [. . .
15 . . .] . . . [. . . . . .] wide, broad . [. . .

---

16 Your [. .] is Adad, who overshadows the whole extent of the lands, dark [. . .
17 [At] whose bellow heaven and earth [. .] . tremble [. . .
18 [. .] . the sea . . . . . [. .] . . . . . . [. . .
19 Canal supervisor of heaven and earth, the open country (?) . [. .] . . . . . . [. . .

---

20 Your [. .] is Nannar . . . [. .] . of day and night, the [. . .
21 [At] his rising he gives decrees [and] raises his symbol [. . .
22 Whose sign no one knows . . . , who is equipped with horns [. . .
23 Whose station [in] heaven is awesome, without whom the fate of the peoples is not decided [. . .

---

24 Your [. .] is Šamaš, the light of heaven and [. .] . . . . the great gods . [. . .
25 [. .] the sum of everything, who directs the [black]-heads, who turns the peoples' darkness to light [. . .
26 [.] . which extends over everything, with splendour [. .] . . . . [. . .

---

27 Your [. .] is Ninurta, the mighty lord . [. . of the storm] flood, the rider of the tornado [. . .
28 [In] whose terrible battle . . [. . .] . . . not . . [. . .
29 [. .] . . fierce Girra . [. . .] . . [. . .

---

2. Literature as a Medium of Political Propaganda in Ancient Egypt

RONALD J. WILLIAMS

THE SPOKEN, AND LATER THE WRITTEN WORD has, from time immemorial, been regarded in the ancient Near East as potent and creative. Its efficacy is well illustrated in Hebrew thought by the divine fiat in the opening chapter of the Book of Genesis, by which the acts of creation were accomplished. A concise summary is contained in Psalm 33:9:

> He it was who spoke, and it came into being;
> He who commanded, and it stood firm.

In Mesopotamian literature the same concept appears in a passage from the *Epic of Creation*, which tells how the royal power of the god Marduk was demonstrated:

> Truly, lord, thy decree is supreme among gods;
> Say but to destroy or create—it shall be!
> Open thy mouth: the garment shall be destroyed;
> Speak again: the garment shall be whole.
> He spoke with his mouth, and the garment was destroyed;
> Again he spoke, and the garment was restored.[1]

This was likewise true for Egypt, where *Ḥū*, authoritative utterance, was regarded as an attribute of both the gods and the divine rulers and was itself deified in early times. With this belief must be associated the tendency to avoid the use of words of dangerous import, such as "death," for which euphemisms were devised.

Another feature of Egyptian culture was an oft expressed admiration for eloquence of speech. This appears as early as the Teaching attributed to Ptaḥḥotpe, the vizier of the Fifth Dynasty King Izezi (*c.* 2414–2375 B.C.). When Ptaḥḥotpe requests that his son be trained to succeed him in office, the king urges him to "teach him first about speaking, so that he will be an example to the children of the nobles."[2]

[1]*Enuma eliš*, IV, 21 ff.
[2]Ptaḥḥotpe, 37 ff. (Dévaud's numbering).

The ensuing instructions of the sage are introduced with the words: "Here begin the eloquent utterances which were spoken by . . . Ptaḥḥotpe, consisting of teaching the ignorant to know about the rules of eloquence, which is profitable to him who will obey, but detrimental to him who will disobey it."[3] Further evidence may be seen in the Tale of the Eloquent Peasant, which derived its popularity from the fact that a humble peasant was gifted with oratorical powers. As Ptaḥḥotpe had said earlier, "Eloquence is rarer than green feldspar, yet it is found with slave-girls at the millstones."[4]

We should not be surprised, then, to learn that the written word was used, not only for its magical power in mortuary literature such as the Pyramid and Coffin Texts or the Book of the Dead, but also as a means of achieving political ends. Let us proceed to examine some of the works which were designed to serve as documents for propaganda purposes, while at the same time ensuring by their literary excellence a wide popularity.[5]

We turn first to the century of civil strife and social revolution known as the First Intermediate Period which followed the downfall of the Old Kingdom *c.* 2154 B.C. In addition to the economic impoverishment of the land by the large-scale activities of the pyramid builders, and the weakened power of the royal house under a series of ephemeral rulers following the death of the centenarian Pepi II, the collapse was brought about by the rise to power of the nomarchs, or provincial governors. These officials had succeeded in making their office hereditary, and sought to establish themselves as petty kinglets. Eventually some of them became strong enough to challenge the royal authority. The rulers made desperate attempts to win and hold their loyalty, thus depleting the treasury still further, but all to no avail. In the ensuing anarchy the nomarch of Heracleopolis in Middle Egypt proclaimed himself King of Upper and Lower Egypt, and swept aside the Memphite ruling house. His royal claim did not go unchallenged, however, for the nomarch of Thebes gained control of the region to the south. Fortunately the nomarchs of Assiut remained

[3] *Ibid.*, 42 ff.

[4] *Ibid.*, 58 f.

[5] Cf. G. Posener, *Littérature et politique dans l'Egypte de la XIIe dynastie* (Paris, 1956); A. de Buck, "La Littérature et la politique sous la douzième dynastie égyptienne," in M. David, B. A. van Groningen, and E. M. Meijers, eds., *Symbolae ad jus et historiam antiquitatis pertinentes Julio Christiano van Oven dedicatae* (Leyden, 1946), pp. 1–28; E. Otto, "Weltanschauliche und politische Tendenzschriften," in B. Spuler, ed., *Handbuch der Orientalistik*, 1. Bd.: "Aegyptologie," 2. Abschnitt: "Literatur" (Leyden, 1952), pp. 111–19.

loyal to the Heracleopolitan royal house, and the Theban nomarchs were held in check, although the latter also assumed royal dignities *c.* 2133 B.C. During all this time the rich Delta farmlands were occupied by invading Semitic nomad tribes.

Toward the end of the period, *c.* 2070 B.C., while tension between Thebes and Heracleopolis still ran high, with sporadic fighting breaking out between the rival forces, a literary work made its appearance at Heracleopolis. Its popularity is indicated by the fact that it has survived on three papyri. It purported to be a treatise composed by the aged King Waḥkarēᶜ Kheti III for the instruction of his son and successor, Merikarēᶜ. However, the king's own words, "Now, by my life, while I was still alive (lit. in existence) . . . "[6] suggest that he was already dead. This is confirmed by the fact that the name Merikarēᶜ is enclosed in a cartouche, a treatment reserved for names of reigning monarchs. We must conclude that the text was actually compiled during the reign of Merikarēᶜ, and ascribed to his father to give it authority. The numerous letters written by Egyptians to deceased persons[7] suggest that the dead themselves might also write letters to the living.[8]

The work begins with a classic expression of the thesis, The pen is mightier than the sword: "Be a craftsman in words, that you may be strong! A king's tongue is his might; words are more powerful than any fighting. No one can circumvent the craftsman of the mind."[9] Speech may also be dangerous in such troubled times, as Merikarēᶜ is warned: "The talker is a trouble-maker. Suppress him! Slay [him]! Obliterate his name! [Destroy] his associates! Suppress his memory and his adherents who love him! The agitator is a (source of) confusion to the citizenry, since he creates two factions among the youth."[10]

A reverence for wise predictions and sayings from earlier times is characteristic of these documents:

A knowledgeable man is a storehouse[11] for nobles. He who knows that he knows does not attack him. [Iniquity] does not arise in his presence, but

[6]P. Ermitage 1116A, verso (misnamed recto by Golénischeff!), 94 f.

[7]Cf. A. H. Gardiner and K. Sethe, *Egyptian Letters to the Dead* (London, 1928).

[8]This was indeed the case when, in the Contendings of Horus and Seth, the deceased Osiris wrote a letter to the divine tribunal naming his son Horus as rightful successor to the throne.

[9]P. Ermitage 1116A, verso, 32 f.

[10]*Ibid.*, 23 ff.

[11]Reading the traces of signs and the clear determinatives as *wg*ǰ with Sir A. H. Gardiner.

maʿat[12] comes to him (well) strained, in accordance with what the ancients have said. Emulate your fathers, your ancestors. . . . See! Their words remain in writing; open, read, and emulate (their) knowledge.[13]

The political aspect of this work appears in the advice to cultivate peaceful relations with the Theban house:

Do not have bad relations with the Southland, for you know the prophecy of the Court concerning it.[14]

You are on good terms with the Southland. The bearers come to you carrying gifts. I did the same as the ancestors, if it had no grain to give. Be kind, since they are weak towards you, and be satisfied with your own bread and beer. Red granite comes to you unhindered, so do not damage the monuments of another, but quarry stone in Ṭūra. Do not build your tomb of plundered material; ‹do not make› what has been used into what is to be used.[15]

As the latter passage shows red granite was quarried at Aswān, in the Theban territory.

A remarkable feature of the document is the "self-criticism" put in the mouth of Kheti:

Egypt fights in the necropolis! Do not destroy the tombs! Do not destroy (them)! Do not destroy (them)! I did the like, and the like happened.[16]

See, a shameful deed took place in my time: the regions of Thinis were destroyed. It happened, but not through what I had done. I learned about it after it was done. See my reward for what I had done! Now, it is shameful to damage, and useless for him to restore what he has torn down, to rebuild what he has demolished, or to refurbish what he has spoiled. Beware of it! A blow is repaid with its like; that is the consequence of everything that is done.[17]

That the divine pharaoh should admit to error in these passages, unique in Egyptian literature, is testimony to the lengths to which Merikarēʿ was prepared to go in making overtures to the Theban nomarchs.

In keeping with the political nature of the work, the accomplishments and benefactions of Kheti are related. These include the re-establishment of control in the western Delta and an enlightened

[12]A term variously translated as "justice," "righteousness," "truth," which means the divinely ordained world order.

[13]P. Ermitage 1116A, verso, 33 ff.

[14]*Ibid.*, 71.

[15]*Ibid.*, 75 ff. [16]*Ibid.*, 69 f. [17]*Ibid.*, 119 ff.

policy of reconstruction, with the result that trade was resumed with Syria:

I pacified the whole of the west as far as the sea-coast. It pays taxes, so that it gives *mrw*-wood, and juniper is (also) seen. It gives it to us. The east, however, is still rich ‹in› foreigners.[18]

It means that rebels will not arise there, that the Nile will not disappoint you by not coming, and the tribute of Lower Egypt will be in your hand. See, the mooring-post is driven in in the region which I acquired in the east, to the borders of Ḥebenu and the Horus-way, furnished with towns and filled with Egyptians (lit. people) of the choicest of the whole land, in order to repulse their attacks. May I see a brave man who will emulate (me) in it, achieving for himself more than I have done![19]

Now, by my life, while I was still alive these foreigners were a (veritable) wall whose strongholds were open. . . . I had Lower Egypt attack them. I captured their inhabitants and seized all their cattle; [I] slew the [people] amongst them so that the Asiatic was filled with revulsion for Egypt. Do not trouble yourself about him. The Asiatic is (but) a crocodile on his bank: he robs an isolated person, but he cannot attack the pier of a populous town.[20]

Kheti also exerted himself on behalf of Middle Egypt, and had a canal dug, fifty-five miles in length, from Memphis to Heracleopolis:

It (i.e., the Memphite area) is the umbilical cord against the foreigners; its walls are defended; its troops are many; the subjects in it know how to take arms, except for the priests within the territory of Djed-sūt.[21] It totals 10,000 men as citizens, free, without duties. There have been magistrates in it since the time of the Court. Strengthen the borders, that its garrisons may be strong. . . . A canal has been made to Heracleopolis.[22]

Kheti's generous policy toward his nobles is outlined, to be adopted as a political "platform" by Merikarēʿ:

Advance your magnates that they may carry out your laws. He who is wealthy in his house will never be partial; the one who does not lack is a man of property. The poor man does not speak his truth, nor is he straightforward who says, "If only I had!" He is partial towards him whom he loves, and leans toward the one who rewards him. The great one (i.e., the king) is great (only) when his great ones are great. A king who has courtiers is strong; he who is wealthy in nobles is rich (indeed).[23]

Advance your magnates, promote your warriors and increase the troops of your following, they being provided with lists (of goods?), presented with fields and endowed with cattle.[24]

---

[18] *Ibid.*, 82 f. [19] *Ibid.*, 87 ff. [20] *Ibid.*, 94 ff.
[21] The neighbourhood of the pyramid of King Teti of the Sixth Dynasty.
[22] P. Ermitage 1116A, verso, 99 ff.
[23] *Ibid.*, 42 ff. [24] *Ibid.*, 60 f.

Similarly the royal attitude towards the underprivileged is stated:

Perform *maʿat*[25] that you may endure on earth. Calm the weeper. Do not shove the widow aside. Do not drive a man from the possessions of his father.[26]

Make no distinction between a well-born son and a commoner, but select a man according to his ability, that every craft may be (well) performed.[27]

Finally, the pharaoh seizes the opportunity to make some pronouncements on ethical conduct which exhibit a high moral tone. The concept of a final judgment after death now finds its first expression:

As for the magistrates that judge the poor wretches, you know that they will not be lenient on that day when the unfortunate are judged, the hour when they exercise their function. The Accuser is disagreeable, being one who knows. Do not trust in length of years, for they regard a lifetime as but a single hour. If a man survives after death, his deeds are set beside him in a heap. Moreover, existence yonder is eternal, and he is a fool who does what they censure. He who reaches it without doing wrong will exist there like a god, striding forth freely like the eternal Lords.[28]

The cake[29] of the upright in heart is more acceptable than the ox of the wrongdoer.[30]

By such a document, Merikarēʿ hoped to win the support of his subjects, and to achieve a "peaceful co-existence" with the Theban royal house.

After the Heracleopolitan rulers had been overthrown by King Mentuḥotpe II of the Theban dynasty *c.* 2040 B.C., prosperity returned to the unified land. Then suddenly civil strife broke out once more for a brief period (*c.* 1997–1991 B.C.), after which order was again restored by Amenemḥet I, founder of the Twelfth Dynasty, who had previously served as vizier under Mentuḥotpe IV. As a commoner who had usurped the throne, his position was at first a precarious one. Soon after his accession a work appeared attributed to a lector-priest named Neferti, who was described as living during the reign of Snofru, more than six centuries earlier. This pharaoh of the Fourth Dynasty was later revered for his humane attitude toward his subjects.

That the document was widely read is clear from the fact that it survives on one papyrus, two wooden writing tablets, and twenty

[25]See *supra*, note 12. [26]P. Ermitage 1116A, verso, 46 f. [27]*Ibid.*, 61 f.
[28]*Ibid.*, 53 ff.
[29]The word *b t* is clearly written in one manuscript with the determinative for "cake." However, a pun on the word *bit*, "character," was certainly intended.
[30]P. Ermitage 1116A, verso, 128 f.

ostraca. At the outset of the text the Egyptian love of eloquence is again displayed: "His Majesty said to them, 'Men, I have had you summoned to have you seek out for me a son of yours who is wise, a brother of yours who is capable, or a friend of yours who has accomplished a noble deed, who may speak a few fine words to me, choice expressions, so that My Majesty may be diverted at hearing them.'"[31] When this priest from Bubastis in the Delta begins his "predictions," for such they are to be, the king himself commits them to writing:

> The lector-priest Neferti said, "Is it to be about what has happened or what is going to happen, sire, my lord?" His Majesty said, "About what is going to happen, of course! Today, indeed, (no sooner) comes into being (than) it passes away!" Thereupon he stretched out his hand to the box of writing materials and took out for himself a papyrus roll and a scribe's palette, and then put into writing what was said by the lector-priest Neferti.[32]

The troubled years of the interregnum are then described, not without some exaggeration:

> What has been done has become like what has not been done, so that Rēʿ must begin to recreate. The land has perished completely—no remnant remains, not (even) the black of the nail survives from what was destined.[33]

> I give you the land topsy-turvy! What has never (before) happened has occurred. They shall take weapons of warfare, so the land lives in an uproar. They shall make arrows of copper and crave the bread of blood. They shall laugh uproariously at pain, and will not weep at death. . . . Every man's heart is concerned with himself. They will not make mourning today, the(ir) minds being completely detached. A man sits still and turns his back while one man slays another. I give you the son as a foe, the brother as an enemy, the man slaying his father.[34]

In the reference to copper arrows in the latter passage the author seems to give himself away, for to date no arrows of this metal have been found anterior to the Eleventh Dynasty. Neferti continues his description: "The land is diminished, but its rulers are many; it is destitute, but its taxes are great. The barley is scarce, but the grain-measure is large, and it is measured to overflowing."[35]

[31] P. Ermitage 1116B, verso (also mistaken by Golénischeff for the recto!), 5 ff.
[32] *Ibid.*, 14 ff.
[33] *Ibid.*, 22 f. This hyperbole contains a pun on the Egyptian name for Egypt, *Kmt*, "the black (land)." The rich soil has disappeared so completely that there is not enough to lodge beneath a finger-nail!
[34] *Ibid.*, 38 ff.
[35] *Ibid.*, 50 f.

Finally the "prophet" comes to the point, as he describes the saviour of the nation:

In fact, a king will arise in the south, Ameny by name, the son of a woman of To-Seti.[36] He is a child of Upper Egypt. He will receive the white crown, will don the red crown, and will unite the two powerful ones (i.e., the double crown). He will satisfy Horus and Seth with what they love. . . . Rejoice, men of his time! The well-born man will make his name for ever and ever. Those who fall away to evil and those who plot rebellion have subdued their mouths for fear of him. The Asiatics will fall before his carnage, the Libyans will fall before his flame, the rebels before his wrath, and the refractory before his majesty. The uraeus which is on his brow calms the refractory for him.

One (i.e., the pharaoh) will build the Walls of the Ruler, not allowing the Asiatics to descend into Egypt. They will beg for water by virtue of supplication in order to let their cattle drink. *Maʿat*[37] shall come into its own, iniquity being driven outside. He who will see and be a follower of the king will rejoice.[38]

His hero is none other than King Amenemḥet, for which Ameny is the well-attested abbreviation. Here we have a clear reference to Amenemḥet's military campaigns in the eastern Delta and Libya, and his construction of the frontier post known as the Walls of the Ruler at the Wādi Ṭummilāt, designed to repel the bedouin tribes from invading the eastern Delta.

A moving account of an attempt on the life of the same king, originating in a harem conspiracy, is contained in the Teaching of Amenemḥet. The wide circulation of this classic in later times is attested by its preservation on four papyri, three wooden writing tablets, and at least fifty-four ostraca. Literary analysis shows it to be a skilful combination of a teaching in the tradition of the earlier didactic works, an autobiography, and a prose narrative.[39]

It commences in the style of the first *genre*:

Here begins the instruction which . . . Amenemḥet, triumphant, composed, when he spoke in a vision to his son, the Universal Lord, and said:

You who have appeared as the god, obey what I shall say to you, that you may be king over the land, govern territories, and exceed the good.[40]

This passage contains two controversial expressions. The first is *mȝʿ ḫrw*, rendered as "triumphant," an epithet which commonly follows

[36]The first nome of Upper Egypt.

[37]See *supra*, note 12.

[38]P. Ermitage 1116B, verso, 57 ff.

[39]Cf. A. de Buck, "La Composition littéraire des enseignements d'Amenemhat," *Muséon*, LIX (1946), 183–200.

[40]P. Millingen, 1/1 ff.

the names of deceased persons. It is significant that the term does not accompany the name of Senwosret, his son and successor, at the close of the document.[41] The second is *wpt mꜣꜥt*, the translation of which as "vision" is supported by its occurrence on the stela of Taimḥōtep now in the British Museum.[42] This would suggest that the assassination attempt was successful, with the result that most scholars are now convinced that the work is a pseudepigraph.[43] This is confirmed by the fact that Senwosret is accorded the title of "Universal Lord," and that his name is enclosed within a royal cartouche, both honours reserved for reigning monarchs. Moreover, the expression "appear as the god" is the technical term for accession to the throne.

However, a defence of the earlier view of the text as a genuine account of an abortive attempt on the sovereign's life has been offered by Anthes,[44] who argues that *mꜣꜥ ḫrw* should here be rendered as "who is acknowledged as (the) right (king)," and *wpt mꜣꜥt* as "in determining the right (for his son)." He regards the fact that Senwosret was associated with his father as co-regent *c.* 1972 B.C. as sufficient reason for the royal honours. Nevertheless, half a millennium later, a writer of the New Kingdom penned an encomium of the scribe Kheti, author of the celebrated Satire on the Trades, who flourished during the reign of Senwosret I, in the course of which he said: "I immortalize his name. It was he who composed a book, the Instruction of the King of Upper and [Lower Egypt] Sḥetepibrēꜥ (i.e., Amenemḥet I), when he had gone to rest, joining heaven and entering among the lords of the necropolis."[45] Clearer evidence that the Egyptians themselves later believed that the work was produced after Amenemḥet's death could hardly be desired.

At all events, in February of 1962 B.C., during the absence of the crown prince on a military campaign in Libya, Amenemḥet was assassinated as the result of a harem intrigue, as we learn from the well-known Tale of Sinuhe:

> In the thirtieth year, the third month of inundation, the seventh day, the god ascended to his horizon, the King of Upper and Lower Egypt Sḥetepibrēꜥ flew off to the sky, being united with the sun's disk, the flesh

[41] *Ibid.*, 3/7.

[42] British Museum Stela No. 147, 9.

[43] Including, among others, Maspero, Gunn, Weill, de Buck, Volten, Otto, Posener, Hayes, and recently even Gardiner.

[44] R. Anthes, "The Legal Aspect of the Instruction of Amenemhet," *JNES*, XVI (1957), 176–91; a further note also in *JNES*, XVII (1958), 208–9.

[45] P. Ch. Beatty IV, verso, 6/13 f.

of the god being merged with him who made him. The Court was hushed, hearts mourned, the great portals were shut, the nobles (sat) with heads on (their) laps, and the patricians grieved.

Now His Majesty had despatched an army to Libya, with his eldest son as its commander, the good god Senwosret, he having been sent to chastise the foreign lands, to smite those in Tjeḥnu-land. Now, indeed, as he was returning, having brought prisoners of the Tjeḥnu and no end of all kinds of cattle, the Companions of the palace sent to the western border to inform the prince of the events which had transpired in the royal chambers. The messengers found him on the road; they reached him at night-time. He did not delay for a moment; the falcon flew away with his henchmen without informing his army of it.

Now the royal children who were with him in this army had been sent for, and one of them had been summoned. While I was standing by, I heard his voice as he was speaking at a distance, since I was near at hand. My mind was distraught, my arms opened wide, trembling having fallen on my whole body. I betook myself with a leap to find myself a hiding-place, and placed myself between two bushes.[46]

Sinuhe's reaction on hearing this distressing news was one of consternation and fear, since he might well have been accused of implication in the plot. Hence he took immediate steps to remain in hiding for a period, but this resulted, as fate would have it, in a sojourn of many years in Syria. It is clear that bold and swift action was required on Senwosret's part to assert his claim to the throne and to punish those responsible for the assassination. This explains the great secrecy surrounding his departure for the capital. It also makes plain why the Teaching of Amenemḥet was composed, as a document attesting to the validity of Senwosret's position as rightful heir.

This latter text continues with counsels reflecting the deep disillusionment of the king whose reign had been a beneficent one, thus evoking sympathy for the murdered ruler, a sympathy which was designed to stir up resentment on the part of the populace against the palace conspirators:

Be on your guard against those who are subordinate (to you) lest that come to pass to whose terrors no thought has been given. Do not draw near to them in your loneliness. Do not trust a brother, do not be intimate with a friend, do not acquire for yourself trusted acquaintances; there is no profit in it. (Even) when you sleep, guard your own thoughts, because a man has no adherents in the day of trouble. I gave to the poor and reared the orphan. I made him that was nothing succeed as well as him who was a man of means. (Yet) it was he who ate my food who made an uprising; he to whom I had given my hands created a threat against me; those who

---

[46]Sinuhe, R, 5 ff.

had clothed themselves in my fine linen regarded me as those who had none.[47]

The work goes on to relate the details of the attack:

It was after supper, when night had fallen. I had taken an hour of repose, and was lying down on my bed. I was weary, and my desire was bent on sleep, when weapons were brandished and enquiry was made about me. I acted like a snake of the hillside. I awoke at the fighting, being alone, and found that it was a combat of the guard. If I had made haste with weapons in my hand, I should have made the cowards retreat in confusion(?). But no man is brave at night; no one can fight single-handed; no success is achieved without a helper.

See, bloodshed occurred while I was without you, before the courtiers had heard that I was to hand over (the rule) to you, before I had taken my seat with you. Let me counsel you, because I did not provide for it (i.e., the bloodshed), nor foresee it, nor had my mind considered the slackness of the servants. Have women ever drawn up in battle array? Has rebellion ever been fomented within the house?[48]

The rhetorical questions refer to the fact that this was a plot within the harem.

The pharaoh then proceeds with a recital of his benefactions, especially his successful campaigns in Nubia and the Delta:

No (such) disaster had overtaken me since I was born. Never had there been the like of my achievement as a warrior. I forced my way to Elephantine, and turned back to the Delta marshlands. Having attended to the frontiers of the land, I surveyed its midst. I attained the limits of the frontier strongholds(?) by my marvellous might.

It was I who created the barley, whom Nepri[49] loved. . . . No one was hungry in my years; no one was thirsty in them. Men sat, because of what I had done, conversing about me. . . . I tamed lions and captured crocodiles: I subdued the people of Wawat and captured the Madjoi. I caused the Asiatics to slink away like curs.[50]

He concludes with a passage which again refers to Senwosret as his legitimate successor, in terms which certainly suggest that Amenemḥet was no longer alive: "<You were my own tongue(?)>,[51] Senwosret, my son, while my feet still walked; you were my own mind, while my eyes still saw. . . . See, I have made a beginning, that I might join the end for you. . . . Ascend (the throne) for a reign which will be superior to mine."[52]

[47]P. Millingen, 1/3 ff.

[48]*Ibid.*, 1/11 ff.

[49]The god of grain.

[50]P. Millingen, 2/9 ff.

[51]The reconstruction follows a proposal of A. Volten, *Zwei altägyptische politische Schriften* (Copenhagen, 1945), pp. 120 f. The text is corrupt at this point in all copies.

[52]P. Millingen, 3/7 ff.

The reign of Senwosret I (*c.* 1971–1928 B.C.) was not without its problems. Chief of these was the fact that Amenemḥet I had gained royal power with the assistance of the nomarchs whom he rewarded by restoring many of the privileges which they had lost under the rulers of the Eleventh Dynasty. This resurgent power of the local governors again posed a threat to the centralized administration, with the result that the office was later to be abolished forever by Senwosret III. Meanwhile Senwosret I sought to retain the loyalty of his subjects by every means possible, not least of which was the power of the pen. For example, the Tale of Sinuhe, to which we have already referred, seized the opportunity of making its hero glorify the sovereign:

Thereupon he said to me, "Whatever will that land be like without him (i.e., Amenemḥet I), that beneficent god whose fear was throughout the countries like (that of) Sakhmet in a year of pestilence?"

I myself said to him in reply, "Undoubtedly, since his son has entered the palace, he has appropriated the inheritance of his father. He is, of course, a god without peer, no other surpassing him. He is a master of sagacity, of worthy counsels and efficient commands. Exit and entry are in accordance with his command. It was he who subdued the countries, whereas his father remained in his palace, while he (i.e., Senwosret) reported that what he (i.e., Amenemḥet) had commanded had been done. He is a mighty man, achieving with his strong arm; a champion, without an equal, when he is seen charging in the conflict or approaching the fray. He is a curber of horns, a weakener of hands. His enemies cannot join battle. He is sharp-sighted, a smasher of foreheads, so that none can stand in his presence. He is long of stride, destroying the fugitive."[53]

"He is gracious, and of great sweetness, having gained love, so that his city loves him more than itself, and rejoices in him more than in its (own) god. Men and women pass by in exultation over him, now that he is king. He conquered while but a youth. . . . He is unique, god-given. How this land which he has ruled rejoices! He is one who expands its borders. He will conquer the southern lands and despise the northern countries. He was made to chastise the Asiatics and to crush the bedouin. . . . Utter no curse against His Majesty. . . . He will not fail to do good to the country which will be loyal to him."[54]

Another literary work in praise of the qualities of Senwosret I was couched in the traditional form of an instruction, although in poetic form. It was addressed to the high functionaries and members of the nobility by some important personage, probably the vizier. Perhaps he is to be identified with Ptaḥemdjedḥuty who, like Kheti,

[53]Sinuhe, B, 43 ff. [54]*Ibid.*, 65 ff.

was commemorated in the panegyric on famous scribes and authors of didactic treatises contained in Papyrus Chester Beatty IV.[55] At any rate, the text was later appropriated by an official named Sḥetepibrēʿ in honour of Amenemḥet III, and its wide distribution is evidenced by its preservation on one stela, two papyri, one wooden writing tablet, and some twenty ostraca. It opens in a sententious style:

I say something of importance:
I make you hear,
I make you know a counsel for eternity,
A manner of living righteously,
Of passing a lifetime in peace.
Adore the king in your inmost being;
Associate His Majesty with your thoughts.[56]

The writer then compares the pharaoh with various deities, among others Sia, the god personifying Perception, Rēʿ, the life-giving sun god, Khnum, the ram-headed creator god, Bastet, a kindly cat-headed goddess, and Sakhmet, the lion-headed goddess of destruction:

He is a Sia who is in the minds:
His eyes investigate the inmost thoughts of all.
He is a Rēʿ:
Life is under his control;
That which exists is beneath his light,
One sees by means of his rays;
He illuminates the Two Lands more than the sun-disk,
He burns . . . more than fire;
He makes verdant more than a high Nile,
Having filled the Two Lands with power and life.
Noses are cold when he gives himself up to anger;
When he is calm one may breathe his air.
He gives sustenance to those who follow him,
He is generous to the one who adheres to his path.[57]

He is a Khnum for all bodies,
A sire who brings mankind into existence.
He is a Bastet who protects the Two Lands;
He who venerates him will be protected by his arm.
He is a Sakhmet against him who has transgressed his command;
He whom he hates will be in misery.[58]

[55]Suggested by Posener, *Littérature et politique dans l'Egypte*, p. 119.
[56]Sḥetepibrēʿ, 2 ff. Cited according to the numbering of C. Kuentz in *Studies Presented to F. Ll. Griffith* (London, 1932), pp. 98 f.
[57]*Ibid.*, 12 ff. [58]*Ibid.*, 29 ff.

The work closes with further admonitions to loyalty:

> Fight for his name;
> Respect the oath made by him (i.e., in his name);
> Keep yourselves free from any act of insurrection.
> He whom the king loves will be a venerated one;[59]
> There is no tomb for him who is rebellious against His Majesty,
> His corpse is thrown into the water.
> Honour the crown of Lower Egypt;
> Venerate the crown of Upper Egypt;
> Exalt him who wears the double crown.
> You are to do this that your body may prosper,
> That you may find it good for ever.[60]

Still another "instruction," entitled the Teaching of a Man for His Son, was in reality addressed to the people, seeking their submission to the authority of the pharaoh. This work has been partially recovered from one leather roll, two papyri, and nine ostraca. It commences: "Here begins the teaching made by a man for his son. He says: Listen to my voice; do not ignore my words; do not let your mind relax from what I shall say to you. Be consistent(?) without transgression in it. No slackness occurs in a wise man."[61] The document attempts to curtail revolutionary movements and anarchy by evincing a concern for the underprivileged:

> He who lacked resources becomes the possessor of a fortune; he who had little becomes the possessor of dependents. He makes the one who had no success succeed. Those who have suffered become possessed of a town. He teaches the dumb(?) to speak; he opens the ears of the deaf. This (occurs) in the space of a lifetime apart from Fate, and without Fortune opposing it. . . . You will have much in your possession (if) you spend your lifetime within the will of your god (i.e., king). Venerate the King of Upper Egypt; honour the King of Lower Egypt. . . . He who lacked a name will be a venerated one.[62]

By these means Senwosret I succeeded in bolstering up his position in the early years of his rule, and laid the foundations for a long and prosperous reign.

Our final example of propaganda literature comes from the Twentieth Dynasty, when Ramesses III (*c.* 1197–1165 B.C.) ruled as a virtual dictator in a totalitarian state. The unrest that seethed among

[59]One who is furnished with a tomb and the necessary mortuary provisions.
[60]Sḥetepibrēʿ, 35 ff.
[61]British Museum Papyrus 10258, 1/1 ff.
[62]See *supra*, note 59. Ostracon Louvre E23561, 1 ff., with P. Amherst XV, 2/1 f.

the populace is reflected in the lampooning of the pharaoh in satirical sketches, in one of which he is caricatured as a mouse. From time to time, however, the discontent manifested itself in more tangible and dangerous forms. During his reign a plot by the vizier at Athribis was thwarted. Later, in his twenty-ninth year, *c.* 1168 B.C., strikes of dissatisfied workers in the Theban necropolis broke out as a result of inadequate or overdue rations. Finally matters came to a head when Ramesses was assassinated *c.* 1165 B.C. in a harem conspiracy engineered by Queen Tiy on behalf of her son. When some persons were later brought to trial, three judges were caught in the act of drinking and plotting with the accused and were promptly arrested and added to the number of the prisoners.

The new king and rightful successor to the throne, Ramesses IV, had the criminals duly punished, and then faced the necessity of establishing himself securely on the throne. Very naturally he too adopted the written word as the means by which to confirm his position. The resulting document was the Great Harris Papyrus, the longest scroll in existence, measuring some 133 feet in length. Although drawn up at the instigation of Ramesses IV, the work was clearly intended to be regarded as the posthumous message and testament of his father.[63] In it the latter exonerates himself of any guilt that could account for his assassination. At great length he recounts his military exploits and his generous benefactions to the temple estates, and invokes the blessings of the gods on his chosen successor, Ramesses IV. Addressing the god Amon-Rēʿ, he says:

> How happy is the one who relies on thee, O god Amūn, the Bull of his mother, Ruler of Thebes! Mayest thou allow me to arrive safely, mooring in peace, and resting in the "holy land" like the ennead. May I mingle ‹ with › the excellent souls of Manu[64] who behold thy rays in early morning! Hear my petition, O Lord, my father. I am unique among the gods who are by thy side. Crown my son as king on the throne of Atum; adorn him as Mighty Bull, Lord of the Two Banks, King of Upper and Lower Egypt, Lord of the Two Lands, Woser-Maʿat-Rēʿ Setepenamūn, Son of Rēʿ, Lord of Diadems, Ramesses Heka-Maʿat Meriamūn, effluence that came forth from thy body. It was thou who didst foresee him as king while he was but a youth.[65]

[63]First recognized as a pseudepigraph by V. Struve, "Ort der Herkunft und Zweck der Zusammenstellung des Grossen Papyrus Harris," *Aegyptus*, VII (1926), 3–40.

[64]The mountains of the West.

[65]P. Harris I, 22/1 ff.

Again he prays:

Mayest thou complete for me the mighty deeds which I performed for thee, O father! I have reached the west side like Osiris. . . . Create peace for my heart, O august father, as I was beneficial to thy *ku*[66] while I was on earth. . . . Adorn my son to be king, as lord of the Two Banks; make him ruler of the Two Lands like thyself, as sovereign in To-Meri: Woser-Maʿat-Rēʿ Setepenamūn, whom thou didst thyself choose to be heir and to magnify thy name. . . . It was thou who didst create him as a youngster that thou mightest appoint him to be the crown prince on the double throne of Gēb. Thou didst say, "He shall become king on the throne of him who begot him."[67]

There follows another clear reference to Ramesses III as deceased:

Thou didst multiply good things for me while I was on earth. Thou didst draw (me) to rest by thy side in the west of the sky like all the mysterious gods of the underworld. . . . When I was ruler on earth as lord of To-Meri, was I not greatly beneficent toward thee so as to seek for all advantages for thine august temple to offer them before thee in thy city of Memphis?[68]

Towards the close of the work, he refers in unmistakable terms to his death, and calls upon his people to serve the new pharaoh:

See, I have gone to rest in the necropolis like (my) father Rēʿ, and mingled with the great ennead in heaven, earth and the underworld. Amon-Rēʿ has established my son on my throne; he has received my office peacefully as ruler of the Two Lands, sitting on the Horus-throne as lord of the Two Banks. . . . Touch his sandals; kiss the ground before him; bow down to him; follow him on every occasion; venerate him; praise him; magnify his beauty as you do for Rēʿ in early morning. Offer him your tribute in his august palace; send him the gifts of the lands and countries. Adhere to his sayings and (his) commands, . . . heed his utterances that you may prosper under his might.[69]

Examples have now been adduced of several literary works designed for the purpose of political propaganda originating in periods ranging from the First Intermediate Period to the late New Kingdom. Were space to permit, it would be possible to speak of still others, such as the Westcar Papyrus, which appears to be a document intended originally to support the claim to legitimacy of the first three rulers of the Fifth Dynasty, or the Admonitions of Ipuwer, composed as an

[66]The word *ku* designates the protective spirit which accompanied every individual through life. It formed part of his personality, and might be regarded, depending on the circumstances, as roughly equivalent to such concepts as "desire," "appetite," "vital force," etc.

[67]P. Harris I, 42/1 ff. [68]*Ibid.*, 44/8 ff. [69]*Ibid.*, 79/4 ff.

attack on the reigning monarch at the beginning of the troubled times of the First Intermediate Period. Enough has been said, however, to make the fact abundantly clear that the ancient Egyptians were keenly aware of the potent force exerted by the written word. This was especially effective when reinforced by the authority of antiquity, or couched in the form of a communication from the deceased god-king.

Small wonder, then, that the Egyptians so prized their literature: "A book is more effective than a carved tombstone or a solidly built tomb-wall(?)"![70] And it was very natural that they should extol the authors: "Their names are pronounced because of their books which they composed, since they were good, and the memory of the one who composed them is eternal."[71] May this ancient maxim serve as a fitting description of the distinguished scholar and teacher to whom this small token of respect is gratefully dedicated!

[70]P. Ch. Beatty IV, verso, 3/1.
[71]*Ibid.*, 2/12 f.

3. The Formal Aspect of Ancient Near Eastern Law[1]

R. A. F. MACKENZIE, S.J.

THIS PAPER AIMS AT SKETCHING, in broad outline, certain formal characteristics of the extant legal collections of the ancient Near East, most of which may be grouped under the convenient rubric of "cuneiform law."[2] That is, taken together, they make up a body of material comparable, in homogeneity and extent, to such fields of study as Roman law or Teutonic law. Territorially, we may conceive this as extending, in its period of widest diffusion, from Elam on the east to central Asia Minor in the west, and from northern Assyria to Palestine.[3] Chronologically, it was operative during the last three millennia B.C., though it so happens that its extant remains, in codes and law-books, practically all fall within the second millennium. Its original centre of development, as far as this can be inferred from the available sources, appears to have been among the Sumerian city-states of Lower Mesopotamia, towards the end of the third millennium B.C. From this point in space and time it radiated, as an integral part of the Babylonian, or rather Sumero-Akkadian culture, over the territory just mentioned; it was adopted by one people after another, and thus, while preserving always a certain unity and the marks of its origin, it changed and developed in various ways, by combination with, or adaptation to, the pre-existing customary jurisprudence and cultural conditions of various communities. It existed in a number of different languages—four, that we know of, though there were probably others

[1]This paper was read before the Oriental Club of Toronto on January 13, 1953. It is a pleasure now to offer it in homage to Professor T. J. Meek. This is especially appropriate, since it was under his tutelage that I was introduced to the subject of cuneiform law. He must not be held responsible however for the views here expressed.

[2]A term devised (as German *Keilschriftrecht*) by Paul Koschaker; cf. his "Keilschriftrecht," *Zeitschrift der deutschen morgenländischen Gesellschaft,* LXXXIX (1935), 1–39.

[3]Its extent is judged of course not merely by the *provenance* of the few law codes with which this paper is concerned but by the periods and areas from which cuneiform legal documents have been recovered. Cf. A. Alt, "Eine neue Provinz des Keilschriftrechts," *Welt des Orients,* II (1947), 78–92 = *Kleine Schriften,* III (1959), 141–57.

as well; and though its principal extant units have in common that they are written in the syllabic cuneiform script of Babylonia, yet this is an accidental and extrinsic characteristic, and we may on other grounds quite legitimately classify a lawbook as cuneiform law, even though it has come down to us in some other writing. However, the diffusion of cuneiform law, as of the Sumero-Akkadian culture in general, does seem to have been intimately bound up with that of the cuneiform script. They went together, as parts of the civilization of the time, adopted in varying degrees by most of the peoples dwelling around the Fertile Crescent, in the Middle or Late Bronze Age.

The materials available so far for study—there is no knowing what further treasures archaeology may some day reveal to us—include five large *corpora* of legislation.[4] These fall chronologically into two groups. The older group comprises the Laws of Eshnunna, from the twentieth or nineteenth century B.C.; the Laws of Lipit-Ishtar, about the nineteenth century; and the Code of Hammurabi, eighteenth or early seventeenth. The later group includes the Hittite Code, from the sixteenth or early fifteenth century, and the so-called "Middle Assyrian Laws," from about the fourteenth century.[5] Finally, with these latter may be associated the so-called "Book of the Covenant" in the Hebrew scriptures (Exod. 21–23), since its first half contains at least a large fragment, somewhat revised, of a code of cuneiform law. This last (that is, the *Urtext* or source of Exod. 21:2–22:17) I would put not later than the thirteenth century.

When we say that all these belong to cuneiform law, we must not misrepresent the nature of their mutual relationship. There is no line of legal development leading from one to another, and it would be very difficult to show, for example, that any single Hittite law owes anything in substance to any paragraph of the Code of Hammurabi. The family resemblance which they do show concerns more their form than their substance, and it may be summed up in two related points: the first is the prevailing use of a conditional, casuistic enunciation for

[4]The oldest code so far known is that of Ur-Nammu (mid–twenty-first century B.C.), founder of the Third dynasty of Ur; but of this, only five fragmentary laws are at present decipherable. See Kramer's edition in *Orientalia*, XXIII (1954), 40–51.

[5]The following abbreviations will be used here for reference: LE, Laws of Eshnunna; LLI, Laws of Lipit-Ishtar; CH, Code of Hammurabi; HC, Hittite Code; MAL, Middle Assyrian Laws. Translations of all these will be found in J. Pritchard, ed., *ANET*, pp. 159 ff., CH and MAL being the work of Professor Meek. In this paper however the translations given are my own.

the separate articles of law; the second is the strictly juridical, and non-religious outlook of the jurisprudence on which thes are founded. It is the former especially that will be considere

Casuistic law is that which determines the procedure to be followed, and the judgment to be found, by a court sitting on a case submitted to it. The form developed for this purpose in cuneiform law consists of a preamble, containing the enunciation of the case to be judged, followed by an enacting clause which pronounces the judgment. The preamble, or protasis, sets forth hypothetically the legal situation in question, described in more or less detail according as in the mind of the legislator more or less precision is required. It must be noted that this situation is a present state of affairs, even though the acts or events which gave rise to it (and which are enumerated) naturally lie in the past. It is not the past act, as such, which the law (*per impossibile*) intends to annul—that, after all, is irrevocably over and done with; it is its effect, the claim or liability resulting from it, as it is laid before the judge, which requires to be resolved or remedied, by some action to be taken in the future. In the second part of the law, the enacting clause, this legal consequence is enunciated, as a judgment framed in apodictic terms, resting on the authority of the legislator, which the judge is to apply to the case before him. To take a simple example from one of the older codes (LLI §29): "Granted that a (prospective) son-in-law has entered the house of his (prospective) father-in-law (and) has brought betrothal-gifts, (but) later they have driven him forth (and) given his wife to his companion:—the betrothal-gifts which he brought they shall restore to him; that wife shall not marry his companion."

In terms of our Indo-European syntax we may conveniently represent the whole article as a conditional sentence, of which the protasis contains the statement of the case and the apodosis its solution. Thus, English translations of cuneiform laws generally begin with "if." This is probably the best we can do in literary presentation, the gain in idiomatic naturalness offsetting the slight inaccuracy. At the same time we have to remember that this casuistic form of the ancient Orient is subtly different from that of our conditional sentence. The protasis is not grammatically dependent on, or subordinated to, the apodosis, as is shown even by the fact that in Akkadian laws the (main) verbs in the protasis never take the subjunctive termination. Rather there are two grammatically co-ordinate statements, two successive affirmations, one of which states what *is*, the other what *shall be*. The nexus between the two is logical, not grammatical.[6] It is the introductory word, or formula, which precedes the first statement that indicates the logical and legal connection in which they stand, and so has a technical meaning more specific than the English "if."

The chosen introductory word in the different languages is itself instructive. As this form was transferred from one language to another (from Sumerian into Akkadian, from Akkadian into Hittite, from Akkadian, probably through the mediation of Canaanite, into Hebrew) a fixed term was chosen from the vocabulary of the receiving language to perform this introductory function. The original Sumerian phrase was *tukum-bi*, which is not a conjunction but a noun coupled with a possessive pronominal suffix: "its case" or "their case."[7] Thus, instead of translating "if," it would be more exact to render it "Their case (is as follows)." Here, in the oldest of the known formulae, the original non-subordinating and demonstrative character of the introduction is most clearly brought out. *Tukum-bi*, of course, is not limited to this legal formulation; it is the introductory formula also in omens and in medical prognoses, and is even used to indicate contemplated contingencies in contracts. It is in this last use that its meaning approaches most closely our English "if."

The corresponding technical term in Akkadian laws is *šumma*. This has been plausibly analysed[8] as a verbal form, the permansive state of the verb *šêmu*—decide, determine—used impersonally, with *-ma* explicative added as the last syllable. It may be rendered literally, "It being determined (namely) that . . . ," or more simply, "Granted that. . . ." That is, this introductory formula in legal contexts refers to the case as laid before the court, the summary of the evidence forthcoming from testimony of witnesses or other sources. This being determined, the legal disposition follows. In Hittite there are two words, *takku* and *man*, which serve in ordinary contexts to introduce conditions or hypotheses: of these only the former is used as an initial term in articles of law. Though its etymology is not entirely clear, it appears to be derived from an Indo-European demonstrative stem *to-*, and is

[6]Cf. T. J. Meek, "The Asyndeton Clause in the Code of Hammurabi," *JNES*, V (1946), 64–72.

[7]Cf. A. Poebel, *Grundzüge der sumerischen Grammatik* (Rostock, 1923) §423.

[8]Cf. Meek, "The Asyndeton Clause." Speiser, in "A Note on the Derivation of *šumma*," *JCS*, I (1947), 321–8, has suggested instead that the word is an old demonstrative, formed from *šu'ma*. This would if anything strengthen our present argument on its demonstrative force.

related to the Hittite sentence-connective *ta*, "and then."[9] Unlike the Sumerian and Akkadian expressions, it is a conjunction; nevertheless the above connections seem to indicate that it too has a demonstrative or deictic force.

In Hebrew also there are two common words available to denote conditions, *kî* and *ʾim*. These are used practically interchangeably for ordinary conditional sentences, but a sharp and quite rigid distinction appears in the formulation of laws. *Kî* always introduces the main statement of the case; *ʾim* always introduces the subordinate alternatives; and these roles are never interchanged.[10] This alone suggests that a special technical force here attaches to *kî*, as the initial formula of casuistic law. Joüon remarks[11] that it differs from *ʾim* by a nuance coming closer to the meaning, "in the case that . . . ," obviously similar to the interpretation of *šumma* given above.

Now to examine more closely the nature of this type of law. First, it is strictly pragmatic; that is, it is quite independent, *per se*, of any religious doctrine or ethical principle. No general principles are appealed to, no axioms laid down. The situation described calls for such and such action, or has such and such consequences, but the validity of this affirmation rests solely on the will of the legislator, and the enunciation of the law prescinds from any intrinsic connection that may exist between the case and its solution. One advantage of this amorality, if we may call it that, is the great flexibility characteristic of this casuistic formulation. It can and in fact did serve as a vehicle of criminal law, of civil law, and even of commercial regulations such as the fixing of prices and wages.

Secondly, in consequence of the foregoing, the casuistic laws do not formally express any obligation laid upon the individual, even when their subject matter is quite clearly ethical. That is to say, he is not forbidden, for example, to steal or to commit adultery; at most, he is warned that if he does these things, certain consequences are likely to follow, consequences of course unpleasant, and at least in part designed to deter him from so acting. It is interesting to note, in the Old Testament, the dissatisfaction of the Deuteronomic writers with this legalistic and profane point of view. The Code of Deuteronomy

[9]Cf. E. Adelaide Hahn, "Some Hittite words in *ta-*," *Language*, XII (1936), 109–113; "The Shift of a Hittite Conjunction from the Temporal to the Conditional Sphere," *ibid.*, XX (1944), 91–107.

[10]Cf. A. B. Davidson, *Hebrew Syntax* (Edinburgh, 1896) §130, n. 5.

[11]*Grammaire de l'Hébreu biblique*, §167 *i*.

includes ten laws[12] in this "standard" casuistic formulation; to five of these there have been added vigorous ethical statements, to supply the moral judgment which was felt to be wanting: "and so shall you root out the evil from your midst," or "for that is abominable to the Lord." Even in the Code of Hammurabi we find here and there a phrase which seems to contain a value judgment and to be inserted to justify or explain a penalty. For example, CH §7: ". . . that noble, being a thief, shall be put to death."[13] But in general the dispassionate legalistic tone is steadily maintained, and ethical, commercial, and procedural enactments follow one another with no perceptible variation in form or emphasis. Thus, CH §195, "Granted that a son has struck his father:—they shall cut off his hand," and CH §257, "Granted that a noble has hired a ploughman:—he shall pay him 8 *gur* of wheat per year," are, as far as the letter of the law is concerned, of equal importance and equally binding.

Thirdly, in so far as these laws are intended to be authoritative and binding, they do indeed express an obligation; but it falls not on the individual citizen but on the judge or judges who are the agents of the legislator in seeing that the latter's enactments are put in practice. By the past act, or complex of acts, set forth in the protasis, an obligation has arisen, a debt has been contracted, or the juridical order of society has been disturbed. That obligation or debt must be discharged, the juridical order re-integrated, by the carrying out of the terms of the apodosis, whether that lays down a penalty, a benefit, or merely some further judical procedure, such as ordeal or appeal to a higher court. In any case, it is the judge who has the responsibility of applying the law and of handing down a decision which expresses the mind of the legislator as applied to the particular case.

Fourthly, as a corollary of the foregoing, it is of the essence of this form that the solution of the case should be indicated. In penal laws, the penalty is specified; in contractual regulations, the obligations binding the parties; in rules of procedure, the action to be taken by the judge—even if it is only to give the ruling: "There is no penalty in that case." Generally speaking, we may call casuistic laws remedial enactments; naturally, they must determine the remedy. This is in

[12]Deut. 21:15–17, 18–21a; 22:13–21a, 22a, 28 f.; 24:1–4a, 5, 7a; 25:1 f., 5–10.

[13]However, the phrase *awīlum šū šarrāq* may be only evidence of the compilatory character of CH; LE §40 (parallel to CH §7) has for its apodosis simply *šūma šarrāq*, "he is a thief." CH may have retained *šarrāq* from an earlier version, and made it circumstantial by adding a final and more explicit *iddâk*, "he shall be put to death."

marked contrast to the categorical and unconditioned mode of expression proper to apodictic law.

What has been said about the pragmatic and amoral character of this style of law must not be understood as extending to the minds of the lawgiver and his subjects. The laws are simply applications of acknowledged principles of *jus* and *fas*. Their limited and drily factual formulation is a natural consequence of their origin, the notation of decisions actually rendered by courts. There was no point in overloading such precedents with abstract principles which judge and litigants took for granted, and which were not subject to rulings by the court. But such abstract principles as the immorality of theft, of murder, of filial rebellion, of adultery are clearly supposed by these different collections of laws, and even formed a prerequisite for the creation of the casuistic formulation. A given court or judge had made such and such a decision, and it was the *right* decision; hence future courts, dealing with the same case, should deliver the same judgment. We may refer, by way of confirmation, to the prologues of Lipit-Ishtar's and Hammurabi's codes, with their emphatic statements of the moral and ethical intentions of the legislators.

The origin of this formulation of casuistic law is most naturally sought among the Sumerians, in the city-states of Lower Mesopotamia at some time during the third millennium B.C. It clearly arose out of a long-continued and fairly stable practice of law; that is, it is a crystallization of jurisprudence, based on the exercise of already customary law. It supposes (we are speaking, it must be remembered, of the form itself, not of any particular legislation expressed in it) a court or courts already functioning, habitually giving certain decisions in certain cases, hence judging according to certain definite legal principles. Further, these courts were (in modern parlance) definitely lay tribunals. This jurisprudence is a function of secular life, a civil and civic activity, distinct from the cultic life of the priesthood and the temples, governed by religious and ritual presuppositions. It is as remote from religion, as untouched by dogmatic or mythological considerations, as the bargaining of the merchant or the tactics of the soldier. Neither the eloquence of Hammurabi's Prologue nor the exhortations of the Deuteronomists can disguise the practical, human, lay character of this form of law, imprinted on it from its origin.

This origin, whenever it occurred, was a distinct achievement—the creation of a tool of the human spirit comparable with the Greek hexameter or the Latin prose period. It is easy to say that this casuistic formulation is merely a decision in a particular case applied to future cases. But the word "applied" involves a great deal. The particular decision would consist only of the apodosis, with demonstrative terms (proper names or the like) indicating the parties concerned: "A shall be put to death," "B shall pay C a mina of silver," and the like. To synthesize such material into a true law, the typical case, of which the judge's sentence gives only the solution, must be indicated more or less fully, the particular data must be generalized, and case and sentence must be bound together to make one law. Finally an act of authority must intervene to make the resulting formula binding, not on one judge or one court only, but on many. These steps, which may seem to us natural and almost inevitable, required considerable reasoning powers, both of induction and deduction, for their execution. The men, presumably Sumerians, who first hammered out this universalized formula deserve credit for a significant advance along the path of civilization.

It would be in place here to say something about the development undergone by this form, a development which we are now in the happy position of being able to trace, at least to some extent, in the first centuries of the second millennium. But considerations of space forbid more than a bare reference to it. A comparison of the Laws of Eshnunna and of Lipit-Ishtar with the Code of Hammurabi shows that the First Dynasty of Babylon, in particular, must have witnessed great activity in the field of law and produced a school of legal draftsmen of considerable technical skill. In the code this standard casuistic formula is so developed that it can be and is applied, with admirable economy and precision, to the most complicated cases and to a great variety of materials, including procedural law, the fixing of prices and wages, and the privileges enjoyed by certain classes of citizens. In the Laws of Eshnunna we find price- and wage-fixing, but in the form of simple enunciations; Hammurabi's legists have ingeniously reduced them to the standard conditional form. For instance, LE §3: "A wagon together with its oxen and its driver—1 *massiktum* 4 *seah* of grain is its rental." How was a regulation like that to be drafted in the casuistic law form? Very simply (CH §271): "Granted that a noble has hired draught-oxen, a wagon, and its driver:—he shall pay 180 *qa* of grain per day." This mention of the subject and the act of hiring really adds nothing to the simple regulation; they are introduced for the purely formal reason of maintaining the familiar casuistic formula.

We turn now to the other formal type of law represented in the ancient Near East: apodictic law. An apodictic article of law lays a command directly on the subject, obliging him to do (or refrain from doing) some particular action judged by the legislator to be desirable (or harmful). It may be identical in form with a precept given by a superior to an individual inferior, but what distinguishes law from precept, at least in intention, is the universalized character of the former. In time, its validity is unlimited; it is intended to be always in force, "until further notice." In extent, it is equally unrestricted (apart of course from express limitations); all those are bound by it who are responsible for the action or omission prescribed and who come under the authority of its author. In its pure form, apodictic law does not contemplate the hypothesis of disobedience or contumacy. Its enunciation, unlike that of casuistic law, makes no provision for the statement of a penalty; this must be added, if at all, in a separate clause.

In passing, it is worth mentioning, for the sake of its possible bearing on the Israelite legal system, that just as the casuistic style is characteristic of Mesopotamian jurisprudence, so Egyptian law, or what passes for it, is conceived always in apodictic terms. Actually, Egyptian law is a highly elusive entity, and we have as yet no sure evidence that a written code or lawbook ever existed in Egypt before the time of the Persian empire.[14] What we do have is a handful of royal decrees and edicts containing *ad hoc* instructions to officials; documents, that is, which are more administrative than legislative. Jurisprudence, as a science, seems never to have been developed by the ancient Egyptians. Still, we may take it that proclamations such as the Nauri stele of Seti I, or the reform edict of Haremhab, were at least intended to have the effect of laws, and in them we find a system of direct commands, and a personal, arbitrary tone, as different as possible from the Mesopotamian sources just discussed. One characteristic that makes it hard to classify these edicts as laws in the full sense is their lack of any set formulation, any fixed juridical mode of expression.

[14]Cf. J. A. Wilson, in *Authority and Law in the Ancient Orient* (Suppl. to *JAOS*, XVII [1954], 5 f.): "Despite all the written documents which have come down to us from ancient Egypt, we possess neither a body of law which is comparable to the Asiatic codes, nor any textual references to such laws elsewhere. . . . Since Egypt was blessed by having on earth a god as king, law proceeded from his mouth, always vitally renewed, and no codification was necessary or even proper."

The main locus of apodictic law in the ancient Near East is the legal system of the ancient Israelites, as represented in the various codes and collections of the Pentateuch. But it is also present, though exceptionally, in the documents of cuneiform law, which are by no means limited to the standard casuistic form we have described. Some incautious statements have been made at times about the uniformity of style found in these lawbooks; it has even been laid down, as an *a priori* principle, that a code of laws, having a single author, must necessarily preserve exactly the same style from beginning to end.[15] But examination of our sources shows that only the Sumerian laws of Lipit-Ishtar are perfectly consistent in adhering to one formulation; and that does not prove much, because we have only one-third of the original text. The Laws of Eshnunna, on the other hand, include almost as great a variety of forms as the Hebrew Book of the Covenant. Of the fifty-odd laws making up the Eshnunna code, just over half have the standard casuistic formula beginning with *šumma.* Ten others are apodictic regulations of prices and rentals. Five more are casuistic, but in a relative construction, beginning with "a noble, who . . ." or "a male or female slave, who . . ." (*awīlum* [*wardum, amtum*] *ša* . . .). For example, LE §13: "A noble who is caught in the house of a plebeian [ ] in the daytime shall pay 10 shekels of silver; one who is caught at night in the house shall die, his life may not be spared." This relative construction is nowhere found in the Code of Hammurabi or in the Hittite Code; it appears in a few sentences in the Middle Assyrian Laws. But, over a thousand years later, it is the exclusive construction in a little group of fifteen laws from the neo-Babylonian period.[16] In the Pentateuch, the same construction (beginning *ʾîš ʾašer*, or the like) is common in the Law of Holiness and the Priestly document generally, but is quite unknown to the older collections, even to Deuteronomy. This is interesting, because it would appear that this relative construction was a normal Semitic idiom, which the Babylonians might have developed as their regular legal formula. But the conservatism of Hammurabi's legists, who insisted instead on preserving the classical *šumma* idiom taken over from Sumerian, suppressed it, till centuries later it appears again at the two ends of the Fertile Crescent—between which the Jewish exile of the sixth century might supply a connection.

[15]Thus A. Jirku, *Das Weltliche Recht im Alten Testament*, 32.
[16]Cf. Pritchard, ed., *ANET*, p. 197 f. (translation by Professor Meek).

There are two main formulations of apodictic law in the Pentateuch, and one of these is sporadically represented in the cuneiform codes. This is the impersonal so-called "jussive" formulation: "So-and-so shall do this" or "such-and-such shall be done." Although this corresponds grammatically to the apodosis of the casuistic formulation (the verb form used is the third person of the Hebrew imperfect or the Akkadian present), yet it definitely comes under the heading of apodictic law, being formally a command or prohibition for the future, not the solution of an existing case. For example, Deut. 17:6: "On the evidence of two or three witnesses shall the guilty be put to death; he shall not be put to death on the evidence of a single witness." This formulation is specially prevalent in the ceremonial legislation of the Priestly Code.

In the Code of Hammurabi there are three sections which contain apodictic decrees in this form. We shall briefly examine the first, §§34–41, a group of laws dealing with the inalienability of royal fiefs. The central law here is §37: "Granted that a noble has bought the field, orchard, or house of a soldier, commissary, or (other) feudatory:—his tablet shall be effaced and he shall forfeit his money; the field, orchard, or house shall revert to its owner." That is typical casuistic law; it supposes the transaction already accomplished and directs the judge in his finding: the property transfer is to be declared null and void, but the money transfer is to stand, by way of penalty. But this article is preceded by §36, which lays down the general principle: "The field, orchard, or house of a soldier, commissary, or (other) feudatory shall not be sold." This is apodictic, forbidding even the contemplated transaction. There follows another apodictic law, establishing a distinction between the fief which the feudatory has received from the crown and other property which he may have acquired by his own industry (§§38–39): "A soldier, commissary, or (other) feudatory shall not deed to his wife or his daughter (any part) of the field, orchard, or house belonging to his fief, nor give it (in payment) for his debt. (But) of a field, orchard, or house which he has bought and possesses (in his own right) he may deed (part) to his wife or his daughter, or give it (in payment) for his debt." Finally, §40 is also an apodictic decree, making an exception from the general law in favour of three classes of persons: "A votary, merchant, or foreign vassal may sell his field, his orchard, or his house; the buyer shall perform the feudal duties attached to the field, orchard, or house which he has bought."

The most plausible explanation of this intrusion of the apodictic form into the otherwise consistently casuistic code seems to be that these apodictic laws were originally royal decrees issued by Hammurabi himself, before the compilation of the code; that they were taken over as they stood by the Babylonian legal draftsmen; and that it was simply respect for the royal formulation that forbade any attempt to recast them in casuistic style.

There are two other places in the Code of Hammurabi where a similar combination of styles occurs.[17] And the Hittite Code and the Assyrian Laws each have a single such locus.[18]

The other, and more important, formulation of Israelite apodictic law is what is called the preceptive imperfect. A verb in the second person singular of the imperfect expresses a command or prohibition, directed to each member of the Israelite community. This is the form, "thou shalt (not) . . . ," familiar to us from the Decalogue, prevailing in the second half of the Book of the Covenant, and indeed found in every section of the Pentateuch. This direct address is entirely unknown to cuneiform law.[19] It is the Israelite formulation *par excellence*, and a brief analysis will demonstrate its great cultural and religious significance.

There is first the legislator who is here speaking. Other peoples put their legal systems under the patronage of the gods and invoke the displeasure of the latter upon transgressors, but nowhere save in Israel is the divinity itself conceived as drafting and dictating actual articles of law. When combined with the singular address, this concept secures an overwhelming immediacy in its impact on the individual conscience. The singular in the casuistic laws is naturally conceived as distributive: "if (any) man. . . ." The singular address in the wisdom literature is directed to the supposed disciple of the sage, "my son." Apart from these two idioms, the natural grammatical construction in

[17]CH §§177 (last clause), 187.

[18]HC §§50–56; MAL §§ 40, 41 (second clause).

[19]A convincing precedent exists however in the form of the suzerainty treaty, which established a covenant relationship between overlord and vassal prince. This is known to us from Hittite sources, and has been brilliantly analysed, and compared with the Israelite covenant tradition, by G. Mendenhall, *Law and Covenant in Israel and the Ancient Near East*, 24–50 (reprinted from the *Biblical Archeologist*, XVII [1954], 50–76). "A striking formal characteristic of this section [the prologue to the treaty] is the 'I-thou' form of address. Since the Hittite king is the author of the covenant he speaks directly to the vassal. . . . The covenant form is still thought of as a personal relationship, rather than as an objective, impersonal statement of law" (*ibid.*, 33).

injunctions addressed to a plurality is the plural, and that is what we find in the Pharaonic decrees and the administrative correspondence of Babylonian and Assyrian kings, when a group is addressed. But in the Decalogue, and other laws in the same form, this unexpected and unprecedented[20] singular establishes contact, at a stroke, between the personal deity and each member of his people. The Israelite listening to these commandments cannot entirely sink his personality in the group. His private conscience is put under obligation, and he is held responsible for his own moral conduct. It is true, of course, that the concepts of collective guilt and collective responsibility remained vivid in Israelite thinking, but these must be balanced against the individual responsibility clearly implied in the Ten Words. From the start, a fundamental tenet of Yahwism was the dignity, and consequent duty, ascribed to each human being to whom God spoke.[21]

In the direct address of this preceptive imperfect form, the stress is laid less on the actual provision of the law, which may be something already long familiar, and more on the duty of obedience to a categorical and unquestionable command. Thus the significance of the Decalogue in the history of religion lies as much in its form as in its content. After all, the ethical commandments which make up its second half were for the most part not new: the prohibitions of neglect of aged parents, of murder, theft, and adultery, are common to most human societies, and certainly were no new revelation to the Hebrew tribes. But—along with the presumably novel prescriptions concerning the exclusive worship of a unique God and the peculiar aniconic character of his cult—they acquire a new meaning, and a new validity and binding force, from the mode of their enunciation. For instance, there was of course a condemnation and sanction for murder before the Decalogue was promulgated, but "Thou shalt not kill" is a new law, all the same, and one that the community as such could never have formulated. For it is uttered, implicitly in the first person, by a superhuman authority. It is true law, prescribing an obligatory norm of action to the members of a community, but its unconditioned and

[20]That is, unprecedented in its use in public law (see the preceding note). The Hittite Code itself makes no use of this direct address, remaining "an objective, impersonal statement of law."

[21]I am supposing an early date for the Decalogue, that is, roughly contemporary with the establishment of the tribal federation. If that be called in question, there is still the Book of the Covenant which can hardly be later than the Judges period. The argument rests not so much on the dating of specific laws as on the early existence in Israel of this preceptive imperfect *form* of law.

categoric character contrasts strongly with the conditioned, juridical, and non-moral character of cuneiform law, which said, equivalently, "If you do this, this will happen to you." If indeed this direct address was taken over from the existing international covenant convention, its adoption remains a stroke of genius on the part of the Israelite lawgiver. Presumably it was his own religious experience that taught him that only some such personal idiom would serve to express the character, and the will, of his God.

4. Yahweh the God of the Heavens

D. K. ANDREWS

"THE GOD OF THE HEAVENS" is a title for Yahweh found both in the Old Testament and in Aramaic papyri. The papyri in which the title occurs are letters and documents of a Jewish colony at Elephantine in Egypt written during the fifth century B.C.[1] Seventeen of the twenty-two instances of the title in the Old Testament occur in the books of Ezra, Nehemiah, and Daniel, and one each in Jonah, II Chronicles, and Psalm 136. The post-exilic date of these writings is either obvious or generally accepted. Thus, with the exception of two examples in Gen. 24: 3, 7, the expression appears only in documents of post-exilic date. The purpose of this paper is to review the use of the title, to inquire into its origin, and to consider its significance for post-exilic Judaism.[2]

I

The title appears in both Hebrew and Aramaic portions of the Old Testament. The Hebrew form *ʾᵉlôhê haššāmayim* is found nine times[3] and *ʾēl haššāmayim* once.[4] The equivalent Aramaic phrase *ʾᵉlāh šᵉmayyāʾ* occurs twelve times in Ezra and Daniel.[5] The papyri from Elephantine provide nine further examples of the Aramaic title.[6] In addition, variant forms of the title are found twice in the book of Daniel, namely: *melekh šᵉmayyāʾ* ("the King of the heavens")[7] and

[1]The papyri containing this title may be found in A. E. Cowley, *Aramaic Papyri of the Fifth Century B.C.* (Oxford, 1923), henceforth indicated by the abbreviation *AP*.

[2]The title has often been remarked by Old Testament scholars. Attention may be drawn in particular to A. Vincent, *La Religion des Judéo-Araméenes d'Eléphantine* (Paris, 1937), pp. 100–42, and O. Eissfeldt, "Baʿalšamēm und Jahwe," *Zeitschrift für die alttestamentliche Wissenschaft*, N.F. XVI (1939), 1–31.

[3]Gen. 24: 3, 7; Jonah 1: 9; Ezra 1: 2; Neh. 1: 4, 5; 2: 4, 20; II Chron. 36: 23.

[4]Ps. 136: 26.

[5]Dan. 2: 18, 19, 37, 44; Ezra 5: 11, 12; 6: 9, 10; 7: 12, 21, 23 (twice). Cf. also Dan. 2: 28, "a God in the heavens."

[6]*AP* 30: 2, 28; 31: [2], 27; 32: 4; 38: [2], 3, 5; 40: 1.

[7]Dan. 4: 34 (EVV 37).

mārēʾ šᵉmayyāʾ ("the Lord of the heavens").[8] It is striking that the latter variant should also occur once in the Aramaic papyri.[9]

It is obvious at once that the title occurs more often in Aramaic texts than in Hebrew. But a further significant fact emerges when the context of the Hebrew examples is considered. In most cases, they derive from and represent Aramaic terminology. Two of them belong to the decree of Cyrus quoted in II Chron. 36: 23 and Ezra 1: 2. Since the Persian kings used Aramaic as the official language for communication with the different parts of their empire,[10] the Hebrew text of this decree must represent a translation of the official Aramaic version or have been composed to imitate the style of such a document.

Four examples of the title occur in the "Memoirs" of Nehemiah. As an official in the Persian administration Nehemiah must have known Aramaic and been familiar with the Aramaic terminology used in carrying on the business of government. When he offered prayer to "the God of the heavens" while he was cupbearer to the Persian king in Susa (Neh. 1: 4, 5; 2: 4), he appears to have been using the language of a court official. It is worth noting that Dan. 2: 4, which states that the official interpreters of dreams at the court in Babylon addressed the king in Aramaic, reflects a popular tradition about the use of Aramaic by officials at the royal court. Later, when Nehemiah as governor of Judah informed Sanballat and other representatives of the Persian administration in Palestine that "the God of the heavens" would prosper the Jews, he was most likely addressing them or corresponding with them in the official Aramaic of the empire.

Even Jonah 1: 9 and Ps. 136: 26 may have an Aramaic context. The sailors to whom Jonah identified Yahweh as "the God of the heavens" would probably be considered familiar with Aramaic for its value as a language of international commerce. When the psalmist invited people to give thanks to "the God of the heavens" for the provision of food for "all flesh" he may have had a wider Aramaic-speaking audience in mind, not merely Hebrew-speaking Jews. Only the two examples in Gen. 24: 3 and 7 seem entirely devoid of Aramaic associations.

When consideration is given to the circumstances in which the title is used, a common pattern comes to light both in the Old Testament

[8] Dan. 5: 23.

[9] *AP* 30: 15.

[10] Cf. F. Rosenthal, *A Grammar of Biblical Aramaic* (Wiesbaden, 1961), p. 6; A. Jeffery, "Aramaic," *The Interpreter's Dictionary of the Bible* (New York, 1962), I, 186–8.

and the papyri. First, the title is used when Persian kings or officials refer to Yahweh. In his decree to the Jews, Cyrus stated that "Yahweh, the God of the heavens," had given him all the kingdoms of the earth (II Chron. 36: 23; Ezra 1: 2). Darius ordered his treasurers in Syria to provide animals, wheat, oil, wine, and salt out of the public treasury for daily sacrifices to "the God of the heavens" in Jerusalem (Ezra 6: 9, 10). Artaxerxes issued an official letter to Ezra describing him as "the scribe of the law of the God of the heavens" (Ezra 7: 12, 21). In it he directed that whatever "the God of the heavens" required for the sacrificial cultus in his temple should be provided by the Persian treasurers (Ezra 7: 23). When Bigvai, the Persian governor in Judah, replied to a petition from the Jews in Elephantine, he also used the title "the God of the heavens" rather than the divine name Yahu which was used by the Jews themselves (*AP* 32: 3 f.). In like fashion, the author of Daniel once represents Nebuchadnezzar speaking of "the King of the heavens" (4: 34; EVV 37).

Secondly, the title is occasionally found when Jews in the service of the Persian administration use the terminology customary to their office. The instance of Nehemiah praying to "the God of the heavens" while he was a palace official in Susa has been pointed out. In Dan. 2: 18, 19, where the context implies that the author had a court of the Persian type in mind, Daniel also prays to "the God of the heavens." In the Aramaic papyri the title is used in a letter by Maʿuziah b. Nathan (*AP* 38: 2, 3, 5) and in a letter by Hoshaʿiah b. Nathan (*AP* 40: 1). Since both were prominent scribes they may have been adopting an official formula.

The remaining examples of the title, with the exception of Gen. 24: 3, 7, occur where Jews are addressing Persian officials or other foreigners. When the Persian governor Tattenai came to Jerusalem to investigate building activities there, the Jews reported to him that they were "the servants of the God of the heavens" but that they had been handed over to Nebuchadnezzar by "the God of the heavens" when their fathers angered him (Ezra 5: 11, 12). In the Aramaic papyri the Jews at Elephantine used the title in addressing a petition to Bigvai the governor in Judah for help in rebuilding the temple of Yahu in Elephantine. They wished Bigvai health from "the God of the heavens," asserted that they prayed to "Yahu, the Lord of the heavens" (*mārēʾ šᵉmayyāʾ*), and promised him merit before "Yahu, the God of the heavens" for his assistance (*AP* 30: 2, 15, 27 f.; 31: 2, 27[11]). Likewise,

[11] *AP* 31 is a copy of *AP* 30.

Daniel informed King Nebuchadnezzar that "the God of the heavens" had given him his worldwide empire, but that in due course he would establish a new and indestructible kingdom (Dan. 2: 37, 44). Daniel also addressed Belshazzar accusing him of lifting himself up against "the Lord of the heavens" (*mārēʾ šᵉmayyāʾ*, Dan. 5: 23). In the case of Jonah 1: 9 it is not foreign officials, but ordinary sailors, who are addressed. In Ps. 136: 26 the invitation to give thanks to "the God of the heavens" is apparently addressed to "all flesh."

One negative observation must be made. Except for Gen. 24: 3, 7, the title is not used by Jews in a purely Jewish context. For the Jewish community God is identified by his name, Yahweh, and by titles such as "the God of Israel." In the book of Ezra, for example, the same Jewish community that told Tattenai they were "the servants of the God of the heavens" (5: 11) were addressed by prophets "in the name of the God of Israel" (5: 1). After the dedication of the second temple the people are described as worshipping "Yahweh, the God of Israel" (6: 21). Whereas Artaxerxes referred to Ezra as "the scribe of the law of the God of the heavens" (7: 12), the Hebrew author in the preceding verse described him as "the scribe of the words of the commandments of Yahweh" (7: 11). A somewhat similar situation exists in the Aramaic papyri. In documents which concern the local Jewish community by itself or in relationship to its neighbours in Elephantine, God is designated merely by his name "Yahu" or by the expression "Yahu the God." For example, *AP* 22 contains a list of men who gave money for "Yahu the God."

Before discussing the origin of the title, the two exceptional examples in Gen. 24: 3, 7 must be considered. If this chapter is correctly assigned to the Yahwist source with or without Elohist revisions, it would provide the only examples of the use of the title before the exile. Furthermore, it is here used by Abraham in speaking to his own servant within the confines of his own household; no aliens or foreign officials are involved. Its use in this chapter does not fit any of the categories for the use of the title in post-exilic times.

But the "title" in this chapter is exceptional in another way: it is only part of a longer expression. In verse 3 Abraham asked his servant to swear "by Yahweh, the God of the heavens and the God of the earth." In verse 7 Abraham promised the servant that "Yahweh, the God of the heavens" would send his angel to further his mission. The text in this verse is somewhat uncertain: one Hebrew manuscript lacks the phrase "the God of the heavens,"[12] and the Septuagint adds "and the God of the earth." In any case, the expression here appears to be a reflection of verse 3. This longer expression should not be confused with the post-exilic title. It provides a striking parallel to older Semitic oath formulae which invoked the great gods together with the gods of heaven and the gods of earth to witness oaths. For example, the stele of Zakir, king of Hamath in the eighth century B.C., invokes Baʿal-shemain, Ilwēr, Shamsh, Shahr, and the gods of heaven and the gods of earth.[13] The expression in Gen. 24: 3, 7 may be a Hebrew adaptation of such a formula, *ʾelôhê haššāmayim wēʾlôhê hāʾāreṣ* being regarded as a description of Yahweh rather than a reference to other gods. There is a subtle difference between designating Yahweh "the God of the heavens and the God of the earth" and calling him simply "the God of the heavens." The first suggests his lordship over the whole universe of heaven and earth; the second associates him with the sky whence he wields his authority over the earth.

II

Three possible explanations for the origin of the shorter post-exilic title present themselves. The first treats the older expression as the exemplar from which the shorter title was drawn. A. Vincent, in his book on the religion of the Elephantine Jews, claimed that the older expression was an early witness to monotheism in Israel, that it was never entirely forgotten by the Jews in Palestine or in Egypt, and that it was brought back into currency after the exile in order to place Yahweh on the same footing as the Persian "god of the sky." Since the Persian rulers regarded Ahura Mazda as a celestial god, the Jews revived the old title of Yahweh to gain favour for the Hebrew religion from the Persian administration.[14]

This explanation, however, overlooks the distinction between the two titles and does not give sufficient weight to the complete absence of either title in pre-exilic writings apart from the one chapter in Genesis. It is true that the Old Testament often states that Yahweh created the heavens and the earth and that he dwells in the heavens. But not once

[12]See O. Procksch, *Die Genesis* (Leipzig, 1913), p. 141, n. b; J. Skinner, *Genesis* (Edinburgh, 1910), p. 342.

[13]Cf. D. W. Thomas, ed., *Documents from Old Testament Times* (London, 1958), p. 247.

[14]"La Religion des Judéo-Araméenes," pp. 104–24, 142.

among these many statements does the epithet "the God of the heavens" appear. It may be significant that the Old Testament avoided localizing the domain of Yahweh. Thus, just as they never spoke of Yahweh as the God of Jerusalem or the God of the land of Israel,[15] so they may have avoided calling him "the God of the heavens" in pre-exilic times.

A second possibility is that, as E. G. Kraeling has suggested,[16] Yahweh absorbed the title of the god Baalshamin. Baalshamin was the great "lord of heaven" whose cult was increasingly popular throughout Syria from the twelfth century B.C. until early Christian times. Baalshamin is listed at the head of the pantheon in inscriptions byYehimilk of Byblos twelfth century B.C.) and by Zakir of Hamath (eighth century B.C.) and in Esarhaddon' treaty with Baʿal of Tyre (seventh century B.C.). The Phœnicians spread the cult of Baalshamin to Carthage and elsewhere in the Mediterranean world. From the first century B.C. until the fifth centuy A.D. inscriptions and literary references attest the worship of Baalshamin in the Hauran and Safa, at Palmyra, at Dura-Europas, and at Haran.[17]

The title *Baʿal Šāmayim* does not occur in the Old Testament. However, Eissfeldt has examined references to the god Baal in the Old Testament where the name occurs in the singular without any qualifying noun or adjective and has concluded that Baalshamin was the god intended in most cases. According to Eissfeldt, it was the cult of this god that posed the great threat to Yahwism in the ninth century under the house of Omri and in the seventh century under Manasseh. The Baal against whom Zephaniah and Jeremiah warned the people at the end of the seventh century would then be Baalshamin.[18]

At first it seems plausible that the epithet "the God of the heavens" was the Hebrew counterpart to the title of this popular pagan god. However, the fact remains that the epithet was not applied to Yahweh in the pre-exilic period. One may surmise that the antipathy towards the cult of Baalshamin was a factor militating against the application of his title to Yahweh. It was, as Eissfeldt points out,[19] only when the conditions of Persian rule rendered the cult of Baalshamin less of a

[15]Cf. W. Eichrodt, *The Theology of the Old Testament* (Philadelphia, 1961), I, 205.

[16]*The Brooklyn Museum Aramaic Papyri* (New Haven, 1953), p. 84.

[17]Eissfeldt, "Baʿalšamēm und Jahwe," pp. 1–14; Vincent, *La Religion des Judéo-Araméenes*, pp. 119–25.

[18]Eissfeldt, "Baʿalšamēm und Jahwe," pp. 14–26.

[19]*Ibid.*, p. 27.

threat to Yahwism that the Jews began to speak of Yahweh as "the God of the heavens."

A third explanation traces the origin of the title to the influence of Persian religion and the policies of the Persian government. As a god of the sky, Ahura Mazda enjoyed a pre-eminent place in the religion of the Persian rulers. From pre-Achaemenid time he was represented on tombs, palaces, and rock inscriptions as a figure emerging from a winged sun-disk and hovering in the air over the king, his foremost worshipper. There is a dearth of inscriptional material from Persia itself reflecting Cyrus' religious views, but in the many inscriptions of Darius and his successors Ahura Mazda is lauded as the great god, greater than all other gods, who made the sky, the earth, mankind, and all the blessings men enjoy.[20] It is obvious that a supreme deity of the character ascribed to Ahura Mazda would merit being called the god of the heavens, though the title does not occur in any extant inscription or written document from Persia.

The Persian rulers, however, did not force subject peoples to accept the cult of Ahura Mazda. Throughout the empire local cults were permitted to continue and were even supported by the government. Cyrus in his Cylinder inscription in Babylon acknowledged the authority of Marduk as the great lord who had made him ruler of the whole world.[21] In Ezra 1:2 he is credited with acknowledging Yahweh as the source of his power. Cambyses is said to have restored the revenues of the temple of Neith, and Darius issued a decree supporting the claims of the priests of Apollo at Magnesia. In general, Persian rulers displayed tolerance towards local customs and religions.

But their recognition of local cults was by no means universal. Cambyses reduced the revenues of many Egyptian temples, making it difficult for them to perpetuate their cults. According to the petition of the Elephantine Jews written a century later, Cambyses had actually destroyed other Egyptian temples (*AP* 30: 13 f.). After his accession, Xerxes banned the daeva cults in his native Persia. Later, in 482, after putting down a revolt in Babylon, he destroyed the temple and statue of Bel Marduk located in that city.[22] Apparently the tolerance of the Persian kings for local cults was tempered by theological and political factors. Their actions represent attempts to regularize the religious

[20]Cf. the tomb inscription of Darius at Naksh-i-Rustam, ll. 1–5. See R. G. Kent, "Old Persian Texts," *JNES*, IV (1945), 41.

[21]J. Pritchard, ed., *ANET*, p. 315.

[22]For the religious policies of the Persian kings, cf. A. T. Olmstead, *History of the Persian Empire* (Chicago, 1948), pp. 91, 156, 231–6.

life of their empire, and they were probably more disposed to recognize the cults of sky gods than those of other deities.

The practice of calling Yahweh "the God of the heavens" belongs in this context. On the part of Jewish petitioners it represents a claim that the cult of Yahweh qualified for recognition and support by the Persians, because Yahweh could be identified with "the God of the heavens." On the part of the Persian authorities it represents a recognition of this claim. The title, "the God of the heavens," represents a definition by which the Persian authorities tested the claims of the Jewish religion and determined its legitimacy. The origin of the title, therefore, should be sought in the diplomatic terminology of the Persian administration. Since it does not occur in any Persian inscription or written document describing the attributes and qualities of Ahura Mazda, it may have been developed specifically for government purposes. It was an apt definition of the character of Ahura Mazda which might be used by government officials to evaluate the deities of subject peoples and relate them to Ahura Mazda. If it were a term used in administrative circles, this would explain its use, not only in correspondence between Jews and Persian authorities, but also by office-bearing Jews like Nehemiah who used the language of a court official.

It is curious that the closest approximation to the title, "the God of the heavens," occurs not in Persian sources but in Herodotus' description of Persian religion. He reported that the Persians offered sacrifice on high mountain peaks to Zeus, "calling the whole vault of the sky Zeus" (*Hist.* I, 131). Herodotus' identification of the Persian sky god with Zeus has been explained on linguistic grounds as an equation of the name of the old Aryan sky god, *Dyēus* (*Diyauš* in Old Persian), with its natural Greek cognate.[23] But the Greek historian may have based his comment on the popular view of Ahura Mazda as the god of the sky which was disseminated by Persian officials. In such case, he was motivated by theological rather than linguistic considerations and presents an early illustration of the practice of identifying Zeus with other sky gods. In the same way, when the Greek language was introduced into Syria, inscriptions and other written documents employed the name Zeus as the counterpart of the Semitic Baalshamin for theological, not linguistic reasons.[24] The statement of Herodotus,

[23] J. H. Moulton, *Early Zoroastrianism* (London, 1913), pp. 391–3.
[24] Vincent, *La Religion des Judéo-Araméenes*, pp. 122 f., 139.

then, would reflect the same impression of the Persian god as those Jewish writings in which Persians acknowledge "the God of the heavens."

III

If the title originated in politico-religious circles as a definition to categorize deities of a certain type, it is pertinent to ask whether it has more than political value. Even Vincent, who regarded the title as an old Israelite epithet for Yahweh and as an early witness to a monotheistic faith, thought that it was used by post-exilic Jews mainly for political reasons. He concluded that it provided an ambiguous formula under cover of which the Jews got their way with the Persian rulers and re-established the cult of Yahweh.[25] This might account for its use in the Aramaic papyri and in Ezra, but it is too narrow to cover the whole range of uses of the title. It would not, for example, explain why Nehemiah in his "Memoirs" said that he offered his private devotions at Susa to "the God of the heavens."

However, it must be admitted that the title in itself did not possess great theological significance. It had a rather circumscribed usage in the Old Testament and never really found its way into the vocabulary of devotional literature of theological disputation. Thus, for example, the author of Daniel did not use it to advance the claims of Yahweh against the god of Antiochus Epiphanes whom he called *hassiqqûṣ m^{e}šōmēm*, "the desolating abomination" (11: 31; cf. 9: 27; 12: 11). Since *siqqūṣ*, "abomination," was used as a substitute to avoid pronouncing the name Baal (e.g. II Kings 23: 13), this abusive title is a thinly disguised corruption of *baʿal haššāmayim*, "the lord of the heavens." Though the author ridiculed the claim inherent in the name of the false god, he did not counter it with the claim that Yahweh was "the God of the heavens," but with the assertion that he was "the God of gods" (11: 36). Attempts to read too much into the title, "the God of the heavens," should, therefore, be avoided.

This title served, in the first place, to identify Yahweh as the supreme deity who is the ultimate source of all power and authority. Thus, Cyrus acknowledged that his authority to rule all the kingdoms of the earth derived from "Yahweh, the God of the heavens" (II Chron. 36: 23; Ezra 1: 2). When Jonah informed the sailors that he worshipped "Yahweh, the God of the heavens," the sailors were the

[25] *Ibid.*, p. 142.

more terrified to learn that Jonah's angry God was no local deity or guardian genius, but the original creator of sea and land (Jonah 1: 9). Even when the title was used by itself it had the same effect. Thus, Nebuchadnezzar was reminded that it was "the God of the heavens" who had made him "king of kings" and controlled the destiny of all kingdoms until his own everlasting kingdom would be established (Dan. 2: 37, 44). Though the deity's name is not given, his absolute authority is clearly stated.

The use of the title has a second implication, that post-exilic Jews recognized a genuine awareness of the true God among the Gentiles. Thus, where Jonah 1: 9 applies the title to Yahweh, it implies that the sailors had some knowledge of "the God of the heavens" and would, therefore, know to whom Jonah was referring. Ps. 137: 26 suggests that "all flesh" who received food from God would know "the God of the heavens" to whom they were urged to give thanks.

Gentile kings were frequently credited with an awareness of this God. According to Ezra 6: 6–10, Darius acknowledged the authority of this high God when he ordered his governor in Syria to permit the erection of a temple for his worship in Jerusalem and when he made provision for sacrifices to be presented there and for prayers to be offered on behalf of the king. Artaxerxes also acknowledged him when he appointed Ezra as "the scribe of the law of the God of the heavens," that is, as a secretary or representative of the king to supervise religious affairs in Judah.[26] He gave Ezra power to regularize the cult of "the God of the heavens" in Jerusalem in accordance with the religious practice authorized by the law of God and to enforce obedience to the law of God and the law of the king. Like Darius, he also ordered that financial support and materials for sacrifice be provided for the practice of the cult of "the God of the heavens" in Jerusalem (Ezra 7: 12–26). According to Dan. 2: 37, 44, Daniel addressed King Nebuchadnezzar as if he knew that "the God of the heavens" controlled the destiny of the nations. Nebuchadnezzar, in his turn, blessed "the Most High" whose sovereignty could not be questioned and gave honour to him as "the King of the heavens" whose ways were just (4: 31, 34 [EVV 34, 37]).

Second Isaiah presents a similar point of view with regard to Cyrus. While Second Isaiah ridiculed the idol worshippers in Babylonia in

[26]H. H. Schaeder, *Esra der Schreiber* (Tuebingen, 1930), pp. 45 f.

the reign of Nabonidus,[27] there is no evidence that the religion of Cyrus came under the same condemnation. Second Isaiah spoke of Cyrus with approval in 44: 28 and 45: 1–3. Many commentators find an allusion to Cyrus in Second Isaiah's description of a person whom Yahweh roused from the east and called in righteousness to his service (41: 2; 45: 13).[28] The reference to righteousness parallels the emphasis that the kings of Persia placed on doing right.[29] Mal. 1: 11, which dates from the early fifth century B.C., also speaks with approval of the sacrificial worship offered by people throughout the world from the farthest east to the west.[30]

But not all Gentiles were credited with a knowledge of "the God of the heavens." Second Isaiah's criticism of the Babylonian idol worshippers under Nabonidus has been mentioned above. Dan. 5: 1–31 describes Belshazzar's insolent attitude toward "the Lord of the heavens." More often the king is reported to have recognized "the God of the heavens," while his officials oppose him. In Ezra and Nehemiah it was the governor of Syria and the Persian officials in Samaria, Trans-Jordan, and the Negeb who carried on investigations, made accusations, and hindered the building of the temple in Jerusalem. In Dan. 6: 1–28, the king did not willingly persecute those who worshipped "the God of the heavens," but jealous and scheming courtiers tricked him into a mistaken religious programme which he later corrected.

These facts suggest that a genuine knowledge of "the God of the heavens" was detected in some people and in some cults but not in others. One may conjecture that the cult of Baalshamin in Syria, the cause of so much religious conflict before the exile, remained anathema to the Jews throughout this period, even before it was forced on Jerusalem in Hellenized form by Antiochus Epiphanes in 168 B.C. Passages which portray a genuine religious knowledge in the Persian

[27]It is significant that Dan. 5: 1–31 condemns Nabonidus' son Belteshazzar for failing to glorify the true God and that both the cuneiform verse account of Nabonidus and the Clergy of Babylon and the Cyrus Cylinder denounce Nabonidus' religious policies. Cf. Pritchard, ed. *ANET*, pp. 312–16. Thus, both biblical and extra-biblical records agree in their censure of the regime of Nabonidus.

[28]Cf. J. Muilenburg, in *The Interpreter's Bible*, V, 449 f., 523.

[29]Cf. Darius' statement in the Naksh-i-Rustam inscription, "By the favour of Ahura Mazda I am of such a sort that I am a friend of the right. I am not a friend of the wrong." See *JNES*, IV (1945), 41.

[30]Cf. R. C. Dentan, in *The Interpreter's Bible*, VI, 1128–9.

kings reflect the situation before the end of the fifth century. In the fourth century the Persian kings appear in the role of vindictive despots rather than benevolent overlords. Religious factors may have played a part in this change of attitude. The cults of Mithra and Anahita had grown in popularity among the Persians and had received official recognition by Artaxerxes II at the end of the fifth century. There could be no tolerance of a religion that included the cults of the sun god Mithra and the mother-goddess Anahita. Obviously, a genuine awareness of "the God of the heavens" was not found indiscriminately in all cults, but only in those that conformed to certain standards.

But, though the title did imply the existence of genuine religious knowledge outside of Judaism, it was used in such a way as to indicate a special knowledge within Judaism. The title, which suggests only a general awareness of a supreme god, was used as a substitute for the divine name in correspondence with foreigners. Within the religious community God was known by the divine name Yahweh and by more distinctive epithets, for example, "Yahweh, the God of our fathers" (Ezra 7: 27). Even the instructions of Artaxerxes to Ezra speak of "the law of your God," knowledge of which distinguished the Jews from the other citizens of the empire (Ezra 7: 25).

Only once in the Old Testament does a foreigner who is not a convert to Yahwism use the divine name as well as the title. This was Cyrus in his decree to the Jews (II Chron. 36: 23; Ezra 1: 2). The genuineness of this decree has been much debated but, whether genuine or not, it does reflect Persian court style and is not inconsistent with other documents deriving from Cyrus.[31] The assertion in this decree that Yahweh had given him his empire is paralleled by the statement on the Cyrus Cylinder that Marduk "pronounced the name of Cyrus, King of Anshan, declared him to be the ruler of all the world."[32] The use of the divine name Yahweh would not be more unusual in writing to the Jews than the use of the name Marduk in Babylonian documents.

That Cyrus did issue decrees with the name of Yahweh may be reflected in the phrase *yiqrāʾ bhišᵉmî* in Isa. 41: 25. This is usually translated, "he shall call on my name." The verse apparently refers to Cyrus. Many commentators interpret it as a reference to the eventual conversion of Cyrus to Yahwism. Skinner wrote, "The clause can

[31]Cf. R. A. Bowman, in *The Interpreter's Bible*, III, 570 f.
[32]See Pritchard, ed., *ANET*, p. 315.

hardly mean less than that Cyrus will acknowledge Jehovah as God."[33] However, as Sidney Smith points out,[34] the idiom does not mean "call on the name" elsewhere in Second Isaiah, but rather "call with the name." The verse really states, "From the east he calls with my name." That is, as in the decree in Ezra, Cyrus made proclamations to the Jews using the name of Yahweh.

Unless the use of the names Marduk and Yahweh by Cyrus is to be discounted as nothing but political propaganda, it must represent an identification of the various gods as local manifestations of one divine being or of a coherent pantheon. The inclusion of the decree in the Old Testament implies that Cyrus identified Yahweh with "the God of the heavens" and it does not question the sincerity of his motives. However, Isa. 45: 3, 4, suggests that the knowledge which Cyrus possessed of Yahweh was still incomplete. This passage speaks of Yahweh calling Cyrus by name, but Cyrus did not realize it. It expresses the hope that the effect of his victories might lead to his recognition of Yahweh's role in history. Thus, even in the case of Cyrus, the difference between the Gentile and the Jew is clear. The one possesses a knowledge of God as the great Sovereign whose power is supreme and universal, embodied in the title, "the God of the heavens"; the other an intimate knowledge of the purposes of Yahweh and of his purpose embodied in the expression, "Yahweh, the God of our fathers." (Ezra 7: 27).

[33]J. Skinner, *Isaiah Chapters XL–LXVI* (Cambridge, 1929), p. 26; cf. Muilenburg, in *The Interpreter's Bible*, V, 462.

[34]S. Smith, *Isaiah Chapters XL–LV* (London, 1944), p. 161.

5. Proto-Septuagint Studies*

J. W. WEVERS

IN 1941 HARRY ORLINSKY published a paper under a similar title which he dedicated to his teacher, the late Max Margolis.[1] The paper was occasioned by a fundamental attack on the positions and methodology of the Lagardian school of Septuagint criticism, of which Margolis was so distinguished a member, on the part of Paul Kahle and his disciple, Alexander Sperber.

Paul de Lagarde devoted a great part of his fabulous career to inaugurating a programme of scholarly textual study and publication which was to eventuate in the recovery of the original text of the Septuagint. From various notices in the Church Fathers[2] it would appear that in the course of the third and early fourth centuries the Greek Old Testament had undergone three extensive revisions. The work of Origen on its text is best known, he himself having described in somewhat cryptic terms his own textual work in his *Commentary on Matthew* and in a letter to Rufinus.[3] His textual work issued in the *Hexapla*, a monument to misguided industry. Origen realized that the Greek Old Testament had undergone extensive corruptions resulting in a text which at times differed widely from the original Hebrew. In order to bring order out of this chaotic state of affairs he prepared his *Hexapla.*

Wherever the Old Greek differed quantitatively from the Hebrew, Origen provided a key. When a word or phrase occurred in the Greek for which no equivalent obtained in his Hebrew text, its onset was marked with an obelus, and its end with a metobelus. Obviously these marks in the text could hardly matter much. Far more serious, however, was Origen's work where the Greek text was shorter than the

*A paper given as presidential address to the Oriental Club of Toronto in March, 1960. In a sense this study is a popular sequel to the author's "Septuaginta-Studien," *Theologische Rundschau*, N.F., XXII (1954), 85–138, 171–90.

[1] Harry M. Orlinsky, "On the Present State of Proto-Septuagint Studies," *JAOS*, LXI (1941), 81–91; incidentally Orlinsky was himself a student of Meek.

[2] E.g., Clement of Alexandria, Eusebius, Jerome.

[3] See also his comments *ad Africanus* 5.

Hebrew. Here Origen would add from one or another of the other three translators,[4] and mark the addition with an asterisk and metobelus as well as with the column(s) from which the reading was borrowed. It is usually presupposed that Origen's work was thus purely quantitative in character. It is also suggested that his knowledge of Hebrew was not overly profound.[5] There is some evidence which seems to suggest that Origen did more than that: that he occasionally changed word order, as well as words where he felt that the Old Greek was in error.[6] One suspects that when the Old Greek was obviously wrong, Origen sometimes changed it to a word found in one of the other three translators. Naturally he could not do this too often, since this would have created a furore in the Church which believed in the inspiration of the Greek Old Testament. Furthermore there was no sign available to indicate changes of this kind.

The *Hexapla* was much too bulky to be copied in its entirety, but some fifty copies of the fifth column were ordered for Constantinople,[7] and this is where real chaos began. Copyists did not always understand Origen's signs; many were thus lost in transcription, others were misplaced, and the resulting work is a field day for modern critics.[8] Somewhat later two other recensions were commissioned, one, in Egypt, and the other in Antioch. About the former little is known; it was undertaken by Hesychius, a shadowy figure reputedly martyred

[4]I.e., Aquila, Symmachus, and Theodotion. For the history of the Septuagint text in greater detail see the author's article, "Septuagint," in *The Interpreter's Dictionary of the Bible*, IV (New York, 1962).

[5]E.g., H. B. Swete, *An Introduction to the Old Testament in Greek*, revised by R. L. Ottley. (Cambridge, 1914), p. 61. For a more recent study, see H. M. Orlinsky, "The Columnar Order of the Hexapla," *Jewish Quarterly Review* N.S., XXVII (1936–7), 137 ff.

[6]An examination of MSS. Alex and x in Samuel-Kings shows a number of instances of word order corrected in the direction of the Masoretic text (MT). Though individually Alex and x show peculiarities, they (together with the Armenian and Syro-Hexaplar) constitute the best evidence in these books for the Hexaplaric recension. It would be interesting to check the text of these MSS. against "the Three" with the possibility of unmarked changes in mind.

[7]Eusebius, *Vita Constantini* iv. 36 f.

[8]Such confusion reigns that even the best manuscripts show mixed readings. For such Hexaplaric materials in Codex Vaticanus (generally considered our best evidence for a pre-Origenian text; cf. S. Silberstein, in *Zeitschrift für die alttestamentliche Wissenschaft* (*ZATW*), XIII (1893), 1–75, XIV (1894), 1–30; H. S. Gehman, "Old Ethiopic Version of I Kings and its affinities," *JBL*, L (1931), 81–114; and note 11 *infra*), but naturally without Origenian signs; see J. W. Wevers, "A Study in the Textual History of Codex Vaticanus," *ZATW*, LXIV (1952), 178–89.

in A.D. 311/2.[9] The latter is universally attributed to Lucian, martyred about the same time as Hesychius.[10] Fortunately for us, two Syrians, Chrysostom and Theodoret, published many of their sermons and commentaries, and since both of them used the Lucianic text as their Greek Bible it is relatively simple to establish which extant manuscripts represent this recensional text. For example, for the books of Samuel-Kings five manuscripts (boc_2e_2; HP 19, 82, 93, 108, and 127) were well known to Lagarde as being Lucianic in character. To this must now be added MS. r (HP 700) for Samuel.[11] The best evidence among the Fathers for Hesychius is the text of Cyril of Alexandria. Unfortunately for Septuagint scholars Cyril occupied himself largely with the New Testament, the Prophets, and with Nestorianism, and the Hesychian text is therefore not yet established for most of the Old Testament as it is, for example, for Ezekiel.

Returning to Lagarde, we note that his programme entailed the unscrambling of these three recensions as the first step towards restoring the original text of the Septuagint.[12] To that end he published his *Librorum Veteris Testamenti Canonicorum, pars prior* in 1883. This presumed to be the Lucianic text of Genesis through Esther. Lagarde, however, did not fully realize that a manuscript which is Lucianic in one book may change its textual character completely in some other book. The result is that though for Samuel-Kings the Lagarde volume is more or less adequate, it is almost useless for the Pentateuch, since the manuscripts mentioned above as Lucianic for Samuel-Kings are not Lucianic for the Pentateuch. Lagarde, however, simply accepted these manuscripts as representive of the Lucianic text throughout.[13]

After the lamented death of Lagarde in 1891, the programme was carried forward by Alfred Rahlfs, and the Goettingen Society has continued to edit various books of the Old Testament in accordance

[9]Eusebius, *Historia ecclesiastica* viii.13.7. Orlinsky wrongly objects to this characterization of Hesychius in "Studies in the Septuagint of the Book of Job, IV," *Hebrew Union College Annual*, XXXIII (1962), n. 6 (pp. 120 f.).

[10]*Ibid.*, ix.6.3. Most of our scanty knowledge about the recensions of Hesychius and Lucian comes from Jerome; for references cf. Swete, *Introduction to Old Testament in Greek*, p. 78 ff.

[11]J. W. Wevers, "A Study in the Hebrew Variants in the Book of Kings," *ZATW*, LXI (1945–8), 46 f.

[12]Cf. his *Ankündigung einer neuen Ausgabe der griechischen Uebersetzung des alten Testaments* (Göttingen, 1882).

[13]Cf. *Librorum Veteris Testamenti Canonicorum*, I, v, vi, where Lagarde quotes with approval Vercellone's statement that HP 19, 82, 93, and 108 "unum idemque ἀντίγραφον ad singularem quandam recensionem spectans repraesentare."

with the principles laid down by Lagarde. At present this work is being carried forward by the indefatigable Joseph Ziegler and his associates.[14]

Basic to the work of this school, which included such outstanding textual scholars as the author's academic grandfather, James Montgomery,[15] and his immediate teacher, Henry S. Gehman,[16] is the working hypothesis that eventually some kind of parent text can be restored. In other words, it is held that behind the recensions lies some kind of common text. It is of course not denied that other translations existed for certain parts of the Old Testament. Origen used three anonymous versions beyond those of Aquila, Symmachus, and Theodotion, called simply the Quinta, Sexta, and Septima. Another anonymous version is the famous version of Hab., chapter 3, in the Codex Barberinus (also found in three other manuscripts).[17] Incidentally a colophon attached to Barberinus reads: "I found the Song of Habakkuk agreeing neither with the LXX nor with Aquila, Symmchus, or Theodotion. You might investigate then whether it be the translation of Quinta or Sexta." De Montfaucon states categorically that remnants of Quinta and Sexta are at variance with the text of Anonymous, though he cites only Quinta readings to prove his point, and suggests that it could be the Septima.[18] The fact is: nobody knows. For the books of Judges and Tobit most scholars believe that rival translations are represented in our manuscripts, and the fact that the Theodotion text of Daniel was adopted by the Christian Church as the canonical text in favour of the Septuagint text is well known to Septuagint scholars.[19] In fact, only two manuscripts, a late Chigi MS. and now the Chester Beatty papyrus (968) represent the

[14]Thus far the following critical editions have appeared: I. *Genesis*; IX.1. *Maccab. liber I*; IX.2. *Maccab. liber II*; X. *Psalmi cum Odis*; XIII. *Duodecim Prophetae*; XIV. *Isaias*; XV. *Ieremias, Baruch, Threni, Epistula Ieremiae*; XVI.1. *Ezechiel*; XVI.2. *Daniel, Susanna, Bel et Draco*. For an evaluation of these cf. Wevers, "Septuaginta-Studien," pp. 95 ff.

[15]Especially in the *International Critical Commentary* (*ICC*) volumes on *Daniel* and *Kings*.

[16]Cf. bibliography in Wevers, "Septuaginta-Studien," 86.

[17]E. M. Good, "The Barberini Greek Version of Habbakuk iii," *Vetus Testamentum* IX (1959), 11–30; M. L. Margolis, "Character of the Anonymous Greek Version of Habbakuk 3," *Old Testament and Semitic Studies in Memory of William Rainey Harper* (Chicago, 1908), I, 133–42.

[18]*Hexaplorum Origenis quae Supersunt.* II. *Notae & variae Lectiones ad Cap. III Habacuc. v.1* (Paris, 1713). The actual text of de Montfaucon is "Esse vero septimam Editionem vix est quod dubitemus."

[19]For a thorough discussion of the Greek texts cf. J. A. Montgomery, *Daniel* (*ICC*), 25 ff.

presumably older text. Thus the fact that other translations existed alongside that of the Septuagint is admitted by everyone.

Kahle and his disciples, however, attacked the basic hypothesis of this classical school of Septuagint criticism. In 1915 Kahle published an article in *Theologische Studien und Kritiken* entitled "Untersuchungen zur Geschichte des Pentateuchtextes." The article deals successively with the Samaritan Pentateuch, the Septuagint, and the Hebrew text. In later articles and finally in *The Cairo Geniza* (The Schweich Lectures for 1941) he restates the problem and his own conclusions in greater detail.

Kahle begins with an analysis and reinterpretation of the Aristeas Letter. The story contained in this letter to Philocrates is well known. Since the work of Hody in 1705[20] (that is, for over two and one-half centuries) this Letter has been recognized as a pseudepigraphon. It was certainly written by a Jew as his devotion to Judaism, his interest in the topography of Jerusalem, the temple and its ritual and furnishings, as well as his general Jewish outlook, conclusively prove.[21] Furthermore there are numerous historical inaccuracies in the Letter. Demetrius of Phalerum was never chief librarian at Alexandria, and particularly not under Ptolemy Philadelphus whose displeasure he had incurred. When Philadelphus became king he promptly banished Demetrius for having been so unfortunate as to have supported the wrong son of Soter for the succession, understandably an unpardonable political sin. Another lapse impossible for a contemporary is the representation of Menedemus of Eretria at the royal banquet, a ghostly affair if true since that worthy had died two years before Soter did. Another observation which is often made is the use of Septuagint phraseology throughout Aristeas' description of the temple furnishings and ritual.[22] It would appear that the Septuagint had been in favour and use for some time when this Letter was written.

In fact the whole tone of the Letter militates against its historicity. That Philadelphus may have been interested in adding a copy of the Jewish laws to his library is plausible, but he would hardly have

[20]H. Hody, *Contra historiam LXX, interpretum Aristeae nomine inscriptam dissertatio*, in his *De Bibliorum textibus originalibus. . . .* (Oxon.). The work originally appeared in 1684, but its inclusion in the later work made Hody's formidable attack well-known to Biblical scholars.

[21]Cf. the succinct summary of arguments for its pseudepigraphic character in *Aristeas to Philocrates* (*Letter of Aristeas*), edited and translated by M. Hadas (New York, 1951), pp. 5–9.

[22]*Ibid.*, 182 ff. Interpreted differently by W. W. Tarn, *The Greeks in Bactria and India* (Cambridge, 1938), pp. 414 ff.

engaged in various theological speculations with the translators,[23] or have admitted the superiority of Jewish monotheism.[24] The origins of the Septuagint are to be sought not in the bibliophile interests of the Egyptian ruler but rather in the needs of the Jewish community of Alexandria in the century following Alexander's conquest. Hebrew was becoming more and more difficult for the Greek-speaking members of the diaspora, and the need for a Greek Targum led to the Septuagint.

Kahle has interpreted this Letter somewhat differently.[25] He believes that the Letter was written *circa* 100 B.C. (which may be true, though I think it a bit earlier) as a piece of Jewish propaganda for a standard recension of the Greek Pentateuch rather than for the original translation. He maintains that an official revision of the text was carried out in the second half of the second century B.C., and that this Letter was written to ensure its popular reception. Propaganda, he states, is only written for something that is contemporary; thus fixing the date of the Letter also gives one the date of the recension. He believes that the Letter actually contains evidence for his theory. In Section 30 occurs a passage in Demetrius' report to the king which Kahle translates as follows: "The books of the Law of the Jews (with some few others) are absent. They are written in the Hebrew characters and language and have been carelessly interpreted and do not represent the original text as I am informed by those who know; for they have never had a king's care to protect them."[26] There are two clauses in this translation which need closer examination: "They have been carelessly interpreted" and "they do not represent the original text."

[23]Cf. H. G. Meecham, *The Letter of Aristeas; A Linguistic Study with Special Reference to the Greek Bible* (Manchester, 1935), 316–24. Meecham has collected 24 apparent instances of borrowing by the Letter as well as a number of possible reminiscences and allusions which are by themselves not convincing, since these merely demonstrate familiarity with the biblical (not necessarily the Greek) text. What is of real importance, however, is the demonstration that the Letter was familiar only wih the Greek Pentateuch, and not with the rest of the Greek Old Testament. In my own comparison of the 3 Kingdoms, chapters 6–7, account of the temple and its furnishings with *Aristeas*, 57–82, I could find no evidence of literary relation between the two accounts, whereas the correspondence between *Aristeas* and Exod. 25:23 f. seems completely convincing.

[24]Cf. particularly Demetrius's reply to the king's query concerning the reason for previous silence by historians and poets concerning *τηλικούτων συντετελεσμένων* (312): *διὰ τὸ σεμνὴν εἶναι τὴν νομοθεσίαν καὶ διὰ θεοῦ γεγονέναι καὶ τῶν ἐπιβαλλομένων τινὲς ὑπὸ τοῦ θεοῦ πληγέντες τῆς ἐπιβολῆς ἀπέστησαν* (313).

[25]*The Cairo Geniza* (The Schweich Lectures, 1941; London, 1947), pp. 132 ff.

[26]*Ibid.*, pp. 135 f.

The original text here reads: *ἀμελέστερον δὲ καὶ οὐχ ὡς ὑπάρχει σεσήμανται.* Kahle maintains that *σεσήμανται* (from *σημαίνω*) refers to earlier translations which in itself is possible. The word is certainly ambiguous and can refer either to careless (*ἀμελέστερον*) transmission of the Hebrew text, or to (careless) interpretations, that is, translations. It is suggested that the reference to careless transmission of the Hebrew text could be of no concern to Ptolemy which is of course quite true but not germane to the argument. It is only germane if the conditions of the Letter are historically genuine, and Kahle quite rightly agrees that they are not. It is a Jewish writer, and such a writer would be very much interested in the state of the Hebrew text. In fact, I would suggest that the poor state of the text to be translated was the actual reason for having a Hebrew text sent for from Jerusalem. Certainly the most natural meaning of *σημαίνειν* is "to indicate." If the Hebrew laws are rather carelessly "indicated," it would probably refer to their present state.

The argument, however, hinges on the explanatory words which intervene—*καὶ οὐχ ὡς ὑπάρχει*—and which Kahle loosely renders by "and do not represent the original text." The words literally mean "and not as they really are"—not a particularly clear elucidation of *ἀμελέστερον*. This to my mind means one of two things: either the Hebrew text is bad and does not represent the pure text as it presumably existed in the holy city, or the Alexandrian Jews are accustomed carelessly to interpret the Hebrew text orally and therefore did not get at the real meaning of the text. As a cornerstone for a theory of diverse translations existing in Alexandra *circa* 100 B.C. this interpretation of Kahle is tenuous.[27]

Kahle also refers[28] to a statement in Section 314 of the Letter where reference is made to Theopompus of Chios, reputedly at home in various exotic literatures. Theopompus "was about to introduce rashly into his history certain material previously translated from the Law"[29]

[27]Hadas, ed., *Aristeas*, translates *σεσήμανται* by "committed to writing." Meecham, *Letter of Aristeas*, as does Frankel, *Vorstudien zu der Septuaginta* (Leipzig, 1841), p. 24, admits the rendering "interpret" as possible, thus as Kahle making it refer to a former translation. But the most natural interpretation in the context is careless *oral* interpretation, such as a written text would obviate. The passage is certainly obscure and ought not to be used as an argument for anything. Cf. also H. M. Orlinsky, in *Crozer Quarterly*, xxix (1952), 205.

[28]*The Cairo Geniza*, p. 136.

[29]*διότι μέλλων τινὰ τῶν προηρμηνευμένων ἐπισφαλέστερον ἐκ τοῦ νόμου προσιστορεῖν*—Hadas, ed., *Aristeas*, 314.

and became mentally ill as a result of his tampering with holy things. This is precisely the kind of high-flown fairy tale which one might expect from the writer of this legend. It is hardly proper to press the point of the previously translated material from the Law. Theopompus lived in the time of Soter, and the matter is pure invention. Furthermore in Section 316 the poet Theodectos is related as also having been afflicted. When he was about to put *τι τῶν ἀναγεγραμμένων ἐν τῇ βίβλῳ* (something recorded in the book) into one of his plays, he was afflicted with a cataract. That too is fancy. It is meaningless as far as Kahle's argument is concerned. But even if such other translations or partial translations were present, it would make no difference. The real point is that they were never accepted.

It should be remembered that Philo records an annual feast held on the Island of Pharos to commemorate the events producing the Septuagint. This feast was not limited to Jews only but also "multitudes of others cross the water, both to do honour to the place in which the light of that version first shone out, and also to thank God for the good gift so old yet ever young."[30] The tradition was apparently an old one, and one feels that more than a recension of the Greek Old Testament was here at stake.

One objection to Kahle's reconstruction which apparently has never been raised is that if the revision was made as late as *circa* 100 B.C. it is extraordinary that the work should have been limited to the Pentateuch. According to the Prologue of the Greek text of Ben Sirach the Prophets were part of the canon. Reference is made to "the Law and the Prophets and the rest of the books." This phrase occurs in the context of a discourse on the difficulties of translation from Hebrew into Greek. The full statement reads: "and not only these, but the Law itself, and the prophecies, and the rest of the books, have no small difference when they are spoken in their original form."[31] This was written in 132 B.C. The Alexandrian canon at this time included the Prophets, and one wonders why, were Aristeas referring to a new revision, he did not include the Prophets. If on the other hand the writer is referring to the event of the original translation, about which by the writer's time all kinds of apocryphal accretions had grown, the reference is clear. The event may well be third century B.C., even

[30] *De Vita Mosis* ii. 41, according to F. H. Colson's translation.

[31] *οὐ μόνον δὲ ταῦτα. ἀλλὰ καὶ αὐτὸς ὁ νόμος καὶ αἱ προφητεῖαι καὶ τὰ λοιπὰ τῶν βιβλίων οὐ μικρὰν ἔχει τὴν διαφορὰν ἐν ἑαυτοῖς λεγόμενα*—*Prolog. Sir.* 14–16.

though the romance itself was written in the latter half of the second century B.C.

Up to this point the argument between Kahle and the Lagarde school has been purely speculative, Kahle's objections hinging on a rather dubious interpretation of an obscure passage. If Kahle's frontal attack is to stand, some evidence of these presumed translations out of which the "standard" text emerged will have to be forthcoming. Kahle bases his argument mainly on two types of text—that of Philo, and that of the New Testament. The most recent work on Philo's text is that of Peter Katz.[32] Most of the following argument in connection with Philo summarizes and is based on Katz's observations.

It has long been known that the dominant Bible text in Philonic manuscripts is Septuagintal. Certain manuscripts, however, particularly MSS. U and F,[33] have a non-Septuagintal text which has been a constant source of trouble to Septuagint scholars. This aberrant text is on the whole much closer to the Masoretic text but it is not to be identified with that of the literalistic Aquila with which it does have a great deal in common. The real question is which is the text that Philo himself had. Most Philonic scholars from Mangey's edition[34] (over 200 years ago) down to the excellent work of Cohn-Wendland[35] have concluded that the UF text is that of an interpolator, an editor who changed the Bible text of Philo to agree with the particular translator or recension which he followed.

One of the most remarkable books on Philo to appear since the Cohn-Wendland edition was the Greifswald thesis of August Schröder.[36] Schröder was guided in his thesis by the Greifswald classicist, Gehrke, who apparently knew neither Hebrew nor anything about Philo. Gehrke had been stimulated by a shortlived attack on Cohn-Wendland by Eberhard Nestle[37] who had supported the aberrant text on the grounds that it was closer to the Hebrew. The Septuagint, Nestle felt, was a later adaptation to Christian usage. Philo on the other hand

[32] *Philo's Bible: The Aberrant Text of Bible Quotations in Some Philonic Writings and its Place in the Textual History of the Greek Bible* (Cambridge, 1950).

[33] Vat. graec. 381 and Laurent. plut. 85, cod. 10 resp.

[34] *Philonis Judaei Opera*, edited by T. Mangey (2 vols., London, 1742).

[35] *Philonis Alexandrini Opera quae supersunt*, edited by L. Cohn and P. Wendland (6 vols., Berlin, 1896–1915).

[36] *De Philonis Alexandrini Vetere Testamento* (Greifswald, 1907). I am here dependent on Katz, having been unable to find a copy.

[37] "Zur neuen Philo-Ausgabe," *Philologus*, N.F. XIII (1900), 256 ff. with which compare his later reflections in *ibid.*, XIV (1901), 271 ff.

was a Jewish author and would be interested in a text closer to the Hebrew. Therefore the text of UF was the text of Philo.

Schröder set out to prove that the text of UF was earlier than the Septuagint. The result is an excellent example of how a dissertation should not be done. First of all, his work is limited to two treatises, viz., *de sacr. Abel et Cain* and *Quod Deus sit immut.* This is hardly sufficient material for a major thesis. Furthermore, the work is incredibly naïve.[38] After five pages of Preface "of a painfully elementary character," filled with errors, there follows the "magna tabula" for 27 pages in which 108 passages from these two treatises are simply listed in 8 columns. In each case the Philonic text is given with its UF variants, then that of the Septuagint with its variants, the ancient versions, including the Old Latin and Samaritan. The context is never consulted. Katz says: "Obviously the idea never struck him that his task was to obtain from Philo's exposition the standards of decision as to which form of quotation might be Philo's own. Thus he is able to deal with the isolated quotations by themselves, without ever considering that they form part of a context. If we call to mind the meticulous adherence of Philo's exposition to the quoted words, down to the very vocables, from which he extricates his special interpretation, we realize that Schröder has utterly failed to see the real implications of his task."

The conclusions of his fifty-page monograph of which over half is simply a listing of passages without comment were as follows:

1. The two forms of text are so different that only the one could have come by a deliberate modification of the other.
2. If the UF text is secondary, the sources for it must have been the same throughout. This could not have been either one of "the Three" or the Hebrew.
3. Since we know of no Greek text from which that of UF could have been modified, it represents the most ancient known form of the Old Testament in Greek. The other MSS. corrected to the Septuagint.
4. From Josephus, the Old Latin, and Justin we know that there were other translations existing at an early date.
5. A Pauline parallel at Eph. 5:2 based on Num. 28:2 where, for *qorbān*, προσφοράν is used (also occurring in the UF text), whereas in the Septuagint δῶρα occurs. (I might add parenthetically that the verb προσφέρετε governs the word which might independently have given rise to the Pauline προσφοράν.)

[38]What follows here simply summarizes Katz, *Philo's Bible*, 134 ff.

6. This Pauline parallel proves the text of UF to be the most ancient and also the one used by Philo himself.

These conclusions of Schröder are obviously worthless. The aberrant text is to be found in the lemmata which head the expositions, a fact which Schröder neither indicated nor took into consideration. Had he noted the context, that is, read the exposition of the lemmata, he would soon have noted that the text presupposed in the exposition was not that of UF but that of the Septuagint. In other words, the problem of which was the actual text which Philo used could have been simply solved by reading the expositions. The position of serious Philonic scholars, namely that Philo's Bible was Septuagint, would simply have been demonstrated once again instead of being challenged in such a fashion.

The question of the origin of the aberrant text is of course still pertinent. It is clear that the text is at least partially dependent on Aquila though not identical to it. Katz believes that its source is the so-called R (or Reviser) source which Rahlfs found in the book of Ruth.[39] Though independent of Origen's work, it does show the result of methods similar to those used by Origen. That this text was a revision is clear from the sporadic character of its text. Apparently it is a revision of the Septuagint on the basis of an Aquila-like text rather than a separate translation.[40]

But what about Schröder's thesis that the texts of Josephus, the Old Latin, and Justin prove that non-Septuagint translations existed alongside that of the Septuagint at an early date? The problem of Justin's text has long been difficult. Many felt that Justin often adapted his text to his argument; in other words, that there never was a received text at the basis of his *Dialogue* and *Apologies*. This suspicion has at least in part been removed by Père Barthélemy who published some fragments of the Minor Prophets in Greek found by the Taʿamire Bedouin.[41] This text has a peculiar affinity to that of Justin, and what

[39]This suggestion is attractive but difficult to demonstrate since this Reviser text for the Pentateuch has not yet been identified (i.e., if it exists!).

[40]Showing that Origen's approach was not unique. Kahle is undoubtedly right in speaking of the existence of various texts. What is being questioned here is that our Septuagint MSS. reflect a welter of independent texts. There is no doubt that the simple accounts in the Church Fathers fail to do justice to the complexity of the textual problem.

[41]"Redécouverte d'un chaînon manquant de l'histoire de la septante," *Revue Biblique*, LX (1953), 18–29. For a detailed evaluation cf. J. W. Wevers, "Septuaginta-Studien," pp. 136 ff. Cf. also P. Katz, "Justin's Old Testament Quotations and the Greek Dodekapropheton Scroll," *Studia Patristica*, I (1957), 343 ff.; J.-D.

may be even more significant, to the text of Quinta. It is thus quite possible that through this new text the problem of Justin's text may now be partially solved.

The problem of the text of Josephus and that of the Old Latin is actually one problem. At least one of the Old Latin versions (the Afra) and the text of Josephus, as well as parts of the Peshitta (or Syriac) version, reflects the non-Hexaplaric Lucianic text. The only difficulty is that Lucian is supposed to have made his recension *circa* A.D. 310, whereas these texts are all much earlier. There was thus a Lucianic text before Lucian, in fact, at least 200 years before Lucian. There is to my mind no doubt that the Antiochian text was an early revision of the Septuagint text. That it was a revision rather than a separate translation can be demonstrated from a careful study of the Lucianic text. No two separate translations could have made the same peculiar mis-translations in so many places. Kahle believes that the text of Josephus was revised by later Christian revisers who brought the Bible text throughout in line with the Lucianic text. This seems to me to be unlikely. It would have meant a systematic rewriting of Josephus' text, a difficult task to say the least. My own belief, though I have not yet been able to test the proposition, is that the Lucianic revision *circa* A.D. 310 consisted primarily of the addition of the Origenian plusses to the Antiochian text. It is a fact that the best Lucianic manuscripts do have asterisked passages. All in all, the so-called proto-Lucianic text is to my mind the most difficult problem in modern Septuagint work.[42]

But to return to Philo and Schröder's work on his text. Kahle has accepted the conclusions of Schröder without himself examining the evidence. Schröder's conclusion that the aberrant text was the actual text of Philo now becomes evidence that other texts besides that of

---

Barthélemy, "Quinta ou version selon les Hébreux," *ThZ*, XVI (1960), 342 ff.; S. Jellicoe, "Aristeas, Philo, and the Septuagint *Vorlage*," *Journal of Theological Studies*, N.S., XII (1961), 261 ff.

[42]For a discussion of the relation of the Old Latin to the Antiochian text cf. H. Voogd, *A Critical and Comparative Study of the Old Latin Text of the First Book of Samuel* (Unpublished Th.D. dissertation, Princeton Theological Seminary, 1947). An abstract of this thesis appears in *Catalogue of Doctoral Dissertations: Princeton Theological Seminary, 1944–1960* (Princeton, 1962), pp. 15 f., where the author states, "The Old Latin texts of the African Fathers represent the Lucianic or Syrian Greek text tradition. Since the African Fathers antedate the text of Lucian, they furnish independent evidence of an Ur-Lucianic source." For literature on "Proto-Lucian" cf. Orlinsky, "Studies in the Septuagint of the Book of Job, IV," n. 5.

Septuagint existed already in the first century A.D. The further conclusion is then made that the two texts involved are independent, whereas it is equally possible, in fact, probable, that the aberrant text is simply a revision of the Septuagint text.

Kahle also calls attention to a statement in the Philonic treatise *de migratione Abraami* which reads: "his father having died there he departed from it."[43] Terah was 70 years old at the time of Abraham's birth according to Gen. 11:26. Abraham was 75 years old when he left Haran (Gen. 12:4). The last verse of Genesis, chapter 11, states "the days of Terah were 205 years; and Terah died in Haran." The Septuagint text agrees throughout with the Hebrew, but the Samaritan Pentateuch has 145 years for Terah's age instead of 205. Now Stephen's speech in Acts, chapter 7, also recounts the tale but in these words: "Now after his father died, God removed him from there into the land in which you are now living."[44] Stephen, like Philo, took for granted a lifetime of 145 years for Terah. Therefore, says Kahle there must have been a Greek text with a reading like that of the Samaritan Pentateuch as a basis for the statement by these two worthies. This presupposes logical mathematical minds. I doubt whether either Philo or Stephen had any actual text in mind. The fact is that the death of Terah is recorded in the final verse of Genesis, chapter 11, whereas chapter 12 begins with the call of Abraham from Haran. I suspect that if one were asked how long after his father's death Abraham had left Haran most would have said "immediately afterwards," and yet the mathematics of the Genesis account which most readers have often seen is perfectly clear. This is certainly not evidence of a variant text.

Kahle adduces a second kind of evidence for the existence of early variant texts. Much is made of the Old Testament quotations in the New Testament. As is well known some of these are widely divergent from that of the Greek Old Testament as we know it. Many of the proofs adduced by Kahle turn out upon closer scrutiny to be tenuous. Much is made of the plural reading for father in the Samaritan Pentateuch at Exod. 3:6. Here the Masoretic text has "I am the God of *ābīkā* (thy father). The Samaritan Pentateuch has *abōthékā* (thy fathers). In Stephen's speech the reference is *ἐγὼ ὁ θεὸς τῶν πατέρων σου*. Kahle thinks that this proves the existence of two different translations. Such a conclusion seems hazardous in the extreme to anyone who has dealt with text critical matters. Let us examine further evidence on this

[43]*The Cairo Geniza*, pp. 143 f.
[44]Acts 7:4.

matter. Justin Martyr at one place[45] has ἐγώ εἰμι ὁ ὤν, ὁ θεὸς 'Αβραὰμ καὶ ὁ θεὸς 'Ισαὰκ καὶ ὁ θεὸς 'Ιακὼβ καὶ ὁ θεὸς τῶν πατέρων σου. Here the word order is different since in the Masoretic text, "the God of Abraham, and the God of Isaac and the God of Jacob" follows "I am the God of thy Father." Elsewhere[46] Justin quotes the passage again but omits the phrase "and the God of thy Fathers" entirely. (This does not mean that Justin suddenly picked up another translation!) Furthermore two Greek cursives, MSS. k and m, as well as the Bohairic and Codex C of the Ethiopic, codices of Eusebius, and the edited text of Cyprian, have the plural reading. Does this motley lot of witnesses prove a variant text? Of course not. The plural in view of the following genitives "I am the God of Abraham, and the God of Isaac and the God of Jacob" (notice three fathers) is the easier reading. *Lectio difficilior preferendum est*!

Somewhat later in Stephen's speech reference is made to Deut. 18:15. This follows a telescoped account of the exodus and wilderness journey, in fact, an account telescoped into one small verse, verse 36. Later Stephen returns to the story of the rebellion at Mount Sinai. In the Samaritan Pentateuch a number of passages from Deuteronomy are introduced into Exod. 20:15–22. Actually Deut. 18:15 is not there inserted though verse 18 is, and that is much like verse 15. Kahle says "we have to reckon with the possibility that he found in his Greek Tora the passage from Deuteronomy inserted in Exodus 20 which we find today in the Samaritan Pentateuch only."[47] Aside from the fact that the latter actually has verse 18 instead of verse 15, the speech at this point becomes very general, is certainly only the barest of summary statements, and simply proves nothing one way or another.[48]

What Kahle presupposes with respect to New Testament quotations, and he could have used far better examples than he does, is that the New Testament writers actually had a Greek text of the Old Testament and quoted it verbatim. This conclusion I find quite unacceptable. The New Testament writers were Semitic speaking. Greek was

[45] *Apologia* A' 63.17.

[46] *Dialogue* 59.3. Here the text is further abbreviated as ὁ θεὸς 'Αβραὰμ καὶ 'Ισαὰκ καὶ 'Ιακώβ.

[47] *The Cairo Geniza*, p. 145.

[48] Stephen is obviously not quoting a text; he is preaching a sermon. No one would suggest that verse 36 represented a variant text to the detailed account of the exodus, Red Sea, and wilderness wanderings. Homiletically he continues by saying, "This is the Moses who said . . . ," quoting the Deut. verse in question. This is certainly not a textual problem whatsoever.

only their second language. Their Bible was the Hebrew Bible; the translation to which they were accustomed was an oral Aramaic Targum. Paul was trained as a Pharisee, and only secondarily in the Greek translation of the Bible. He and his fellow-writers wrote in Greek, it is true, and quotations from the Old Testament had therefore to be made in Greek. But manuscripts were not readily available to the New Testament writers. One doubts whether Paul took a copy of the Greek Old Testament along with him on his travels. On the other hand, the New Testament writers were well acquainted with the Old Testament in Hebrew, and it would be far simpler to translate *de novo*. What is surprising actually is not how often the quotations depart from the Septuagint text, but rather how often they agree. One further point ought to be mentioned in this connection. Some of the New Testament quotations follow the text of Theodotion, or as the author would prefer to call it, the Palestinian text to which the name of Theodotion was later attached. This is particularly true of the quotations from Daniel in the Apocalypse. Apparently an oral Palestinian interpretation of the book of Daniel arose which Theodotion later adopted and edited and which gradually replaced the Septuagint or Alexandrian version almost completely in the Christian church. That this was an oral Targum is made more likely by the fact that it was known to New Testament writers and quoted by them. An oral Targum seems far more likely than another Ur-Document, in this case an Ur-Theodotion. One Ur-Document, an Ur-Lucian (or better, the Antiochian text) which cannot be avoided, is enough!

In general, Orlinsky's criticism of Kahle's *The Cairo Geniza* is valid. He says: "In his eagerness to find support for his theory of many independent Greek and Hebrew texts, Kahle has ignored the important role that oral tradition, oral quotations and interpretations, played in those days. Thus, e.g., the Nash papyrus is hardly more than some kind of liturgical fragment copied memoriter; the Rabbis in the Talmud cited biblical passages from memory, with the resultant errors and differences. . . ."[49] Memory plays an extremely important role in a manuscript culture. Manuscripts were very expensive, and only the wealthy could afford to have them. Biblical manuscripts would be the property of churches and synagogues rather than of individuals. The kind of manuscript factory which apparently existed at Qumran in Jesus' day was a rarity; from that point of view members of the Qumran community were a privileged group.

[49]A review of *The Cairo Geniza* by Orlinsky in *JAOS*, LXIX (1949), 165.

It should also be kept in mind that biblical manuscripts were not paginated, nor was the text nicely divided into chapters and verses. A modern writer wishing to quote a biblical passage simply looks it up and quotes chapter and verse verbatim. The writers of the gospels and epistles were not so fortunate. They had to depend almost wholly on their memory. Most of these writers would know favourite passages by heart. Paul, for example, in view of his Rabbinic training, knew much of the Hebrew Old Testament and certainly all the Torah by heart. His knowledge of the Greek text would have been somewhat more imperfect, as his quotations from the Old Testament show. This same principle applies to the early Church Fathers. A study of biblical quotations in Justin's *Dialogue with Trypho* will soon convince one of its relevance. Numerous quotations occur more than once. But the quotations are not always word for word the same. I have already mentioned one such quotation: Exod. 3:6 which occurs in different forms in the *Dialogue* and the first *Apology*. Others could be cited with similar results.[50] It is only those Fathers who are commenting exegetically on the Old Testament whose biblical quotations can actually be trusted as textual evidence. Such writers as Cyril of Alexandria on the Prophets, Chysostom and Theodoret, Jerome, Origen, *et al.* have commented on the text and their quotations are solid evidence for textual variants. Why? Because they used manuscripts. They were explaining the text. Hortatory writers such as the apologists simply quoted from memory. The same thing may be true for Josephus. The case of Philo is different. Philo was allegorizing the Torah. His Greek Bible was the Septuagint and he undoubtedly quoted from a manuscript. Thus his text is good evidence. *A priori* the conclusion that all kinds of written translations of the Greek Old Testament existed out of which a "standard" Septuagint eventually emerged is most unlikely. In fact, a standard text did not emerge in the early Christian centuries, but revisions and recensions did.

The Kahle hypothesis has been carried to much greater extremes by his disciples. The story of Franz Wutz and his *Transcriptionstheorie*

[50]E.g., Gen. 19:24 is quoted in the *Dialogue* four times. The quotations are as follows: 56.23–*κύριος ἔβρεξεν ἐπὶ Σόδομα καὶ Γόμορρα θεῖον καὶ πῦρ παρὰ κυρίου ἐκ τοῦ οὐρανοῦ*; 60.5—*κύριον παρὰ κυρίου τοῦ ἐν τοῖς οὐρανοῖς*; 127.5—*καὶ κύριος ἔβρεξεν ἐπὶ Σόδομα πῦρ καὶ θεῖον παρὰ κυρίου ἐκ τοῦ οὐρανοῦ*; 129.1—*ἔβρεξε κύριος πῦρ παρὰ κυρίου ἐκ τοῦ οὐρανοῦ*. All four citations differ. But these readings are largely valueless for textual purposes. Dozens of such variants could be found in the *Dialogue*.

is well-known.[51] At one time it had a great vogue, but his early death brought an end to his brilliant but baseless conjectures. Within a year of his passing almost everyone had abandoned if not forgotten his theories. Another of Kahle's disciples has done far more damage. Alexander Sperber published numerous monographs and lengthy articles on Septuagint studies. His best known work entitled *Septuagintaprobleme*[52] was severely and rightly attacked by Orlinsky.[53] Rather than repeating his criticisms it might be better to review a hundred-page article of Sperber entitled "New Testament and Septuagint."[54] In fairness to Kahle, it should be said that he does not endorse all of his disciple's conclusions.

Sperber begins by pointing out well-known differences between New Testament quotations and the Septuagint. These differences he believes to be based on a "Bible of the Apostles." The article is intended to define this text. Concerning what Swete, in his *Introduction to the Old Testament in Greek*, had to say about the problem (in which he presents the usual solution to the problem more or less as it is discussed in this paper), Sperber comments: ". . . I may say that Swete was far from realizing the problem as such, and that all his remarks are consequently to be put into the discard."[55] After such an auspicious beginning we are prepared for great things, and we are not disappointed. The major part of the article deals not with New Testament quotations but with Origen's *Hexapla.* After dismissing Lagarde's archetype theory in a few words as already refuted by his earlier work, Sperber continues with a statement on the current view of Origen's work and his refutation of it. The refutation consists of four statements. (1) The Septuagint is a translation of Hebrew into Greek, and "like all other ancient translations no doubt follows slavishly the Hebrew original." Since there were great differences in Origen's days, it must mean that the Hebrew had undergone great change.[56] The only thing that can be said about this proposition is that

[51] *Die Transkriptionen von der Septuaginta bis zu Hieronymus.* (*Texte und Untersuchungen zur vormasoretischen Grammatik des Hebräischen* II: BWAT, 2e Folge: Heft 9) (Stuttgart, 1925). It should be noted that Kahle does not necessarily follow Wutz's later absorption "in his special ideas," *The Cairo Geniza*, 233.

[52] *Texte und Untersuchungen zur vormasoretischen Grammatik des Hebräischen* (Herausg. v. P. Kahle; BWANT, 3e Folge, Heft 13) (Stuttgart, 1929).

[53] "On the Present State of Proto-Septuagint Studies."

[54] *JBL*, LIX (1940), 193–293.

[55] *Ibid.*, p. 204, summarizing Swete, *Introduction to Old Testament in Greek*, pp. 392–8.

[56] "New Testament and Septuagint," p. 208.

Sperber's surprising statement does not make it so. (2) The argument of unfairness to the Jews hinges on the presupposition that the Septuagint is more Christian than the Hebrew. But cases can be cited in which the opposite is true, that is, where the Hebrew could be used, much more tellingly than the Greek. Since Christians of the second and third centuries normally could not read Hebrew it is hard to see the relevance of this statement. (3) Origen did not have the "requisite knowledge of Hebrew to restore the Septuagint to its original purity, that is, to the Hebrew veritas." (4) And what is the Hebrew *veritas*? This could only be the Hebrew Bible of Origen, and not the Vorlage of the Old Greek. No one doubts this, but it is an irrelevancy.

Sperber thereupon outlines his own "New Approach." All the evidence about Origen's work in the Church Fathers is set aside and "we shall, therefore, go back to the original sources, and base our conclusions solely on the evidence of Hexaplaric statements themselves." By taking into account only the materials collected by Field, Sperber maintains that "in this fashion *we base our conclusions on Origen's work alone*."[57]

With tremendous industry Sperber has collected and classified materials under the obelus and under the asterisk. From this he concludes that what Origen really did was to compare two Septuagints. One was the obelus Septuagint. This was then compared to the asterisk Septuagint. Divergences were noted with an asterisk on the margin (not in the text). These when eventually copied into the text led to numerous doublets which are particularly apparent in the Old Latin as well as in Theodoret. It does not occur to Sperber, working as he does in lofty isolation, that these texts have long been identified as Lucianic by scholars, and therefore have nothing to do with the work of Origen. All of Origen's work can thus be subsumed under the presupposition that he compared these two Septuagints of his. This thesis is then tested by comparing the texts of MSS. B and A for the Pentateuch. Sperber is naturally able to do this because he has rejected all the work of former Septuagint scholars to whom classification into recensional families was a prior task. This comparison leads Sperber to the conclusion that the texts of these two codices go back to different sources. B is really the product of the obelus text, and A, that of the asterisk type. Similarly for the texts of Judges he says "the only conclusion to be drawn must be that no 'genuine' LXX (in the singular!) existed in Origen's days, but two independent translations

[57]*Ibid.*, p. 209 f.

of the Bible into Greek, both of which held an equal claim to be called 'Septuagint.' "[58] The same conclusion, namely that "B shows close affinity to the obelus type, and A to the asterisk type" is held to be sound for the rest of the Old Testament as well (specifically, Hosea, Ezekiel, I Samuel, and Psalms are examined in a few places).[59] This astounding conclusion is then carried forward to apply to the so-called "Bible of the Apostles." Sperber has thus far concluded that "we saw that as late as in the days of Origen two different translations of the Old Testament into Greek were known as LXX. In combining their variant readings in the fifth column of his *Hexapla* he indicated the source, from which these variants came, by marking them with an obelus or asterisk, respectively. But the very fact that he incorporated these readings in the fifth column proves that he considered the two translations as genuine LXX."[60] The difficulty which Sperber feels has been present with those who concern themselves with Old Testament quotations in the New Testament is that they think of the Septuagint as that of a single text (that of B). The fact is that the "Bible of the Apostles" was really the asterisk Septuagint.

It is quite unnecessary for twentieth-century scholars to refute Sperber's conclusions. Sperber may be able to work in complete isolation of Septuagint scholars on Origen's *Hexapla*, but it is rather too much for him to work in isolation from Origen himself. Origen explains his signs clearly and carefully in his *Commentary on Matthew*.[61] The obelus is put at the beginning of a Septuagint passage for which no equivalent word or words are present in the Hebrew. Whenever the Hebrew had a word or words not found in his Septuagint, he would insert under the asterisk ἀπὸ τῶν λοίπων ἐκδοσέων the necessary phrase. Naturally the passages under the asterisk will be closer to the Hebrew. And of course the so-called "Bible of the Apostles" would seem closer to the later so-called asterisk Septuagint, because the Old Testament quotations in the New Testament which diverged from the Septuagint were simply translations *memoriter*.

Since Origen himself has contradicted Sperber, nothing further need be said on the matter. One doubts whether Kahle would be happy to

[58] *Ibid.*, p. 259.
[59] Section xiv, pp. 263–6 of *ibid.*
[60] *Ibid.*, p. 279.
[61] Ad 19:16 ff. in *Die griechischen christlichen Schriftsteller der ersten drei Jahrhunderte*, Bd. 40, edited by E. Klostermann (Leipzig, 1935). This has now been reprinted in *Bibliotheke Hellenon Pateron kai Ekklesisastikon Sunggraphon*, Vols. XIII f. (Athens, 1957–8). The relevant passage is in Vol. XIII, p. 356, ll. 7–40.

accept some of the wild statements of his disciple, and yet this is the kind of chaos that can result from theories inadequately founded in fact. Kahle has done a service in calling attention once again to the Targumic character of ancient Greek translations. He has, however, not succeded in upsetting the basic approach towards Greek Old Testament textual criticism in which one attempts to classify readings recensionally and thereby tries to determine earlier readings.

Kahle concluded his first major paper on the subject as follows:

> Die Geschichte der griechischen Pentateuchübersetzung its gleichbedeutend mit einer allmählichen Angleichung von Uebersetzungen, die dem alten Vulgärtext nahestanden. . . . Die älteste Form dieser Uebersetzung rekonstruieren zu wollen, ist eine Utopie. Man wird im besten Falle eine oder die andere Revision dieser Uebersetzung mit einiger Sicherheit bestimmen können. Die weitere Verbreitung einer Textgestalt ist zumeist erst die Folge von Ueberarbeitungen und steht an Abschlusse einer gewissen Entwicklung, nicht am Anfange. Ich glaube nicht, dass die Uebereinstimmung der hauptsächlichsten, aus dem dritten nachchristlichen Jahrhundert stammenden Textgestalten dem "ursprünglichen" Text der griechischen Uebersetzung nahebringt, trotzdem dies seit Lagarde als ein Art Evangelium gilt.[62]

This Lagarde *Evangelium* has been independently tried in the field of detailed and sustained textual criticism by such great masters as Margolis in his edition of Joshua,[63] by Montgomery in his work on Daniel and Kings,[64] by Ziegler in his editions of the Prophets,[65] and by my own great teacher, Gehman, in his work on various versions,[66] and they have found it true. The future of proto-Septuagint studies depends on the classical line, with some necessary modifications to be sure, rather than on the general lines of Kahle's approach.

[62] "Untersuchungen zur Geschichte des Pentateuchtextes," *Theologische Studien und Kritiken*, LXXXVIII (1915), 399–439.

[63] M. L. Margolis, *The Book of Joshua in Greek*. Pts. I–IV (Paris, 1931–8); for an appreciation of Margolis, cf. H. M. Orlinsky, *Max Leopold Margolis, Scholar and Teacher* (Philadelphia, 1952).

[64] J. A. Montgomery, *A Critical and Exegetical Commentary on the Book of Daniel* (*ICC*) (New York, 1927); *A Critical and Exegetical Commentary of the Books of Kings* (*ICC*), edited by H. S. Gehman (New York, 1951).

[65] Bände XIII, XIV, XV, XVI.1 u. 2 of the volumes listed *supra*, note 14.

[66] E.g., H. S. Gehman, "The 'Polyglot' Arabic Text of Daniel and its Affinities," *JBL*, XLIV (1925), 327–52; "The Sahidic and the Bohairic Versions of the Book of Daniel," *JBL*, XLVI (1927), 279–330; "The Hesychian Influence in the Versions of Daniel," *JBL*, XLVIII (1929), 329–32; "The Old Ethiopic Version of 1 Kings and its Affinities," *JBL*, L (1931), 81–114; "The Armenian Version of I. and II. Kings and its Affinities," *JAOS*, LIV (1934), 53–9; "The Relations Between the Hebrew Text of Ezekiel and that of the John H. Scheide Papyri," *JAOS*, LVIII (1938), 92–102; "The Relations between the text of the John H. Scheide Papyri and that of the Other Greek MSS. of Ezekiel," *JBL*, LVII (1938), 281–7.

6. The Life and Works of Joseph Ḥazzāyâ

E. J. SHERRY, S.J.

THERE ARE TWO MAIN SOURCES for the life of Joseph Ḥazzāyâ. One contains some contradictions; the other is based on a confusion of two Josephs with somewhat similar surnames but quite dissimilar histories.[1] From these sources, the notice on Joseph Ḥazzāyâ in the *Book of Chastity* by Îshôʿdenaḥ and the observations on Joseph Hūzāyâ in the *Bibliotheca Orientalis* of Assemani,[2] scholars have drawn their accounts of this author's life. Usually little attempt has been made to separate fact from fiction and in truth the effort to do so is not too satisfying for we have few facts and much fiction. Most modern writers have been content to give a synopsis of Îshôʿdenaḥ's remarks, quote selected passages from Assemani, and assign Joseph to a vague period ranging anywhere from the early seventh to the late eighth century. A notable exception is Mgr. Addai Scher's article in the *Rivista degli Studi Orientali.*[3]

The rather summary treatment accorded to Joseph Ḥazzāyâ may be attributed to three causes: (1) Our information about him is quite meagre. What we have is not clear and those details are lacking which would help us to fix his date. Joseph himself did not help matters any by writing under the name of his brother ʿAbdîshôʿ. (2) It was long thought that all his works had been lost or destroyed. Hoffmann, however, in 1880 knew of two fragments among the manuscripts of the India Office Library, London, England.[4] (3) Although Addai Scher indicated some titles and translated a few short passages from Joseph's extant works in 1910,[5] these and other works by Joseph were

[1]Cf. J.-B. Chabot, in *Mélanges d'Archeologie et d'Histoire,* XVI (1896), 225–92.

[2]Cf. J. S. Assemani, *Bibliotheca Orientalis.* III. *De Scriptoribus Syris Nestorianis* (1725–8), 1. 100. Hereafter cited as *BO.*

[3]Cf. *Rivista degli Studi Orientali* (*RSO*), III (1910), 45–63; J.-B. Chabot, in *Journal asiatique* (*JA*), Dixième Série, VIII (1906), 265–7.

[4]Georg Hoffmann, *Auszüge aus Syrischen Akten Persischer Märtyrer* (Leipzig, 1880), p. 117, n. 1057; W. Wright, *A Short History of Syriac Literature* (London, 1894), 127–9.

[5]Scher, *RSO*, III, 54 f.

not readily available to European scholars until the acquisition of the Vatican Codex 509 in 1928 and the Mingana Codex 601 in 1932.

The life of Joseph as given by Îshôʿdenaḥ is as follows:

The Holy Aba Joseph Ḥazzāyâ, who was ʿAbdîshôʿ, was a Persian by race and his city was called Nemrod. His father was a Magian, indeed a chief of the Magians. When ʿUmar-ibn-al-Khaṭṭāb ruled the kingdom of the Arabs, he sent a force to give battle to the Turks. The city of Nemrod, which Nemrod, the king, had built and called by his name revolted against him (ʾUmar). It did not open (its) gate to him. Joseph happened to be outside the gate and was taken captive along with one hundred and thirty persons. He was seven years old when taken captive. A certain Arab from the city of Shengar bought him for three hundred and seventy *zuz*, circumcised him with own sons and made him a pagan. He stayed with him three years and when his master died, the sons sold him to a Christian named Cyriacus from the village of Dadar in the region of Qardu for five hundred and ninety *zuz*. He (Cyriacus) brought him to his home and made him steward over all his possessions (house), for he had no son. Cyriacus frequently urged him to become a Christian but he was not persuaded. Cyriacus having taken him to the monastery of Kamul, which was near the village, the young man saw the monks, was inflamed with love of our Lord, and received baptism in the convent of Mar John Kamul. When Cyriacus saw that he was constant in prayer and wished to become a monk, he gave him his freedom.

He then went to the monastery of Aba Ṣeliba in the region of Beth Nūhadra. He was received by Cyriacus, the head of the monastery who later became Bishop of Balad. He practised the monastic way of life and was especially diligent in reading the Psalms and the Scriptures. He then came to the country of Qardu and lived there many years.

Then the faithful came after him and made him superior of the convent of Mar Basima in the country of Qardu. He directed the monastery for a period and then came to Mount Zinai and settled there for a time. On the suggestion of Mar Kardhawi, Bishop of Haditha the faithful made him superior of the monastery of Rabban Baktishôʿ which is called (the monastery) of Marga and is in the neighbourhood of Zinai. He did not cease the labour of composing books. He had a natural brother whose name was ʿAbdîshôʿ who came from the City of Nemrod, received baptism and became a monk. From that time he wrote all his books under the name of his brother ʿAbdîshôʿ. He wrote (spoke) four treatises (*mîmrâ*) in his works which were not approved by the doctors of the Church and Mar Timothy held a synod and excommunicated him in the year one hundred and seventy of the kingdom of the banu-Hisham. One may learn whence Joseph Ḥazzāyâ took (his) doctrine from his history which Nestorius, Bishop of Beth Nūhadra, set down. I think the reason of the Katholikos was jealousy. God knows the truth.

After he had directed the monastery of Marga for a very long time, while still superior he died at a very advanced age. The brethren buried him in the monastery of Mar Athen until the Lord comes to raise him up. May his prayers and the prayers of all the saints mentioned in this book be a wall and a protection for the wretch (its) owner and for his parents. Amen.

The publication of the text[6] in 1896 from which the above translation is made cleared up some of the obscurities connected with Joseph Ḥazzāyâ but left many points as vague as they were before. The account has many details that were probably of interest to those for whom it was written but are not very helpful to us. We learn where he was born, the locality in which he lived, the conditions of his earlier life, the offices he filled, and the names of some of his contemporaries.

Through this text the surname and penname of Joseph have been established and are now generally accepted. Hoffmann thought Ḥazzāyâ was a derivative of Ḥazza (Arbela) and that Joseph of Ḥazza, not Joseph the Seer, was the name. Wright held the same opinion.[7] J.-B. Chabot[8] and subsequent scholars have accepted Assemani's translation, Videns the Seer, which appears to be correct since we know that Joseph came from Nemrod not from Arbela. The statement that after the entrance of ʿAbdîshôʿ into the monastery Joseph "wrote all his works under the name of his brother ʿAbdîshôʿ" seems to settle the doubt expressed by Hoffmann. M. A. Mingana held that ʿAbdîshôʿ was an author in his own right,[9] but his reasons are not convincing. In view of Îshôʿdenaḥ's remark and of the identification mentioned in the manuscript of the India Office Library as well as that referred to by Addai Scher[10] it would seem that M. Mingana's opinion is less probable. Moreover, if it is borne in mind that the term Ḥazzāyâ is not a patronymic or place name but rather a title of esteem it would seem a little strange that the title should have been given to both brothers. Furthermore, in the lists that have come down to us there is no mention of this ʿAbdîshôʿ as a writer. Finally, a comparison of the works written under the name of ʿAbdîshôʿ Ḥazzāyâ and those of Joseph show such marked similarity in style, thought, phrasing, and Scripture quotations as to justify the conclusion that they were written by the same author. The evidence that we have makes it likely that Joseph was the brother with the literary gift.

If we assume, and it seems reasonable to do so, that the Nemrod mentioned in the text as Joseph's native city was Nemrod on the Tigris,

6Chabot, *Mélanges*, XVI.
7Hoffmann, *Auszüge*, p. 116, n. 1054; Wright, *Syriac Literature*, p. 129.
8Chabot, *JA*, X, 265.
9Cf. *Woodbrooke Studies*, VII (1934), 145.
10Cf. Scher, *RSO*, III, 48; Mingana, *Woodbrooke Studies*, VII, 146.

and if we consider the other place names given in his history, a glance at the map will show that he passed his life in a rather restricted area in northeastern Mesopotamia. After his manumission and introduction to the monastic life he seems to have spent some time as a solitary, a short period and then a very long one as superior of two monasteries, and considerable time at writing for it is said he composed nineteen hundred works. We know, then, where he lived and we have some account of how he lived but about when he lived we are not so certain.

It is stated that he was taken captive at the age of seven by the troops of ʿUmar-ibn-al-Khaṭṭāb. That he was taken captive is no doubt true but that it happened in the Caliphate of ʿUmar-ibn-al-Khaṭṭāb seems unlikely for several reasons. During the Caliphate of ʿUmar-ibn-al-Khaṭṭāb (A.D. 634–44), the campaigns of the Arabs were directed chiefly against Syria, southern Mesopotamia, and Persia.[11] Mosul was captured in 641 but fighting in the north was intermittent. The sale of the captive to "an Arab of the City of Shengar" implies that Arabs were settled in the area, but it is doubtful if there were such settlements in this region during the second Caliphate. Cyriacus, Bishop of Balad, and Nestorius, Bishop of Beth Nūhadra, both of whom, as we shall see, were younger contemporaries of Joseph Ḥazzāyâ, lived at a much later date.

It is much more likely that ʿUmar II, that is, ʿUmar-ibn-ʿAbd-al-ʿAzīz (A.D. 717–20) is meant. If so, why was ʿUmar-ibn-al-Kaṭṭāb written? Addai Scher suggests[12] that originally the name was written *ʿmr br ḥem* and that a copyist changed the *ḥem* to *ḥṭb* (Scher writes *ḥṭp*) and accounts for his opinion by saying that ʿUmar II was ʿUmar-ibn-ʿAbd-al-ʿAziz, ibn-Marwān ibn-al-Ḥakam. He might have gone even further and suggested that *br ḥṭb* was the original writing because ʿUmar's maternal great-grandfather was the second caliph, ʿUmar ibn-al-Khaṭṭāb.[13] However, both suggestions are improbable and contrary to normal Arabic nomenclature. A consideration of the historical circumstances of the time points to ʿUmar II rather than to ʿUmar I.[14]

Ishôʿdenaḥ says, "when ʿUmar ibn-al-Khaṭṭāb seized the sceptre of the kingdom of the Arabs, he sent a force to do battle with the Turks. The city of Nemrod, etc." The phrase *ʾḥid ʾtūdâ* is the usual Syriac expression meaning "he who bears rule, he who seizes the sceptre" and is very apt with regard to ʿUmar II who succeeded to the Cali-

[11]Cf. P. Hitti, *History of the Arabs* (London, 1937), pp. 147–59.
[12]Scher, *RSO*, III, 46.
[13]Hitti, *History of the Arabs*, p. 234.
[14]Chabot argues for ʾUmar II in *JA*, X, 267 but in his *Littérature syriaque* (1934) says "Joseph fait prisonnier par les troupes du calife Omar (634–644)."

phate by trickery.[15] During the reign of ʿUmar's predecessor, Sulaymān (715–717), there had been trouble in the eastern provinces of the Caliphate. Discontented elements in these areas would naturally take advantage of the confusion consequent on a change of rulers, especially when the succession was disputed, and their hopes for a successful revolt would be buoyed up by the news that ʿUmar had ordered Maslamah, the former Caliph's brother, who had been besieging Constantinople, to withdraw his forces. This would be taken as a sign of Arab weakness. Word of the disaster that overtook the Arab fleet in its withdrawal (such news would travel fast and probably reach the interior in a short time) would give further encouragement to any who were inclined to rebellion. Although ʿUmar II was opposed to "booty wars"[16] and concerned himself chiefly with financial and religious reforms, he none the less maintained Arab supremacy wherever it had been established. There is no published record of his having "sent a force to do battle with the Turks" but it may well be that he sent troops to maintain order in the restless eastern provinces. Towns like Nemrod may have felt themselves to be far enough away from the centre of government to make it safe for them to close their gates against his troops. The territory around Nemrod had been overrun under ʿUmar I, it is true, but to say that the city "revolted" suggests rather that the Arab domination had been well established and this applies to the reign of ʿUmar II much more than to that of ʿUmar I. The phrase "against the Turks" probably means no more than against the people living to the east, just as we are prone to name all peoples living east of the Germanic lands, Slavs. Such speculations are interesting and even necessary to help clear up the confusion, but a much better argument for placing the date of Joseph Ḥazzāyâ's birth seven years before the reign of ʿUmar II can be drawn from the names of Bishop Cyriacus, N̍estorius, and the Patriarch Timothy.

When Joseph came to the monastery of Aba Ṣeliba, he was received by Cyriacus "who later became Bishop of Balad." Cyriacus was made bishop by Mar Cyprian of Nisibis who died in A.D. 767.[17] Thus it was sometime about the middle of the eighth century that Joseph Ḥazzāyâ lived in the monastery of Aba Ṣeliba. We are told in the *Book of Chastity* that N̍estorius, Bishop of Beth Nūhadra, wrote a history of Joseph Ḥazzāyâ. It would seem that the excerpt on Joseph in the

[15]Cf. C. I. Huart, *Histoire des Arabes* (Paris, 1912), I, 269.

[16]Cf. *ibid.*, I, 270.

[17]J.-B. Abbeloos et T.-J. Lamy, éds., *Barhebraei Chronicon Ecclesiasticum* (Paris, Louvain, 1877), III, col. 162.

Book of Chastity was taken from the history by Ṅestorius, for its contents indicate that the writer was either personally acquainted with his subject or knew those who were. Ishô'denaḥ (*d. c.* 900) does not give such intimate details of any other of the "one hundred and forty founders." It argues a certain familiarity when a writer, especially a Syriac writer, tells us that Joseph was taken outside the gate with one hundred and thirty other persons; that he was seven years old at the time; that a pagan Arab of Shengar bought him for three hundred and seventy *zuz*; that he circumcised him along with own sons; that the sons sold him (at a profit) for five hundred and ninety *zuz*; that his new master was a Christian, had no sons, and put Joseph in charge of his estate. We may wish that some of these rather irrevelant details had been omitted and more useful data handed down; at least these items indicate more than hearsay knowledge. Ṅestorius could have had such knowledge. We have a letter signed by him and others and dated in the year 174 of the Arabs (A.D. 790) in which he protests his orthodoxy and abjures the Messalian heresy and other aberrations of which he was suspected.[18] When Joseph was excommunicated by the Patriarch Timothy I, he was accused among other things of Messalianism; even his biographer was obliged to make a formal renunciation of the same charge before his consecration as bishop. This does not prove that Joseph and Ṅestorius were contemporaries but it leads one to suppose that they were. It need occasion no surprise that Timothy excommunicated the one and promoted the other. He was more inclined to be guided by expediency than by principle. Thus through Ṅestorius Joseph is linked to the eighth century.

Timothy I, Nestorian Patriarch from A.D. 780 to A.D. 823, held two synods. In the first, held in 790,[19] John of Dalyata, John of Apamea, and Joseph were condemned. In the second, held in 804, the condemnation was re-affirmed thus: "just as the Catholicos Sabrîshô' (596–604) condemned the writing of Henana of Adiabene (*d.* 610) and Îshô'yahb III (647–58), the fictions of Sahdônâ (*c.* 650) and the commentaries of Isaiah of Taḥal (650?),[20] so we proscribe the blasphemies of this Apamaean (*illius Apamaeensis*) and of Joseph and of John of Dalyata."

18Cf. O. Braun, in *Oriens Christianus*, II (1902).

19The Synod was held 174 A.H. not 170 A.H. as the *Book of Chastity* has it. See Scher, *RSO*, III, 47; J.-B. Chabot, *Synodicon Orientali* (Paris, 1902), pp. 599n f.

20We know very little about Isaiah except that he was a disciple of Henana; see A. Baumstark, *Geschichte der syrischen Literatur* (1922), p. 134. Also *Patroligia Orientalis* (*PO*), XIII, 511, 535.

We shall discuss later the reasons given for the condemnation and need not dwell on that topic here except to say that the above quotation is taken from the part of the synodal legislation stipulating that books before being "published" should be submitted for the Patriarch's *imprimatur*. There is no statement that Joseph was alive at the time of this condemnation but there are indications that he was.

Timothy cites the examples of his predecessors and it is to be noticed that they condemned contemporaries. We know that John of Dalyata was living between 760 and 780 because he received a visit from Saloman who was Bishop of Hadit(h)a during that time. We know too that when he had arrived at a very old age he gathered the faithful and the monks together and gave them instructions concerning the monasteries, etc.[21] As we do not know when John was born, we have no way of estimating in what year he may have been considered to have been "very old." We can be sure, however, from the dates of the Bishop who visited him that if he were not alive when condemned, he was not long dead. From the preamble to the denunciation, it would seem that those censured were still alive.

We may wonder who *hū ʾpmyâ* was. Even in the formal document he is not given a name. ʿAbdîshôʿ and others following him say it was John of Apamaea. But there were several who bore that name and we have no clue to help us determine which is referred to here. Was he so well known and yet of such little consequence that a contemptuous reference to "that fellow from Apamaea" was sufficient designation? Or was he the Apamaean, that is, John of Apamaea, mentioned by Bar Hebraeus,[22] who lived in the sixth century and taught a peculiar doctrine that was a mixture of dualism, pantheism, and Platonism? This is hardly likely unless we suppose that Mar Timothy was indulging in the Semitic penchant for numbers, that is, the first Patriarch mentioned condemned one, the second two, the third three men. Very improbable but not impossible. Or are we to suppose with Chabot[23] that John of Apamaea is some third party so far known only from this reference? There seems to be no satisfactory answer.

What reason have we for thinking that Joseph was alive at the time of the Synod? There is the remark by Îshôʿdenaḥ with reference to

[21]Cf. Chabot, *Littérature syriaque*, p. 106; also Chabot, *JA*, X, 267–8; R. Duval, *La Littérature syriaque* (1907), p. 226; *Book of Chastity* para. 126.

[22]*Chronicon Ecclesiasticum* 1. 222.

[23]Cf. Chabot, *JA*, X, 259–66. I. Hausherr, trans., *Orientalia Christiana*, CXX (1939).

Timothy's motive for the condemnation. "I think the Catholicos was moved by envy (jealousy)." There would be little point to being envious of a corpse. As pointed out above, Ishôʿdenaḥ was too young to know either Joseph or Timothy personally, but he was old enough and close enough in time to these men to have heard bits of gossip on which he would form an opinion. We can surmise that Ishôʿdenaḥ had some grounds for his view. ʿAbdîshôʿ says that "Timothy excelled in vision and in all virtue."[24] Such a man may well have felt some chagrin that he with his gifts and dignities should be known merely as the Patriarch Timothy, while a monk off in the hills was known as Ḥazzāyâ; especially as this title too might have been his, for he came from Ḥazza. If anyone had hinted that the term as applied to him was more than geographical, Timothy was not the man to quibble. However, the title had been pre-empted. There are four or five passages in the *Discourse on Providence* that would lead one to think it had been composed after Joseph's condemnation. If that seems too extreme a position, one can at least see that Joseph was being careful in his discourse not to give occasion for any statement that might be used against him. In the title he says "let discerning readers take heed—let them clear the mind of all envy—all that we say is true and we do not turn aside from the way of the interpreter." Neither the general style of the discourse nor the particular context in which this passage occurs calls for such emphasis. In the section dealing with the building of the Ark he says—"God infused the spirit into three men just as he inspired Basliyel and Elyahb, the artificers of the tabernacle. If it were not for the jealousy (or envy) which holds sway in our generation, I would have mentioned the names of these men but there is no need."[25] Such reticence seems strange, especially since the reason given for it is so bold. It looks as though Joseph had an eye to the censors when he slipped in this sly remark which is innocuous enough to be passed and sufficiently pointed to annoy. Finally, in a passage about the Incarnation he states that God, the Word, "descended not in Nature but made a dwelling place for the descent of His love, I say, and not of His Nature. Let no impious heretic think that I agree with his opinion."[26] Who was the unnamed "impious heretic?" It may have been John of Dalyata who was condemned for saying that the humanity of our Lord was united with his

[24]Cf. A. Mai, *Script. Vet. Nov. Coll.*, X (165), 327. ʿAbdîshôʿ is a late (*d.* 1318) and not impartial witness.

[25]Cf. *Discourse on Divine Providence* f. 232a.

[26]Cf. *ibid.*, f. 236b.

divinity.[27] Why would Joseph have felt it necessary to protest the orthodoxy of such an obviously Nestorian enunciation unless he had already been accused or suspected of heterodoxy?

During the early years of his patriarchate Timothy had more troubles than Martha and was much more concerned with internal and external politics and the consolidation of his position than with dogma.[28] During this period, when writers could, and apparently did express opinions that would not stand critical examination, they would not be likely to insert in the body of their works protestations of good intentions. Timothy, whatever his faults, was a good administrator and able leader. Once assured of his position he turned his attention to discipline and doctrine and in his first synod put a check on questionable teaching and banned unorthodox writings in general and those of three men in particular. Henceforth these and others would be expected to show more care in their statements. This consideration seems sufficient reason to explain why Joseph was so ready with defensive statements in the *Discourse on Divine Providence* and why one may place its composition after 790.

It may be asked—if Joseph were excommunicated while still alive—what explanation is offered for Îshôʿdenaḥ's words "while still superior, he died at a profound old age."[29] We should bear in mind that, though Joseph was excommunicated, the decree was directed primarily against his works and, as we are told, against four treatises in particular. These may have been withdrawn and the sentence against their author mitigated. Timothy was a hard man but not an unjust one. The reiteration of the injunction in the Synod of 804 would then be a reminder to any who may have had copies of these works that they were "on the index." If such a retraction were made Joseph may have been left in office in his monastery. Secondly, it must be remembered that at the time of the Synod in 790 Joseph was an old man. There would be some time and in the conditions of the period probably a considerable time before the decrees of the Synod would be put into effect. Joseph may have died before this happened or he may have died before a successor had been appointed. In either case it would be true to say that he "died while still superior."

Before bringing the discussion of Joseph's date to a close there are

[27]Cf. *Book of Chastity* para. 126.

[28]Cf. Assemani, *BO*, II, 433; III, 1.158–60; *Chronicon Ecclesiasticum* 11. 166 f.; Braun, *Oriens Christianus*, I (1901), 138–52.

[29]Cf. *Book of Chastity* para. 125.

two points that merit some attention, not because of their intrinsic importance but because all commentators remark on them. In the catalogue of ʿAbdîshôʿ,[30] there is listed among the works of Babai, the Great, who died in 628[31] this phrase: *w ʾgrn dysp ḥazzî.* Most Orientalists have translated this: "letters to (or against) Joseph Ḥazzāyâ." As Addai Scher has pointed out[32] this translation is not normal. The Syriac for letters "to or against someone" would be *ʾgrn dlôt pln.* As a matter of fact the item immediately preceding the one in question reads: *hū dlôt shruyʾ* "likewise a book (or instruction) to novices." So ʿAbdîshôʿ's entry must be translated "letters of Joseph Ḥazzāyâ." We have no means of knowing whether Babai wrote a commentary on such letters or made a collection of them or what he did with them. Neither do we know who this Joseph Ḥazzāyâ was. Addai Scher holds that *ysp* is an error for *yḥnn,* that is, John, the Seer and Prophet of the Thebaid.[33] This explanation, though not altogether satisfying, is as good as any other. We can be sure that the "Joseph" mentioned (if the text is correct) is not the Joseph condemned by Timothy. For even if, against all probability, we should place Joseph Ḥazzāyâ in the reign of ʿUmar ibn-al-Khaṭṭāb and if he were captured at the age of seven in the first year of that Caliph's reign, he would have been an infant of a year old when Babai died. Against or to or about such a one Babai would scarcely have written.

Then there is the confusion of names in Assemani, who writes: "Joseph from the region of Huzita, a priest and the third Rector and Master of the school of Nisibis after Narsai, so great was the reputation he enjoyed among the Nestorians because of the nineteen hundred tracts he published that he was given the surname Ḥazzāyâ, the Seer or Prophet."[34] Joseph Hūzāyâ is credited with being the author of the first grammatical work in Syriac and of having introduced the vowel points and accents in use among the Nestorians.[35] Assemani claims that he wrote poems in nine syllable lines. He may have, or perhaps this is a further confusion because he used a system of nine accents or punctuation points to guide readers, especially readers of

[30]Cf. *BO*, III, 1.97.

[31]Cf. Baumstark, *Geschichte der syrischen Literatur*, p. 137; Chabot, *Littérature syriaque*, p. 61; Duval, *La Littérature syriaque*, p. 222; Wright, *Syriac Literature*, p. 169.

[32]Cf. *PO*, XIII, 533n.

[33]Cf. *RSO*, III, 47 and *PO*, XIII, 533. In the Arabic *yḥnʾ* is written and the Paris MS. from which the text in *PO* is taken the *yḥnʾ* is certain.

[34]Cf. *BO*, III, 1:100.

[35]Cf. Chabot, *JA*, Neuvième Série, VIII (1896), 58 f.

the Scripture.[36] Joseph Hūzāyâ died sometime around 580. Apart from the grammar and a book on words that are spelled alike but have different meanings and the poems mentioned by Assemani no other writings are attributed to him. On the other hand, Joseph Ḥazzāyâ was a prolific writer. There is no knowing why Assemani confused the two Josephs. It is quite clear that the Joseph condemned by Timothy in 790 was not the one who died in 580. This latter would, if condemned at all, have been condemned by Sabrîshôʿ and his name joined with Henana. Besides Joseph Ḥazzāyâ was never Rector of the school of Nisibis nor, as far as we know, did he ever have any connection with it.

From what has been said in the foregoing paragraphs, it would seem safe to conclude that Joseph Ḥazzāyâ belongs to the eighth century. The evidence we have is circumstantial, but without twisting the texts at our disposal or putting on them an interpretation that strains credulity, we are brought to this conclusion. Thus, until further study has uncovered newer and more direct evidence, we suggest that Joseph's dates should be 710 (or 712) to 792 (or 795).

According to ʿAbdîshôʿ, Metropolitan of Nisibis and Armenia (*d.* 1318), Joseph composed nineteen hundred works. While this is an improbably large number, in his extant works the author is sufficiently prolix that we may well believe that he was correspondingly prolific. ʿAbdîshôʿ enumerates those given below as being worthy of mention. Out of so many we need not be surprised that so few are named. Timothy anathematized all "who should read or keep in the monastery library or in their cells" any of Joseph's writings. This anathema would account for the loss of a good number and the passage of time would, in any event, occasion the disappearance of many whose intrinsic worth would be too slight to insure their preservation. In such a volume of writing there must have been a fair amount that had little value so that we need not regret the loss of some of it, although, it must be admitted, that the tone of Joseph's extant works is in general high, both in style and content. Here is the list of those titles that were considered worthy of mention by ʿAbdîshôʿ.[37]

1. On Theory and Practice[38]
2. The Book of the Treasurer (Steward) containing an explanation of abstruse questions

[36] Cf. Duval, *La Littérature syriaque*, p. 288.
[37] Cf. *BO*, III, l. 102–3; Scher, *RSO*, III, 45.
[38] Cf. *Discourse on Divine Providence*, ff. 201b, 203a, 232b.

3. On Misfortunes and Chastisements[39]
4. A Commentary on the Book of the Merchant[40]
5. An historical book, the Paradise of the Orientals, a two-volume work in which ecclesiastical matters are interspersed[41]
6. A Commentary on the vision of Ezechiel
7. An Account of the (more) notable Feasts
8. A Commentary on the "Sententiae"[42]
9. A Commentary on the vision which Mar Gregory saw[43]
10. A Commentary on Dionysius[44]
11. Letters on the exalted character of the monastic life

These works except for a few fragments are lost. The titles of the extant works of Joseph Ḥazzāyâ, as far as they are known and where they are to be found, are given in the following list. The first ten items are contained in the Codex preserved in the monastery of Notre Dame des Semences at Alqosh and in the copies derived from it. The folio numbers noted after the first ten items are those of the Vatican Codex, 509. The notices following the other titles are self-explanatory.

1. The Fifth Letter of Rabban Joseph to one of his friends who asked him to inform him of the virtue by the practice of which a man draws especially close to God, and which is the shortest way by which a man may find God among the rest of the many ways which lead to God. Vat. ff. 61a–64b. This letter is also found in the British Museum, Wright's Catalogue No. 875, Add. 12167, p. 774, no. XV where it is listed simply as "Letter of one monk to another." There is no name in the British Museum manuscript.

2. By Mar ʿAbdîshôʿ Ḥazzāyâ—(*a*) On the different operations of Grace in relation to pious (souls) (Vat. ff. 102b–103a); (*b*) On the

[39]Cf. the underlying theme of the *Discourse on Divine Providence* which is that the misfortunes of mankind and their punishment is an evidence of God's providence.

[40]Isaiah of Scete who was the son of a merchant and probably himself a merchant before he became a monk. He lived in the latter part of the fourth century.

[41]Cf. the authority given to stories from the Lives of the Fathers in the *Discourse on Divine Providence* ff. 210a, b, 214b.

[42]Literally, Heads of Knowledge—"Capita Scientiae"—that is, of Evagrius Ponticus; cf. references to this work in *Discourse on Divine Providence* ff. 199a, 203b.

[43]Gregory Nazianzenus, cf. *BO*, III, ll. 103, note 3.

[44]Pseudo-Dionysius the Areopagite; cf. Bardenhewer, *Patrologie* (Freiburg im Breisgau, 1910), pp. 462–8; English translation, pp. 535–41. Cf. also J. Stiglmayr, S.J., *Bibliothek der Kirchenväter*, 11:11.

second operation of Grace on the mind (Vat. f. 103a, (10 lines); (*c*) On the third operation of Grace on the mind (Vat. ff. 103a–103b); (*d*) On the various other operations of Grace (Vat. ff. 103b–104a).

3. By the same Mar ʿAbdîshôʿ—On contemplation which attracts the mind in time of prayer above the motions of the senses and considerations and thoughts of material things and on the illumination (fiery impulse) which transforms the soul to its likeness whenever this contemplation attracts the mind to itself (Vat. ff. 104a–106a).

4. By the same—On the prayer the mind experiences in the sphere of serenity. (Vat. ff. 106a–112b).

5. By the same—On the operation of the motions which in time of prayer affect (dawn on) the mind. Which are composite: which are simple; which have no bounds and (do not conform to any) type (Vat. ff. 112b–114a).

6. By the same—From the Book of Questions—How the Spirit which works in us is known and in what His power is revealed and what is the sign of the Spirit when He manifests in us His operation (Vat. ff. 114a–115b).

7. Letter of the same Mar ʿAbdîshôʿ—To one of his friends on the operations of Grace (Vat. ff. 115a–119b).

8. By Rabban Joseph Ḥazzāyâ, The Wise.—On Spiritual prayer (Vat. ff. 190a–191a).

9. From the "Sententiae" (chapters) of Rabban Joseph (Vat. ff. 191a–191b).

10. From the same Rabban Joseph—A discourse on the nature of the Eternal Being and on the distinction of the Persons of the Trinity and on Their Properties and on the origin of creation and on the Judgment and on the Providence and on the Mercy of our Lord God, and on the love which He has manifested in latter times toward rational creatures and on everything He has done and is doing for them from the beginning of their creation even to the end along with other subjects (Vat. ff. 191b–241a).

11. Questions, Answers, and "Sententiae" of Mar ʿAbdîshôʿ and his disciple (three dialogues). Vatican Library, Rome, Fondo Borgiano siriaco 88:4.[45] Notre Dame des Semences, Alqosh, cod. 45:5: from quire 30, p. 14—quire 31, p. 20.[46] Library of the India Office, London, England, MS. 9 ff. 293a–310a.[47]

45Cf. A. Scher, *JA*, X (13) (1909), 249–87.

46Cf. J.-M. Vosté, *Catalogue de la Bibl. Syr. Chald. du Couvent de Notre Dame des Semences*, p. 20.

47Cf. Wright, *Syriac Literature*, p. 129; Hoffmann, *Auszüge*, p. 117, n. 1057.

12. Book of Questions and Answers composed by Joseph Ḥazzāyâ. Patriarchate of Mosul at Mosul—20 cm. by 15cm., 24 quires, 480 pp., 20 lines to the page.[48]

13. Six short tracts of ʿAbdîshôʿ, the Seer, on the different operations of Grace on the pious. Selly Oak Colleges, Birmingham, England, Mingana, 47rr ff. 248b–252a. See also item 2 above.

14. Fragments of Joseph Ḥazzāyâ are found in a work by Isaac Shebadnaya. This work is an acrostic. In it the author frequently cites other writers textually in order to explain difficulties in his own text. Selly Oak Colleges, Birmingham, Mingana 57—Joseph Ḥazzāyâ f. 41b; ʿAbdîshôʿ Ḥazzāyâ 91b. (It is interesting to note here that five of the authors cited by Isaac are found in Cod. Vat. Syr. 509 & Ming. 601.) Cambridge University,[49] Add. 1998—ʿAbdîshôʿḤazzāyâ ff. 182b, 190b, 208a, Joseph Ḥazzāyâ f. 83a (105a *ysp dʾrbīl*).

15. Prayer attributed to Joseph Ḥazzāyâ. Selly Oak Colleges, Birmingham—Ming. 564R ff. 178b–181b.

16. The answer given to the question, how Enoch and Elias received Communion. Selly Oak Colleges, Birmingham—Ming. 566F ff. 77b–78b.

17. A fragment on Zachariah 4:10. India Office Library, London, England—MS. 9 f. 241b.

Mgr. Addai Scher gives a list of the works of Joseph that were in the library at Seert in his *Catalogue des manuscrits syriaques et arabes conservés dans la bibliothèque épiscopale de Seert.* This library was pillaged and the works probably destroyed during the bitter vindictive fighting of World War I. However, some volumes may still be scattered about. Some wandering scholar or scholarly wanderer may, perchance, run across one or another of them at some time.

[48]Cf. J.-M. Vosté, in *Le Muséon*, L (1937), 349. This work is C.100 in Addai Scher's "Notices sur les manuscrits syriaques et arabes à l'Archevêché Chaldéen de Diarbékir," *JA*, X (10) (1907), 385–431. This manuscript and 21 others were moved to Mosul before the library at Diarbékir was plundered. See Vosté, *Le Muséon*, L, 349. See also, Scher, *RSO*, III (1910), 48–50.

[49]Cf. W. Wright, *Catalogue of Syriac Manuscripts in the Library of the University of Cambridge* (1901), I, 428–44.

7. Zeus in the Hellenistic Age

F. W. BEARE

THE HELLENISTIC AGE is that long period beginning with the career of Alexander the Great (*d.* 323 B.C.) during which Greek influences were widely diffused through the ancient lands of the Middle East–Anatolia, Syria, Egypt, the Mesopotamian regions, and the farthest territories of the Achaemenid Persian empire, even to Bactria and Sogdiana and the frontiers of India. Until the time of Alexander, the Greeks had lived largely on the margin of this Oriental world. They had important points of contact with it in the Greek states of the Asian coast, which had long been subject to Persian rule, but even these had succumbed only in minor measure to the assimilative pressures of the vast Oriental empire to which they were attached. They prided themselves on their Hellenism and never lost touch with the tradition which was so brilliantly sustained at Athens and in other cities of the peninsula and the islands and the Greek states of Sicily and southern Italy. A certain measure of cultural unity had been achieved in western Asia as the result of centuries of imperial expansion and the large-scale movement of populations, as Amorite and Hittite, Assyrian and Babylonian, Egyptian and Persian strove for dominance. But the Greek states, in spite of many cultural borrowings from the far more ancient civilizations of Egypt and western Asia, had succeeded in maintaining their independence and in creating a culture profoundly different in spirit and in aims from anything that was represented in the Oriental conglomerate. As a consequence, when Alexander led his Greek and Macedonian armies through the east in his career of meteoric conquest, the Greek culture which followed in his wake struck into the life of the Orient with a freshness and vigour that had not been felt for centuries and created a new fusion of cultures which was to affect the life of the world for the ages that followed.

Alexander looked upon himself not as a military adventurer but as the standard-bearer of Greek civilization, and the brilliant culture of the Greek world was actively promoted by him, and by his successors, in all parts of their dominions. For a hundred and fifty years it exercised a peculiar dominance. City life was reshaped along the lines of the Greek *polis*, not only in the new foundations—the Alexandrias, the Antiochs, the Seleucias—but even so far as was possible in the imperial cities which were ancient before any Greek dreamed of *synoecismus*. Greek literature was studied; men learned to use the Greek language as the ordinary medium of commercial and political intercourse; artists and craftsmen took the Greek masterpieces as models for imitation; new temples were built and old ones reconstructed on the traditional Greek lines; young men of the Oriental cities—not excepting Jerusalem—flocked to the Greek *gymnasia*; and Greek cults were instituted in regions once sacred to Oriental gods.

In the whole long process of interpenetration that had been going on through the centuries, no single culture had succeeded in imposing itself as did the Greek. Yet, in the long run, this spectacular dominance passed, and the Hellenic contribution became just one more among the manifold elements that made up the Hellenistic complex. The Orient, made captive, gave laws to its conquerors. In the course of the second century B.C. the old Oriental influences make their power felt once again, forcing themselves into and through the Hellenized surface. (There is a remarkable historical parallel in our own era, in the resurgence of the ancient religions and cultures of the Far East after centuries of European dominance.) A symbol of the changing balance of forces may be seen in the differences between the Rosetta Stone, containing a decree in honour of Ptolemy V Epiphanes (dated 196 B.C.), and the decree of Canopus, in many respects similar, issued in the ninth year of Ptolemy III Euergetes (238 B.C.). Both are trilingual inscriptions, the text being given in hieroglyphic, demotic, and Greek. Both are issued by the corporation of the priests of Memphis, in honour of the reigning monarch. Even in the earlier document it is evident that "the indigenous forces were beginning to react with their usual obstinacy upon the intruding Hellenism" (J. P. Mahaffy); but in the reign of Euergetes, the primary language is still Greek and the whole tone and feeling are Greek. In the Rosetta inscription, little more than forty years later, it is the Egyptian text that is primary and the very formulae of the royal name are cast in Egyptian terms, literally translated into Greek. In the decree of Canopus, the reigning king is described simply as "Ptolemy the son of Ptolemy and Arsinoe the Brother Gods"; in the Rosetta text his grandson is proclaimed in the most elaborate fashion as "Ptolemy Everliving, beloved by Ptah, the youthful King who has received the kingdom in succession to his father the glorious lord of kingdoms . . . lord of the thirty-year festival like Hephaestus (i.e., Ptah) the Great; King like Helios (Rēʿ), that great monarch of the upper and the lower regions; offspring of the Father-loving Gods, whom Hephaestus has glorified, to whom Helios has given the victory; the Living Image of Zeus (i.e., Amon), son of Helios (Rēʿ)." The strong resurgence of native forces is here unmistakable, and illustrations of the same trend could be supplied from the archaeology of Dura-Europos on the Euphrates and from numerous sites in Asia Minor and Syria.

Nor was it in their own territories alone that the powers of the ancient Orient were regaining their sway. More and more they were invading the Hellenic world itself. The movement of populations, with the settlement of Oriental groups in the Greek seaports, would alone have sufficed to bring this about. Egyptian residents in Athens had built a temple for Isis even before Alexander's time; and Socrates could accompany his friends down to the Piraeus to see the procession in honour of the Thracian Bendis in 412. The Phoenician Adonis has his devotees in Athens in the fifth century; the Anatolian Sabazios is established there early in the fourth. All these cults were introduced by aliens, not as missionary stations to win Greek converts, but to meet their own religious needs. Even so, it is clear that they made some appeal also to native Athenians. If a Sophocles could offer his home as a shrine for the holy snake of Asclepius, it is not surprising to find that other Athenians were ready to afford a welcome to gods from more distant lands. But it is not until the Hellenistic age that the Oriental cults begin to pour in like a flood, and to become acclimatized. By that time, the old gods of Greece had lost much of their authority. The criticisms of the philosophers and the jests of the comedians had undermined the sense of awe with which men had once regarded them, and the loss of independence together with the decline of political vitality in the city-state had deprived them of most of their essential meaning. Moreover, as the horizons of the Greek widened through his participation in the far-ranging conquests of Alexander, he could not but feel the need of a divinity corresponding in some measure to the vastness of his universe—a divinity who could make some claim to universal worship. The old forms of religion in Greece, rooted as they were in the life of the city-state, were as inadequate to the life of a world community as was the assembly of citizens to the rule of an empire. Nor could they any longer afford satisfaction to the personal religious needs of men in the loose and unstable social structure of the

Hellenistic kingdoms. The influx of the Oriental cults was a response to the shaking of the foundations of the traditional religion of Greece.

The Roman conquest of the East did not make any fundamental change in the religious situation, though certain Roman and Italian cults were introduced, especially in the "colonies" which were settled with veterans of the armed forces and to some extent by Italian farmers displaced from central Italy to make room for a reserve of veterans near the capital. Roman religion itself had already been largely Hellenized and had begun to witness the introduction of Oriental cults especially during and after the wars with Hannibal. Religion in the provinces of the Roman empire, accordingly, displays the continuance of the same kind of phenomena that are to be seen in the Hellenistic kingdoms. Even the worship of the emperor is no more than the substitution of a new object in the general framework of Hellenistic ruler-cults. Rome does not interfere with the religious beliefs or practices of her subjects, except where they appear to affect public morals. It will be recalled that the Roman penetration of the East begins in a significant way with the battle of Magnesia in 198 B.C., when Roman armies inflicted a decisive defeat on Antiochus III of Syria; and this means that when Rome came into the picture, the Hellenistic world was already beginning to be Orientalized. The Oriental resurgence in religion and culture advanced westwards as the Roman armies consolidated the imperial power in the East.

The religious quests of the age took many and diverse forms. Some men took refuge in philosophy, and philosophy tended more and more to take on the character of religion, as in Stoicism, Neo-Pythagoreanism, and above all Neoplatonism. Even Epicureanism, despite its frontal attack on "religion," has an essentially religious quality in the hands of its greatest exponents. None of these philosophies is political in any sense that Plato or Aristotle would have recognized. They are concerned with man in the cosmos, not with man in any limited social nexus such as the *polis*—not with man as Athenian or as Hellene, but with man as human being. "No man is an alien to me," writes Menander, "if only he be a good man. Nature is one in all men, and it is character that establishes kinship" (fr. 602). Their aim was to teach the individual how to live as he ought in a world swayed by forces which were beyond his control; how to forge for himself an armour of imperturbable tranquillity (*ataraxia*) or of a disposition steeled against all pity, fear, and desire (*apatheia*), and so to pursue the true end of man (however that end might be conceived in his school) with the resources which he possessed within himself, in independence of outward circumstances. The primary concern of philosophy was thus ethics, and the ethics of the self-sufficient individual at that; and there was no function left for the gods. But more and more the end was conceived in transcendental terms, and the philosopher taught man to think of his true self as a fragment of deity imprisoned in a physical and material environment from which he must seek to flee to those higher realms of the spirit which are his proper home. The soul, a fragment of the divine fire that contains and transcends the world, must seek salvation in flight, in escape, in regaining its original likeness to God. But the god of such a system is not Zeus or any traditional divinity, but pure discarnate Intelligence—the totality of which the mind of man is a fragment.

In another direction, religion is marked by an enormous development of cults of deified men, hailed as "lords" and "saviours." Asclepius, the deified physician, almost supplants Apollo as the god of healing. Heracles, the Averter of Evil (*Alexikakōn*), who after a life of toils had been exalted to heaven, receives an immense and widespread access of popularity. Living men too were accorded divine honours. At the end of the Peloponnesian wars the victorious Lysander had been granted "honours equal to those of the gods" (*timai isotheoi*) by a number of Greek states. Philip of Macedon had a statue of himself carried in procession with the Twelve Gods. Greeks and Macedonians generally shrank from granting to Alexander the divine honours which he was receiving in the East, yet in their laws they acknowledged his divinity and their ambassadors to him were called *theōroi*—a title normally reserved for envoys to a shrine or an oracle. It is not strange that the Ptolemies and the Seleucids should quickly come to be recognized as divinities, as they fell more and more into the traditional pattern of Egyptian or of Babylonian monarchy; but what are we to say of the council and *demos* of Athens solemnly passing a decree to exalt Demetrius Poliorketes to the ranks of the Immortals on the ground that his power had been effectually present to deliver them when they had called upon the Olympians in vain? Such developments as these are in part a reflection of the doctrine, imperfectly but widely apprehended, that the substance of divinity dwells in some sense in every man and is present in especial potency in the great man; but even more they reflect the weakening of the traditional religion and the decline of faith in the old gods. The ancestral deities of Greece could survive, if they were to survive at all, only by becoming universal gods—gods not of the Greeks alone, but of all nations. There is accordingly an increasing tendency to regard them as local manifestations of the divine power which is known under other names elsewhere. There is a general *theokrasia.* There are no longer rival pantheons, but the gods of every nation are systematically identified with the gods of all the others.

Under such circumstances it is only natural that Zeus, the undisputed master of the Olympians, should become the universal god *par excellence* and the symbol of the idea of deity in every conceivable form. The Zeus of classical times is already straining at the limits of traditional conceptions. In the sixth century, Heraclitus could say that the power which is above all "both wills and does not will to be called Zeus." In a well-known passage of the *Agamemnon* of Aeschylus (170 ff.), Zeus is invoked as a symbol of the mysterious power which rules the universe and is the sole refuge of man:

> Zeus, whoever he be—if it please him to be invoked by this name—thus I call upon him. Nothing can I liken to him, when I have weighed all, nothing apart from Zeus, if the burden of vanity is in truth to be cast from the laden mind. . . . It is Zeus who leads men to wisdom, in that he has made "Learning through Suffering" his established law.

And in a fragment of the *Heliades* which has been preserved, the same poet anticipates the grandeur of the Stoic pantheism which will exalt the name of Zeus in the poems of Cleanthes and Aratus:

> Zeus is *Aither*, Zeus too is Earth, and Zeus is Heaven;
> Zeus is the sum of things and all that doth transcend it.

In Hellenistic times Zeus undergoes a twofold development. In the hands of the philosophers his name becomes merely a symbol for the divine. Even though anthropomorphic language may be used, the name is no more than a convenient traditional designation for the highest principle of being; it can be used in alternation with ὁ θεός or τὸ θεῖον with no perceptible difference of meaning, and the Stoics can speak indifferently of Zeus or Heimarmenē, Pronoia, Orthos Logos, Koinos Nomos, Mind, Spirit, or Fire. In popular usage, on the other hand, his name is given to a host of gods of other lands and peoples—agricultural gods of Anatolia whose former names are unknown to us, high gods of Egypt and of Syria (Amon, Hadad), the Wise Lord of Zoroastrianism (Ahura Mazda–Zeus Oromasdes), the Phrygian Sabazios, the Egyptian Serapis, the Hebrew Yahweh, some minor sun gods of Syria, and even the Roman emperor. With all this, Zeus continues to be honoured in the old cults of the Greek states in much the same way as before. Bulls and rams are still offered upon his altars, and men go to Dodona in quest of his oracles as late as the fourth century after Christ. The Olympic games were still celebrated in his honour until about the same period; in the time of Pausanias (*c.* A.D. 150) there were no less than seventy altars at Olympia, most of them dedicated to Zeus. Nor was the traditional worship limited to the older institutions. In the third century before Christ the Island of Cos provided games and sacrifices in honour of Zeus Soter and Athena Soteira, established a priesthood to serve them, and set aside a generous endowment to maintain them. Early in the second century, after the defeat of the Galatae, Pergamum built for Zeus the most enormous altar ever known—no less than four hundred feet long and seven feet high. (In the matter of new foundations, however, Zeus did not fare so well in Hellenistic times as did Athena, Apollo, and Aphrodite.) The general conception of Zeus continued to be compounded of the vivid word-pictures drawn by Homer, the statue by Phidias which was erected at Olympia, the recipient of the house-cult (Zeus Herkeios, Zeus Ktesios, Zeus Meilichios—represented under the latter two epithets in the form of a snake), the guardian of the city (Zeus Polieus) and of the council chamber (Zeus Boulaios), and not least, the weather god, who can bless or curse with rains and can destroy with his terrible weapon of the thunderbolt. People can still think of Zeus in animistic terms, as the divine Sky; a Greek peasant in Egypt can complain that he has had trouble getting in his harvest "because Zeus rained and the winds blew fiercely," and Marcus Aurelius can quote with approval the Athenian prayer: "Rain, rain, dear Zeus, upon the ploughlands of the Athenians and upon their pastures." In speaking of Zeus in the Hellenistic age we must not lose sight of the substantial carryover from earlier times.

To some extent, of course, this survival of earlier religious matter was a handicap to belief in Zeus. Like the other Olympians, he was the subject of numerous myths, some of them of the most revolting crudity, which represented him as acting in ways that outraged the moral sense of a more civilized age. The earlier philosophers had denounced the poets for ascribing to him all manner of adulteries and deceits and deeds which would be accounted shameful in a man. But in Hellenistic times the philosophers were more inclined to explain away the myths by allegory and to allege that "in these impious fables a really not inelegant scientific theory is contained."[1] But it must be admitted that these explanations rescued the moral character of Zeus by depriving him of every semblance of personality at all. The Zeus of the philosophers could not be an object of worship.

We may now survey in some detail the manifold identifications of Zeus with Oriental deities. This is one of the most remarkable aspects of the general Hellenistic *theokrasia.* Often enough there is no particular point of resemblance between the Greek Zeus and the various gods with whom he comes to be identified, unless it be that they are male. In some cases the only epithet is toponymic, and it may be that the local god had no name of his own until he was identified with Zeus; occasionally he is represented by a statue or relief, with insignia which give some indication of his nature. He is generally identified with the high god of the region; and with the all-encompassing advance of astrology in Roman times he receives ever more frequently the identification with Helios Aniketos, "the Unconquerable Sun." Thus he becomes the focal point of a pronounced tendency in the entire religion of the Empire to develop in the direction of a solar monotheism. From the days of Augustus, emperors are often honoured with a Zeus-title. Seleucus I had been styled Zeus Nikator three centuries before. Now Augustus is called Zeus Eleutherios ("the Liberator"), and even Zeus Soter ("the Saviour"); Nero is hailed as Neos Zeus ("the New Zeus"); Hadrian is honoured as Zeus Olympios in the great temple which he completed for the god at Athens, and then by statues in many other cities of Greece and of Asia. In the sun theology of the later Empire the sun is taken to be the visible form of Zeus in the heavens, and the emperor as his manifest form upon earth, while the high god himself is conceived as the invisible Mind that rules the universe. At this stage the personal name of Zeus disappears among the Greeks, and the supreme being is called simply Hypsistos ("the Most High") or occasionally Pantokrator ("Ruler of All"); but Latin writers continue to use the name Jupiter, with the epithets *summus exsuperantissimus.*

In Egypt, Zeus had long been identified with Amon, the great god of Thebes. From the time of the Middle Kingdom, when Thebes replaced Memphis as the capital, Amon had been the head of the pantheon. In priestly theory he was identified with Rēʿ, the great sun god of On (Heliopolis). His oracle at the oasis of Siwa in the western desert was

[1]Cicero, *De natura deorum* II. 63.

originally a shrine of the Syrian Baʿal-ḥamman, the god of Amanus, who was carried abroad by Phoenician colonists during the second millennium;[2] but it was inevitable that he should very soon be identified with the great Egyptian deity. At the oasis, he was adopted into the state cult of Cyrene shortly after its foundation by Greek colonists from Thera towards the end of the seventh century; in the sixth century his head appears on their coins, and his image is set up in the temple of Apollo Carneios, the principal divinity of the city. Through Cyrene, the cult of Zeus Ammon spread widely through Greece even before Alexander. He was worshipped at Thebes in the fifth century; the renowned poet Pindar dedicated a statue for him and composed a hymn in his honour "for the Ammonians of Libya." Early in the fourth century he had a public cult and a state priesthood at Athens. Alexander travelled to the oasis at the cost of much time and trouble to hear himself acknowledged as son of the god—son of Zeus, for Greeks and Macedonians, in so far as they could be brought to acknowledge his divinity at all; son of Amon, for his Egyptian subjects, who saw in the greeting of the priest the divine recognition of Alexander as their Pharaoh.

Even greater interest attaches to the identification of Zeus with Serapis, that extraordinary—and astonishingly successful—creation of Ptolemy Soter. There is still much disagreement about the early history of this cult; but it is now known that Ptolemy introduced a cult statue of the god in an ancient temple of Isis and Osiris in Rhakotis (the native suburb of Alexandria) while he was still satrap of Egypt under Alexander, and that the great Serapeum was not built until the time of his grandson Euergetes (*post* 247). In the intervening years his cult had been actively promoted in the islands of the Aegean and in the Greek cities of the Asian coast and of the Greek peninsula. Soter is said to have brought the cult statue from Sinope, but a new image was created for the god by a Greek sculptor. The iconography is essentially Greek, not Egyptian, and the rites were almost certainly a composition of Egyptian and Greek elements, since they were ordered by the Egyptian priest Manetho in association with the Eumolpid Timotheus of Eleusis. Cult hymns were composed for him by the philosopher-statesman Demetrius of Phalerum. For all that, Serapis was never looked upon as anything but an Egyptian god. Despite his Greek appearance he remains a foreigner in Greek lands and is usually accompanied by such unmistakably Egyptian attendants as Isis, Horus,

[2] O. Eissfeldt, *Kleine Schriften*, II, 58.

and Anubis. His sanctuaries were always served by Egyptian priests. It is probable that he was worshipped first by Greeks at Memphis under the name of Oserapis; this was the cult name of the god who was worshipped in the shrine attached to the burial chambers of the Apis bulls on the edge of the desert plateau west of Memphis (Sakkarah). Serapis has many attributes. Like the Egyptian Osiris, he is lord of the realms of the dead and men look to him for the gift of a blessed immortality; like Osiris again, he brings fertility to the soil. But he is also—and in Greek lands, predominantly—a healer, a giver of revelations through dreams, and a saviour of those in peril on the sea. In Roman times he is more and more identified with the divine Sun, Helios. The formula "Zeus Helios Sarapis" is found quite frequently from the second century onwards; it is very often inscribed on gems, almost certainly as a magic charm. Inscriptions in this name are found in many places, not only in Egypt but far abroad in different parts of the Mediterranean and beyond. In later centuries his titles are multiplied, and at least once, in a magical papyrus of the fourth century, he is called Zeus Helios Mithras Serapis Aniketos. Sometimes these titles are attached particularly to the Serapis of Canopus, who was renowned for miracles of healing, and we find dedications "to the good god Zeus Helios great Serapis in Canopus."[3] Through the general identification of Zeus with Jupiter, we find Latin dedications in Crete and in Italy to Jupiter Optimus Maximus as both Sol and Serapis (*Iovi Soli optimo maximo Sarapidi*) from the time of Trajan onward.

References to Zeus in the Greek papyri are surprisingly infrequent, and in several volumes of the Oxyrhynchus papyri[4] his name is not found at all, or is found only in oaths, most often in the form "by Zeus, Earth, Sun" (*na Dia Gēn Hēlion*). But it is a papyrus that gives us one of the most interesting of all our Zeus-Serapis documents. On the verso of a papyrus which contains a tax account of the reign of either Hadrian or Antoninus Pius (*P. Oxy.* 1445), there appears the last part of a wonder tale writen "in a large uncultivated hand of the same century" (*P. Oxy.* 1382). A colophon describes it as "The marvel (*aretē*) of Zeus Helios great Serapis regarding Syrion the helmsman." It has to do with the consent of the god to a gift of healing water from his shrine for the people of Pharos, whom we may suppose to have been afflicted by a plague. It begins with the gracious words of the

[3]Friedrich Preisigke, *Sammelbuch griechischer Urkunden aus Aegypten* (4 vols., Leipzig, 1915–31), no. 349.

[4]*The Oxyrhynchus Papyri* (London, 1898–), hereafter *P. Oxy.*

god, which would probably be communicated in a dream. "He said, 'For your sake I now give the water to the Pharites.' And he (that is, Syrion) saluted him and sailed forth and gave the water to the Pharites and received from them for its price one hundred drachmas of silver. And this marvel is recorded in the libraries of the Mercury quarter (one of the wards of the city of Alexandria). All that are present, say, 'One Zeus Serapis.' "

From Ptolemaic times in Egypt we have a number of dedications to Zeus Soter, who receives worship both private and public in countless cults of the Greek world from early times as protector of the house and of the state. Another traditional title, Zeus Olympios, is found chiefly in dedications at Olympia itself (at least until we come to the many dedications to Hadrian under this title in the second century). There is, however, an inscription from the reign of Ptolemy III Euergetes which has a peculiar interest in that it couples with this the otherwise unknown title Zeus Synomosios.[5] Certain altars, precincts, and the land pertaining to them are dedicated "to the Brother Gods and Zeus Olympios and Zeus Synomosios," by Cleon and Antipatros, the priests of Zeus. Zeus is here introduced, in all likelihood, in his traditional function as the sanctioning power of the oaths sworn to make a treaty binding; but in this capacity his usual title is Zeus Horkios. In 2 B.C. a cult statue of Zeus Phrygios was erected in Alexandria by Gaius Julius Hephaistion, "acting as priest of the politeuma of the Phrygians (*OGIS*, II, 658). This "Phrygian Zeus" may have been Sabazios, but it is perhaps more likely that he is a form of a local agricultural deity who was worshipped under the name of Zeus in many towns and villages of Phrygia.[6] Finally we may mention, from the tenth year of Trajan (A.D. 106/7), a dedication by Leonidas, helmsman of the Nile, "to Zeus called Nephotes the Megistos" (*OGIS*, II, 676). The name Nephotes is a transliteration from the Egyptian Nep-pet, "lord of heaven"—probably a local divinity of the Fayum. With all this, there is nothing in Egypt that approaches the multiplicity of Zeus cults that come before us in Syria and Anatolia.

In Syria, Zeus is identified with the baʿals of all the principal cities. Hadad, the great god of Damascus, consort of the "Syrian goddess"

[5]W. Dittengerger, *Orientis Graecae Inscriptiones Selectae: Supplementum Sylloges Inscriptionum Graecarum* (2 vols., Leipzig, 1903–5), I, 65. Hereafter cited as *OGIS*.

[6]W. Calder, *et al.*, eds., *Monumenta Asiae Minoris Antiqua* (8 vols., Manchester, 1928–62), VII, xxxii ff. Hereafter cited as *MAMA*.

Atargatis (Derceto), and like her marked strongly with Anatolian traits, could not fail to suggest Zeus to a Greek, for the thunderbolt was most prominent among his insignia. His Greek cult title of Zeus Damascenos passes to the Romans as Jupiter Damascenus. The Hadad of Baalbek-Heliopolis is likewise Hellenized, and subsequently Romanized, as Zeus (Jupiter) Heliopolitanus. On the island of Delos, a sanctuary was erected in 128 B.C. for Hadad and Atargatis, and not much later we have a dedication to Zeus Adados. The Syrian Baʿal-shamēm is identified with Zeus Ouranios and an attempt is made to identify him with the God of Israel, when Antiochus Epiphanes makes offerings (of swine!) to him in the temple at Jerusalem.

Even more remarkable is the identification of Zeus with a large number of minor local deities of Syria, generally sun gods of no particular renown. From the third century A.D. we have an inscription of Palmyra which honours a certain Septimius Vorodes as "symposiarch of the priests of the [god] Zeus Belos" (*OGIS*, II, 646). More frequently the baʿal is given a toponymic, as when an altar is dedicated to the baʿal of Bosra as "Holy Zeus Beelbosoros and Helios" (*OGIS*, II, 620). It seems probable that the Helios of this inscription is not a second divinity, but Zeus himself as sun god. The epithets Hagnos and Hagios are quite frequently given to Syrian deities, and do not carry any affirmation of moral qualities in the god but merely indicate that he is not to be approached without ritual purifications. On occasion a traditional cult title of Zeus is given. The gymnasiarch Athenion, at Jerash, records what he has spent on the building of the temple of Zeus Olympios (*OGIS*, II, 620); and Agathangelos of Abilene in the Decapolis dedicates a dining-hall to Zeus Megistos Keraunios (*OGIS*, II, 631). ("Megistos," however, is not a traditional cult title of Zeus in the Greek world, though it is found very frequently as an epithet, from Homer on.) Occasionally a local name is preserved and the solar aspect made explicit. From the age of Constantine we have a dedication from Trachonitis to "the lord (*despotēs*) [Zeus] Aniketos Helios the god Aumos" (*OGIS*, II, 619). (In this inscription the name Zeus is restored with certainty by the aid of another inscription to the same god.)

An inscription of exceptional interest tells a good deal about the changing fortunes of the god of the village of Baitokaiké in northern Syria. It begins with the copy of a letter issued by "King Antiochus" (one of the later Seleucids) granting a request for the transfer of the village together with all its property and possessions, which were formerly owned by a certain Demetrius, to "the god Zeus of Baitokaiké."

This is followed by a decree of the city (Apamea?) which had been sent to the "god Augustus," concerning the commercial dealings of the temple; and concludes with a statement that these documents have been set up in public by "the *katochoi* of Holy Zeus Ouranios." Above these Greek inscriptions is a rescript of the emperors Valerian and Gallienus confirming the temple in the undisturbed enjoyment of its ancient privileges; this gives us a final date of A.D. 253–9. It is significant that the god of Baitokaikê has now become not only Zeus, but Zeus Ouranios, in keping with the general growth of solar religion in the later Empire. The letter of Antiochus justifies the grant of the village and its lands to the god, on the ground that from it "the power (*dynamis*) of the god goes forth." Clearly enough at that stage he was not looked upon as a god of heaven.

Some few of these local baʿals were destined to attain a wider fame. The priest of Elagabalus, the god of Emesa, was raised to the imperial throne by his troops, and used his power for the glory of his god. He himself took the name Elagabalus, and he caused the black stone which he adored to be transported to Rome and honoured as the chief god of the state under the cult title of Sol Invictus Elagabalus (A.D. 218). This innovation had no lasting success, partly because it was premature and even more because all this ruler's acts were annulled through the *damnatio memoriae* which was pronounced by the Senate at his death. But in 274 the Emperor Aurelian, after the defeat of Zenobia, transported the Bel of Palmyra to Rome and gave him a temple and a priesthood and a college of *pontifices* as Sol Invictus; December 25 was set apart for the celebration of his birth and the founding of this temple—it was the *dies natalis Solis Invicti* long before it was recognized as the birthday of our Lord. It would appear that this Bel was worshipped by Greeks at Palmyra under the cult title of Zeus Hypsistos, which appears on the vast majority of Greek dedications there.

The Baʿal of Mount Kasios, near Antioch on the Orontes, where he was worshipped in the form of a conical stone, received a cult in many parts of the Hellenistic world under the name of Zeus Kasios (Jupiter Casius). He has been identified with the Baʿal Zaphon ("Lord of the North") of the Ugaritic texts, and under this appellation he had established himself in Egypt many centuries earlier, in the middle of the second millennium. He had a notable sanctuary near Pelusium, on a low ridge a little more than thirty miles east of the town, which was also known as Mount Kasios, and it was from there that his cult spread more widely still in the Hellenistic Age. He was a storm god (like all the Syrian baʿals) and a sea god; as early as the seventh century he is invoked in a curse formula, along with Baʿal-shamēm and the otherwise unknown Baal-malagê and other Tyrian gods, to cause the destruction of ships in case of the violation of a treaty. Greek seamen and merchants carried his cult from Pelusium to Delos, Corcyra, Epidaurus, and Athens; and Latin dedications to him are found at Corcyra[7] (*Iovi Casio*), and even as far away as Heddernheim (*CIL* xiii.2.7330–*Deo Casio*). The earliest Greek documents of his cult come from Delos, and are probably to be dated in 88 B.C. The most interesting of these is made on behalf of a Roman official, Lucius Granicus, "to the great god and Zeus Kasios and Tachnepsis." This inscription is found in the earliest of the three Serapeums on Delos. The dedicant bears an Egyptian name; the sanctuary in which it is found is Egyptian, and the name Tachnepsis is a further Egyptian touch, so that there can be no doubt that it is the god of the Pelusiac sanctuary that is thus honoured. The "great god" will then probably designate Serapis. The dedicant has taken his action *kata prostagma*–"in accordance with a command"–that is, by order of the god himself. Zeus Kasios is a god who makes revelations of his will for men, probably in dreams. The phrase and equivalent expressions (in Latin, *ex iussu, ex praecepto*) occur frequently in dedications to the Syrian gods. The same inscription includes ritual requirements–no woman may approach the shrine, and no man may come near it clothed in wool.[8] Evidence for the cult at Athens and Epidaurus, always in association with Egyptian gods, is much later. Corcyra went so far as to put Zeus Kasios on her coins, making use of a traditional Greek representation; but among the furnishings of his temple there was a marble ship, and the ship is one of the constant insignia of the old Syrian deity.

Seleucia in Pieria was founded by Seleucus Nikator to serve as the port of Antioch, about the end of the fourth century B.C. According to the foundation legend, the site was indicated to him by the god him-himself, as he was offering a sacrifice on Mount Kasios. The baʿal of the mountain was the tutelary deity of Seleucia from the beginning, and the conical stone which was his principal symbol appears on its coins. Strangely enough, however, there is no direct evidence for a Greek cult of him in this area until the second century A.D. In Egypt, as in Syria, it is likely that he was at first represented in the form of a

[7]*Corpus Inscriptionum Latinarum* iii. 576, 577. Hereafter cited as *CIL*.
[8]An Egyptian prohibition; cf. Plutarch, *Isis and Osiris* 352DE.

conical black stone; but at some later time, perhaps in connection with the temple built for him by Hadrian, an image of a Greek type was created for him. It is described by Achilles Tatius, who tells us that he was represented as a youthful, beardless deity, "resembling rather Apollo," holding a pomegranate in his outstretched hand; there is a *mystikos logos* having to do with the pomegranate. The pomegranate is a symbol of immortality; it is not mentioned elsewhere in connection with this cult, nor is it an Egyptian symbol. It may be that we should see in it some evidence of Anatolian influence.

Still greater popularity was to be attained by the god of the little town of Dolichē in Commagene. Centuries earlier he had been the chief deity of the Hittites in the time of their ascendancy; they knew him as Teshub. Before that he seems to have been the patron deity of the wandering metalworkers called Chalybes, and traces of this early character survive in the Roman description of him as *natus ubi ferrum nascitur*. Recognized by the Greeks as a form of Zeus, under the title of Zeus Dolichaios or Dolichenos, he became a great favourite of the armies in the second and third centuries of our era. With his name Latinized as Jupiter Dolichenus, he was carried to Rome in the time of Hadrian (perhaps even earlier) by soldiers of the Commagene cohorts, and from there his worship spread to the farthest outposts of the Empire. He actually comes to be identified with the supreme deity of the state cult under the title of Jupiter Optimus Maximus Dolichenus; and with the trend towards solar monotheism in the later Empire he receives resounding additional epithets—Eternal, Preserver of the Whole Heaven, Pre-eminent Numen, Providence, and (inevitably) Sol Invictus. None the less, he continues to be served by his own priests, and admission to his cult is reserved for those whom he calls into his service (probably through dreams or omens) after a period of novitiate and ceremonies of initiation.[9]

The Kingdom of Commagene also provides us with an identification of Zeus with the great Zoroastrian deity Ahura Mazda, "the Wise Lord." Here in the first half of the first century B.C., Antiochus I, who describes himself as "Great King Antiochus, the Righteous God Manifest, Philoroman and Philhellene," erected a great cairn at the summit of the highest mountain in his kingdom, the Nemrud-Dagh. To the east and to the west of the cairn he constructed wide terraces, and on each terrace he caused a group of five colossal statues to be set up. In

[9]H. Dessau, ed., *Inscriptiones Latinae Selectae* (3 vols. in 4, Berlin, 1892–1916), no. 4316; cf. K. Latte, *Römische Religionsgeschichte* (Munich, 1960), p. 348.

the centre of each group was Zeus Oromasdes. His insignia were chiefly those of Zeus—eagles, oakleaves and acorns, and thunderbolts—but there is a considerable use of astral motifs, which are not truly Zoroastrian, but Babylonian—later Zoroastrianism is deeply impregnated with the astralism of Babylonia. Zeus Oromasdes wears a diadem thickly sprinkled with stars and a tiara bordered with pearls, which are probably also meant to represent stars. Oriental motifs are seen also in the adornment of his throne, which is supported on lions' feet and has chimaera heads mounted on the arms. On the left of this Zeus stand the Tyche of Commagene and a deity who bears the compound title of Apollo Mithras Helios Hermes; on his right stand Antiochus himself represented as a Zeus incarnate, and another compound divinity—Artagnes (Verethraghna) Herakles Ares. Priests are depicted in Persian dress. In the accompanying inscription the king proclaims his descent from Persian and Greek stock and tells the world that he has always shown by his outstanding piety that he regarded his kingdom as "a dwelling common to all the gods." In the cairn which he has erected "close to the thrones of heaven," his body is to sleep to eternity while his devout soul ascends "to the heavenly thrones of Zeus Oromasdes." He promises a blessed immortality to those whose minds have remained pure and who have walked in the ways of the gods. They will see close at hand the great celestial home of Zeus Oromasdes. But punishments of "hostile fire" await the priest or *steganomos* (warden) who dares defile the sacred land of the gods. All this indicates that a remarkable fusion of Mazdaean and Greek eschatological doctrines was attached to the cult of Zeus Oromasdes, and Cumont suggests that similar ideas were carried from Commagene to a wider world in connection with the cult of Jupiter Dolichenus.[10]

When we move into Asia Minor, we find ourselves in lands where Greeks had been in contact with Oriental peoples for centuries. The Greeks of Ephesus had long since made the Anatolian mother-goddess their own under the title of "the Artemis of the Ephesians," though she continued to be served by a caste of professional priests and thousands of hierodules, male and female. Artemis Leukophryene, of Magnesia on the Maeander, is another form of the Great Mother. The very name Artemis is not Greek, but Lydian in origin. Other Olympian gods were adopted by the Greeks from the Asiatic peoples. Hephaestus, Ares, Aphrodite, familiar figures as they are in all Greek literature and art, were introduced to the Greek world only through the colonization of

[10]F. Cumont, *Lux Perpetua* (Paris, 1949), pp. 226, 271–2.

the Asian coast and its islands. Apollo himself, who seems to many to be the very spirit of Greek civilization, is in origin an Asiatic. And long before the Hellenistic Age, the Greeks had identified many Asiatic gods with Zeus. The tutelary deity of the Carian confederacy, for instance, was known to the Greeks as Zeus Stratios—"the Zeus of the armies"; and also, from the double-headed axe (*labrys*) which he carried, he was often called Zeus Labrandeus. In the latter case, it would appear that the god was first called Labrayndos, "wielder of the double-axe," that he gave this name to his sanctuary Labranda (near Mylasa), and from it in turn received the epithet Labrandeus. In Mylasa itself there was a sanctuary of another Carian god whom the Greeks identified with Zeus under the cult title of Zeus Osogoa. As his insignia included a crab and a trident as well as an eagle, the Greeks thought of him as a blend of Zeus and Poseidon and we find the name Zenoposeidon given to him in local inscriptions after the third century B.C. It would appear that the *theokrasia* of the Hellenistic age was largely anticipated by the Greeks of the Asian coastlands.

Asian inscriptions of the Hellenistic age provide us with many references to Zeus under traditional titles. At Sardis, there was a temple and an eponymous priest of Zeus Polieus. At Pergamum, glorying in its Greek character, we hear of Zeus Soter, Zeus Philios, Zeus Boulaios, and Zeus Olympios; several of these epithets occur in other cities of Ionia. In these instances, it is the Greek Zeus who is honoured with traditional forms of Greek cult abroad. More significant is the manifold identification of minor local gods with Zeus in all parts of the region. Often he is distinguished only by a toponymic, and it may well be that the local god never had a native name. We have, for instance, an altar dedicated to "the ancestral god Zeus Bonitenos," from an otherwise unknown village of Bonité in Pontus. At Tralles, there was a sanctuary of Zeus Larasios; his priest was a person of high distinction and great influence. One of them, Menodorus by name, was put to death by one of Antony's commanders on suspicion that he had been inciting the sailors of the fleet to go over to Octavian.[11] Two hundred years later we hear of a Roman knight, son of the High Priest of Asia, or Asiarch, who is priest of Zeus Larasios for life; again it appears that the holder of this priesthood was a person of consequence in civil affairs. The book of Acts mentions "the priest of the Zeus-before-the-city" (14:13); and the circumstances indicate that this was a native Lycaonian deity identified with Zeus.

[11]Strabo, *Geographica* XIV. 1. 42.

More than a hundred and fifty dedications to Zeus Bronton have been found in the neighbourhood of Dorylaeum, in northern Phrygia. Natural though the epithet is for a god who wields the thunderbolt, it does not occur as a cult title anywhere except here and in places to which it has been carried by people of this area. The Phrygian Zeus of the *politeuma* in Alexandria (*vide supra*, p. 102) may have been Bronton; and five inscriptions of the cult have been found at Rome, probably reflecting the devotions of Phrygian slaves. About half of the Phrygian dedications are on tombstones. The ornamentation seldom shows the traditional eagle or the thunderbolt; it consists chiefly of symbols of agriculture—plough, mattock, heads of oxen, vine and grape-clusters. "The Thunderer," accordingly, is a god of agriculture, of the vineyard and the ploughed land, and at the same time a guardian of graves. Almost certainly, this is not a Greek cult, but the worship of a Phrygian deity under the Greek name. He is found once or twice in association with a Zeus Bennios or Benneus ("of the car"—*benna*), who appears more frequently in an adjacent region of Phrygia Epictetus. Some of the tombstones note that they were set up by the dedicant during his lifetime, for himself and sometimes for other members of his family, frequently *kat' epitagēn*, "by command" of the god. In other parts of Phrygia the old agricultural deity of the native population is given epithets which more distinctly indicate his concern for the cattle and the crops; he is Zeus Phatnios (*MAMA*, I, 7); Zeus Epikarpios (*MAMA*, VII, 476); or Zeus Eukarpos (*MAMA*, VII, 453). Sir William Calder has recently drawn attention to the exceptional interest of the Phrygian epitaphs for the history of early Christianity. "But for this Phrygian method of placing graves under divine guardianship, Phrygia would not make the unique claim it makes on the attention of the Christian epigraphist" (*MAMA*, VII, xxxvi ff.). The same formulae of imprecation are used, but God and Christ take the place of Zeus Bronton (or Men, or the Mother), and the eagle and the lion give way to the Cross.

In many places of Asia Minor the temples of Zeus, like those of the Great Mother, were wealthy landholding corporations with estates cultivated by thousands of hierodules. The priesthoods were hereditary in powerful families. The priest of Zeus Olbios, near Olba in Cilicia Aspera, claimed descent from Ajax, son of Teucer, one of the Homeric heroes; and the names of Ajax and Teucer were used in alternation by the "great High Priest of Zeus," as he termed himself. But behind this Teucer lies the name Tarkyaris, formed upon the name of the ancient Anatolian god Tarku, who is almost certainly the original god of this sanctuary. It is most unlikely that the identification with Zeus made any difference to the rites of worship. The temple of Zeus at Vesana, in western Cappadocia, was likewise possessed of large estates and ruled by a priest who was recognized as the third-ranking person in the kingdom (after the king himself and the priest of the Ma of Comana).

These Anatolian Zeus cults, unlike those of Syria, did not achieve any great significance beyond the immediate locality. Only the Phrygian Sabazios succeeds in winning a wider renown, and he seems to have travelled abroad chiefly under his own name, not reduced to a cult title of Zeus. Originally he was closely related to Dionysos; these two are really twin forms of the one Thraco-Phrygian god of vegetation. Both cults have the same orgiastic character; the *bacchoi* of Dionysos have their counterpart in the *saboi* of Sabazios. There was a cult of Zeus Sabazios at Pergamum, of which we hear in a decree of King Attalus III Philometor (138–133 B.C.). It was introduced, he tells us, by his mother Stratonice, who brought it with her from her homeland (she was a daughter of King Ariarathes IV of Cappadocia); she was the most pious of all women, and showed her reverence for all the gods but especially for Zeus Sabazios. By decree of the king, his mother's favourite god is now given a place in the temple of Athena Nikephoros, and his priesthood is entrusted to Athenaeus, son of Sosandros, and made hereditary in his family, to be held in conjunction with the priesthood of Dionysos Kathegemon, the god of the royal house. The king is at some pains to emphasize that the priesthood is "held in the highest honour among us," and is conferred on Athenaeus as a reward for his fidelity (*OGIS*, I, 331). At Pergamum, then, the cult of Zeus Sabazios was part of the apparatus of the state religion. The few dedications to him which have been found elsewhere (Delos, Epidaurus, Lydia) have nothing to indicate a connection with Pergamum; those from Lydia are chiefly confessions of sin, prompted by the misfortunes which have come upon the dedicant by reason of his failure to respect the god.

Zeus Ourios, giver of the fair wind (*ouros*), had a sanctuary on the Asiatic side of the Thracian Bosporus, at the entrance to the Euxine Sea. Hellenistic writers refer to it as Hieron, "the Sanctuary," as if this alone were enough to identify it. The epithet is found as early as 475 B.C. in the *Suppliants* of Aeschylus (594); but in this passage it is not a cult title, nor is there any reason to see in it a reference to the god of Hieron (*contra* A. B. Cook[12]); it simply honours Zeus as the god who brings to a prosperous issue the ventures of his worshippers—*ourios* had long since passed into a metaphor which was not limited to sailing. According to legend, the temple had been founded by Jason or by Phrixos; Jason plays the role of founder of Greek temples abroad in much the way that Abraham is made the founder of sanctuaries in Palestine. Old the sanctuary may have been; it is indeed not unlikely that behind Zeus Ourios stands a more primitive sea god of the Euxine people; but we have in fact no references to the cult until the Hellenistic age. Cicero tells us of a statue of this god which was brought to Rome from Macedonia by Flamininus in 197 B.C.; he mentions another which was in Syracuse, but was stolen by Verres (*Verrines*, II. 4. 128f.). There are a number of dedications from Delos, chiefly from the closing years of the second century B.C., which indicate that the cult was carried by merchants trading into the Euxine and adopted by other seafarers. One of them is made on behalf of Mithridates Eupator and his brother and their ventures (*OGIS*, II, 368); Mithridates put his brother to death shortly afterwards. All the Delos dedications were found in a sanctuary of the Egyptian gods to the northwest of Mount Kynthios, and several of them are dedicated to Zeus Ourios in association with Isis and her train. A certain Eutyches makes an offering "to Zeus Ourios, Sarapis, Anubis, Harpokrates, gods who share the temple and the altar, on behalf of himself and his son Euboulos and all who sail the seas."[13] The Egyptian gods are worshipped here in their capacity of helpers of those at sea; the same sanctuary includes dedications to Isis as Isis Euploia, and to the Dioscuri. Late in the second century B.C. we find a dedication to Zeus Ourios by three cult associations of Roman merchants trading into the Euxine—Hermiasts, Apolloniasts, and Poseidoniasts; to them the Latin equivalent of his name is Jupiter Secundanus. This epithet reflects the broader metaphorical sense of *ourios* as "bringing to a prosperous issue."

We have had occasion to notice a number of instances of the straight translation of the name Zeus into Latin as Jupiter. Much less frequent

[12]A. B. Cook, *Zeus: A Study in Ancient Religion* (3 vols. in 4, Oxford, 1914–40).

[13]P. Roussel, "Les cultes égyptiens de Délos du IIIe au Ier siècle avant Jésus Christ," *Annales de l'Est*, XXIX–XXX (1915–16).

is the translation of the Latin Jupiter into Greek as Zeus, but it does occur in the Roman colonies in Greek-speaking lands, such as Philippi and Corinth. Jupiter Capitolinus turns up more broadly as Zeus Kapetolios. It is impossible, however, to find any trace of influence of the Latin conception of Jupiter on Greek ideas of Zeus. On the contrary, the great Italian numen was effectively made over in the image of Zeus. The Jupiter of Vergil is nothing else than a stately and rather stolid Zeus *togatus*, and the statuary of Jupiter is wholly derived from Greek traditions of sculpture. In this one identification, it should be remembered, we have a return to a prehistoric unity; for both Zeus and Jupiter are forms of the Indo-European sky god, the only god who is found in every division of this far-flung racial family.

The name of Zeus covers a multitude of gods of the most diverse origin and character, and it is impossible to find any unifying or determining element that could issue in the conception of Zeus as the one God exalted over all. Tendencies towards monotheism there certainly were in the ancient world, but they take shape more and more in the adoration of the sun, who may be called Zeus or Jupiter but really owes little or nothing to the manifold object of the ancient cults. Thoughtful men among the Greeks were not in the least concerned to affirm that the name of the high god is Zeus, and that he will not share his glory with another. The "True Word" of Celsus may be taken as the viewpoint of most cultivated Greeks of his time. "It makes no difference," he tells us, "whether we call the most high God Zeus or Adonis or Sabaoth or Amon, as do the Egyptians, or Papas, as do the Scythians."[14]

ADDITIONAL BIBLIOGRAPHY

GENERAL

FARNELL, L. R. *Cults of the Greek States*, Vol. I, Oxford, 1896.

MAGIE, D. *Roman Rule in Asia Minor to the End of the Third Century after Christ*, 2 vols., Princeton, 1950.

NILSSON, M. *Geschichte der griechischen Religion*. II. *Die hellenistische und römische Zeit*, Munich, 1950; 2nd ed. rev., 1962 (not available to me).

PRÜMM, K. *Religionsgeschichtliches Handbuch für den Raum der altchristlichen Umwelt*, Rome, 1954 (reprint of edition of 1943).

VON WILAMOWITZ-MOELLENDORF, U. *Der Glaube der Hellenen*, 2 vols., Basel, 1956 (reprint of edition of 1932).

[14]Origen, *Contra Celsum* V. 41.

SPECIAL STUDIES

EISSFELDT, O. *Baal Zaphon, Zeus Kasios und der Durchzug der Israeliten durchs Meer* (Beiträge zur Religionsgeschichte des Altertums, Heft 1), Halle a/d Saale, 1932.

KAN, A. H. *Iuppiter Dolichenus*, Leiden, 1943.

ROBERTS, C. H., T. C. SKEAT, and A. D. NOCK. "The Gild of Zeus Hypsistos," *Harvard Theological Review*, XXIX, 1 (January, 1936), 39–76.

SALAC, A. "Ζεὺς Κάσιος," *Bulletin de Correspondance hellénique*, XLVI (1922), 160–89.

8. The Molten Sea of Solomon's Temple

GILBERT BAGNANI

THE DESCRIPTION OF SOLOMON'S TEMPLE as given in I Kings and II Chronicles is extremely detailed and elaborate, but all the innumerable attempts, both ancient and modern, to reconstruct it from the given data at once encounter fantastic difficulties—historic, artistic, practical, and technical. Some discouraged scholars have therefore concluded that the whole description is a product of post-exilic imagination, and that trying to reconstruct Solomon's temple is like trying to draw a map of Coleridge's Xanadu. Such scepticism seems excessive. If, as seems probable, I Kings was written *c.* 550 B.C.[1] the writer and compiler must have known people who had seen the temple before its destruction in 586. Their memories may have been vague and inexact, they will naturally have tended to amplification and exaggeration, but their evidence cannot be summarily dismissed. It should not be impossible to distinguish reality from post-exilic hyperbole.

A case in point is "the molten sea" described in I Kings 7:23–26 and in II Chronicles 4:2–5. It was a colossal bronze vessel said to have been cast—I note in passing that the adjective "molten" does not appear in the Septuagint version of Kings—by Hiram of Tyre on the banks of the Jordan[2] and set up in the temple court presumably, as indicated in Chronicles, for priestly ablutions. As described in Kings it was "round all about" with circumference of thirty cubits, a diameter of ten cubits, and a height of five cubits. Its elaborate rim decorated with gourds is described in considerable detail. It was a handsbreadth, that is to say a span, in thickness, and was supported by or rested upon four groups of three bronze bulls. Its capacity was of 2000 "baths." This description and these dimensions are repeated without substantial difference in Chronicles, except that the capacity is said to have been of 3000 "baths."

[1]S. Szekszai, *The Interpreter's Dictionary of the Bible* (New York, 1962), III, 34–5.

[2]According to II Chronicles 2:13 his name was Huram-abi; I believe that some persons consider him to have been the first freemason.

This description has given rise to some quite fantastic reconstruction; the most recent and sensible discussion of the data is the study by C. C. Wylie[3] dealing chiefly with the metrology. Of the two possible cubits, the standard of measurement mentioned, he rightly preferred the royal cubit of 20.9 inches to the short cubit of 17.6 inches. He then went on to examine the value of the "bath" as a measure of capacity, concluding that it was equivalent to about four imperial or five American gallons. This would seem to be in accordance with physical probability. In Egypt water for my workmen was brought by girls from the canal about a mile away in four-gallon petrol tins, and forty pounds of water in an earthenware jar is about as much as one person can manage. Considerably more could be carried in skins that could be slung on donkeys and this may account for the "royal bath" measure which is about double. Noting that the rabbis calculated eight baths to the cubic cubit, he then considered the discrepancy of a thousand baths in the capacity as given in Kings and in Chronicles. Neither figure was based on actual measurement—the omission of the capacity in the Septuagint version would seem to confirm this supposition—but was arrived at by calculations from the linear data. The writer of Kings assumed that "round all about" meant that the "sea" was hemispherical. He then applied to the data for the circumference and depth the formula $V = 1/3\ Cr^2$, that is to say $V = 1/3\ 30.25$, or 250 cubic cubits. And since eight baths are equal to a cubic cubit he finally reached the figure of 2000 "baths." The scribe of Chronicles, arguing on the same data, assumed that the "sea" was cylindrical and the formula $V = 1/2\ Crh$ gave him 1/2 30.5.5 or 375 cubic cubits or 3000 "baths." Since a hemispherical shape is less hopelessly improbable than a circular one, Wylie finally concluded that the scribe of Kings was right and that the "sea" contained something like 10,000 American or 8,000 imperial gallons.

This is a definite advance over the previous fantastic estimates of up to 20,000 gallons, and Wylie's reasoning is, I think, both ingenious and correct, but it still does not make sense. The statement that Hiram's foundries were on the banks of the Jordan is almost certainly correct.[4] Even admitting that Hiram had not only the technical knowledge, but also the material possibility and resources that would enable him to cast such an enormous mass of metal, how could such a monstrosity have been taken from the river bank to the temple

[3]C. C. Wylie, in *Biblical Archaeologist*, XII (1949), 90: cf. A. Parrot, *Le Temple de Jérusalem* (Neuchâtel, 1954), p. 32.
[4]A. Parrot, *Le Temple de Jérusalem*, p. 37.

court? And how could it have been used? It would have been difficult to fill and almost impossible to empty. Even by Wylie's calculations it would have held some forty tons of water. Since the rim of the vessel would have been at least eight feet above the surface of the court how could the priests have used it for their ablutions?[5] If they used a ladder to get up to it there was the risk of drowning if one lost one's footing. It is not a "sea" but a tank or reservoir.

The term "sea" is only applicable to something that exhibited to view a large expanse of water, that is to say visitors to the temple must have been able to look down and over the surface of the water, which must therefore have been below, not above, eye level. Moreover the rim is the only part of the vessel that is described in detail and we can therefore suppose that it was the only part that could be easily inspected. Since no one could possibly know what the thickness of the vessel was, the thickness of a handsbreadth almost certainly refers to the thickness of this rim. The bulls that must have been equally conspicuous and accessible are not described in the same detail, but they had been melted down and replaced by masonry supports in the reign of Ahaz. By the middle of the sixth century there must still have been many persons who remembered and could describe the "sea" and its rim but none who could remember the four groups of bulls. I suggest therefore that the compiler of I Kings derived his acount from oral descriptions of the rim of the vessel, with its thirty gourds placed at regular intervals of a cubit. From these he deduced a circumference of thirty cubits, a diameter of ten cubits, and a depth equal to the radius.[6]

If we jettison the wholly preposterous figure of five cubits in depth but retain the rest of the description there is no difficulty in reconstructing a vessel that could be made technically and used practically. If the "sea" was a very shallow bowl, saucer, or patera of some nine or ten cubits in diameter but only a cubit or little more in depth at the centre, it would when filled with water give the impression of a

[5]Perrot and Chipiez, *HGA*, IV, 327 in their reconstruction (reproduced by Parrot) get round the difficulty by providing it with an opening at the bottom but do not seem to have given it a tap or spigot!

[6]There is no point in discussing whether or not the scribes believed ii to be equal to 3 (the writer of the Septuagint makes the even more preposterous assumption that it is 3.3): that the ratio of the radius to the circumference was approximately 3 1/7 must have been known empirically to every wheelwright and certainly to a first-rate artisan such as Hiram.

"sea," it could be used for ablutions, and its rim could be easily observed. A parabolic bowl of nine cubits in diameter—I allow something for the rim—and one cubit in depth would contain 31.82 cubic cubits. A capacity of between thirty and forty cubic cubits would be equal to between 240 and 320 "baths" or between 960 and 1280 imperial gallons, a much more probable figure. Such a bowl will not have been cast but, like the crater of Vix, the largest bronze vessel that has come to us from antiquity,[7] hammered out cold from a sheet of bronze, and this could be and almost certainly was done in the temple court itself. The rim was cast separately in sections of a cubit from the same mould and, as in the case of the Vix crater, riveted to the rim. The joins between the sections and with the rim were carefully concealed and the visitors, seeing that the rim was indubitably cast, will have assumed that it was in one piece with the bowl, whence the epithet "molten." The bottom of the bowl will have rested directly on the pavement of the court and the four groups of bulls did not support it but merely steadied it. Since these groups will have been cast nearly solid they contained proportionately by far the largest mass of metal, enough to satisfy the Assyrians. Their replacement by masonry piers presented no difficulty, indeed it could be accomplished without even emptying the bowl itself.

[7]On the crater of Vix and its technical construction see R. Joffroy in *Monuments Piot*, XLVIII (1956), 6–7. G. Garbini in *Enciclopedia dell'Arte Antica* (Rome, 1961) IV, 41 also assumes that the vessel must have been hammered.

9. In Search of the Divine Denis

JOHN M. RIST

NEARLY TWO YEARS AGO a paper read to the Oriental Club of Toronto on the subject of fakes and forgeries was published in *Phoenix*.[1] Much to my disappointment I found no reference there to one of the most famous literary frauds ever perpetrated: a fraud which not only passed almost undiscerned for a thousand years and unconvicted for four hundred more, but which during a large part of that period exercised a very considerable influence over the philosophical, theological, and mystical doctrines of European man. I refer to the body of writings which has been transmitted to us as the work of St. Denis, the "divine Denis," that Dionysius the Areopagite, who, as we read in Acts 17, was a convert of St. Paul in Athens.

Besides a number of additional spurious works, the writings that bear the name of Dionysius the Areopagite are the treatises on the *Divine Names* (*DN*), on *Mystical Theology*, on the *Celestial Hierarchy*, and on the *Ecclesiastical Hierarchy*, plus ten letters, some of them to well-known Christian figures, the tenth for example is to St. John the Evangelist, in exile on Patmos. Dionysius forecasts that his exile will eventually be brought to an end.

Thus we see that Dionysius—for we will not deprive him of the name by which he wishes to be called—has no scruples about citing the most important Christian figures as evidence for his belonging to the Apostolic Age and for his claim to be the disciple of St. Paul. In addition to the letter to John, we may mention that the treatises open with an address as follows: From Dionysius the Presbyter to his fellow Presbyter Timothy; and that in chapter one of the *Mystical Theology* (1020D) Dionysius appeals to the teachings of St. Bartholomew, of which we know very little.[2] Bartholomew says, according to Dionysius, that the subject matter of theology is both great and minute, and that the gospel is both great and broad, and at the same time con-

[1] G. Bagnani, "On Fakes and Forgeries," *Phoenix*, XIV (1960), 228–44.

[2] On the supposed connection of Bartholomew with the Gnostic *Book of the Resurrection of Christ* see J. Doresse, *The Secret Books of the Egyptian Gnostics* (London, 1960), p. 95.

cise (συντετμημένον). Again, in the seventh letter (1081B), Dionysius tells us that when the sky was darkened at the time of the crucifixion of Jesus he himself was at Heliopolis and saw the miracle there. Finally here is a passage from his description of the scene at the death of Mary: "When, as you know, Hierotheus and many of our holy brothers and ourselves met together to see that body, Source of Life and Receiver of God (Θεοδόχου), and James the brother of God was there, and Peter, the chief and senior of the Sacred Men, and then after we had seen her, all the hierarchs celebrated the omnipotent goodness of the Divine weakness, each according to his capabilities; on that occasion Hierotheus surpassed all the initiates apart from the Apostles and was wholly transported, wholly outside of himself, and experienced communion with the mysteries he was celebrating" (*DN* 681CD).

Such passages as these once inclined me to wonder if perhaps the sections of Dionysius which claimed apostolic authority were later insertions in the work of a man who himself originally made no such claims. Most of his references to Paul could be taken as references not to Paul's spoken but to his written teachings; but it appears impossible to adopt this solution. The claims to authenticity are built into the work too elaborately and carefully to be mere interpolations. One must assume that, whatever the origin of the Dionysian writings, they were at least all composed by one man.

For such an important, nay apostolic authority on Christian doctrine, fame reached the writings of Dionysius late. We first find references to his works in the letters and treatises of Severus, Patriarch of Antioch, in the early sixth century A.D.[3] Severus, who seeks to bolster his views with the support of the Areopagite, was a leading Monophysite, though not of the most extreme variety. Not the best of company, we may suppose, for the divine Denis. But worse was to follow at the Conference of Constantinople in 533, for when the followers of Severus adduced the Dionysian writings as support for their position, the authenticity of these writings was challenged by Hypatius, the spokesman of the Catholic party, who held them to be Apollinarian.

This accusation in fact meant simply that they were Monophysite, but to use the term Apollinarian was to put the Dionysian writings alongside works which had been condemned as early as the time of Augustine. Apollinaris died in 390 and his teachings, perhaps be-

[3]See *infra*, p. 134 and note 29.

cause of the weight of the opponents who arose against him, collapsed almost immediately. It was the view of Apollinaris first that Jesus as man possessed no soul, and later that he possessed only an irrational soul, the rational part being replaced by the Logos-Christ. It is in opposition to such a view that Augustine in his *Commentary on St. John*, chapter 23, writes that "there was also in Christ a human soul, a whole soul, not merely the irrational part of the soul, but also the rational, which is called mind." Some Apollinarians, says Augustine, dare to claim dogmatically that Christ is only the Logos and flesh and maintain that he did not assume a human soul, while others have him possess an irrational soul, but not a rational. To accuse the apostolic Dionysius of keeping company of this kind was a most serious and damaging charge.

Yet Dionysius' redress was soon to come. It appears that a commentary on his writings had already been completed in 533 by John of Scythopolis, and that they were at about this time translated into Syriac by Sergius of Rešaina. By the next century their fame was secured and spread by the extensive commentary of Maximus Confessor (who apparently based his work on that of John of Scythopolis[4]) and their authority was invoked at the Lateran Council in 649. Later still we find Hilduin writing a *Passio Sanctissimi Dionysii* (*PL* 106) in which our author is distinguished as convert of Paul, bishop of Athens, and finally bishop of Paris. While holding this latter office, we are told, he obtained the glorious crown of martyrdom.

Yet the great days of his fame were still to come. Translated again into Latin by Scotus Erigena, the would-be convert of Paul looms large among the writings of Albert the Great and Thomas Aquinas, and later in those of the Rhineland mystics and St. John of the Cross. During the whole period from the sixth to the fifteenth century there were few to reject his authority. The learned still dispute about the opinion of Photius, but there is no doubt that Dionysius' writings were generally acknowledged.[5]

It was Lorenzo Valla, that great destroyer of accepted truths, who first seriously questioned the authenticity of the Dionysian writings in 1457. His objections were stylistic, as were those of Erasmus who

[4]Cf. U. von Balthasar, "Das Scholienwerk des Johannes von Scythopolis," *Scholastik*, XV (1940), 16–38.

[5]Cf. J. Stiglmayr, "Hielt Photius die sogennanten areopagitischen Schriften für echt?" *Historisches Jahrbuch*, XIX (1898), 91–4, and I. Hausherr, "Doutes au sujet du 'Divin Denys'," *Orientalia Christiana Periodica*, II (1936), 484–90.

published Valla's *Remarques sur le Nouveau Testament* in 1504. Luther however smelt paganism. *Plus platonizans quam christianizans*, he declared, and received the rebuke of the Sorbonne for doing so in 1520. But the doubts that were raised could not be stilled and the struggle between the Areopagites and the anti-Areopagites went on until the end of the nineteenth century, when the publications of two Jesuit scholars, Koch and Stiglmayr,[6] who worked on the problem quite independently, convinced all but the most convinced lovers of departed glory that what the world had for so long supposed to be the writings of the convert of St. Paul were not of the first century A.D., nor indeed purely of Pauline inspiration, but had in fact made extensive use of the commentaries of the Neoplatonic philosopher and head of the Academy, Proclus, whose life spanned the years between 410 and 485 A.D.

Koch and Stiglmayr first demonstrated that the latter part of chapter four of Dionysius' treatise on the *Divine Names* was taken, frequently with almost no alteration, from Proclus' treatise *De malorum subsistentia*. And this was only the beginning of the evidence that began to pile up against the apostolicity of Dionysius' work. Large parts of his structure of the universe, including the main philosophical principles of his work on the *Celestial Hierarchy*, his doctrines of the Good, Unity, Love, Providence, the contemplative life, and the divinization of man and his union in mystic ecstasy with God were shown to depend on Proclus, and—either through Proclus or independently—on Plotinus and ultimately on the whole Neoplatonic tradition of the interpretation of Plato's *Parmenides*. Not that I should wish to give the impression that the author of the Dionysian writings is a mere copyist of the Neoplatonists, although Koch and Stiglmayr sometimes verged upon this opinion. On the contrary, his synthesis of Christian and Neoplatonic elements is highly original and well thought out. Yet his knowledge of both Proclus and Plotinus is certain, and with that certainty his claim to be the convert of Paul disappears.

Apart from his knowledge of Proclus, there are many other problems to be faced if Dionysius is supposed to be a writer of the first century A.D. The most obvious difficulty is that there is no reference to his

[6] H. Koch, "Proklus als Quelle des Pseudo-Dionysius Areopagitica in der Lehre vom Bösen," *Philologus*, LIV (1895), 438–54, and *Pseudo-Dionysius Areopagitica in seinen Beziehungen zum Neuplatonismus und Mysterienwesen* (Mainz, 1900). J. Stiglmayr, *Das Aufkommen der pseudo-dionysischen Schriften und ihr Eindringen in die christliche Literatur bis zum Laterankonzil 649* (Feldkirch, 1895), and "Der neuplatonischer Proklus als Vorlage des sogennanten Dionysius Areopagita in der Lehre vom Uebel," *Historisches Jahrbuch*, XVI (1895), 253–73, 721–48.

writings in the first five hundred years of the Christian era, although his status as a pupil of Paul would, one must suppose, have given his works a considerable authority. We can return to this question when dealing with Severus, Patriarch of Alexandria, who, according to Stiglmayr, is himself Dionysius. For the moment let us content ourselves with saying that attempts to demonstrate references to the Dionysian writings before A.D. 510 have failed. The only contrary evidence of any worth is the remark of Liberatus of Carthage that in about 438 Cyril of Alexandria made use of the writings of Dionysius to refute the heretical positions of Theodore of Mopsuestia and Diodore of Tarsus. But these references to Dionysius were almost certainly attributed to Cyril in the light of the proceedings of the Conference of Constantinople in 533.[7] All other attempts to suggest that the Dionysian writings could have possibly been composed before, at the very earliest, 476 are nugatory. Naturally there has been an attempt to suggest that Dionysius is in fact none other than Ammonius Saccas,[8] that teacher of Plotinus of whom posterity knows nothing, though many scholars think they know so much;[9] but such suggestions can be dismissed out of hand. We may give similar short measure to the idea of the Dominican scholar Pera that the works of Dionysius show similarities to those of Basil of Caesarea. The argument on which Pera places the most emphasis is that Dionysius makes use of the word *θεομαχία*, a common Basilian term.[10] Dionysius does use this word—once, at *DN* 597C, according to van den Daele's *Index*. In brief, we may say that there is no reference to Dionysius' writings in the first five centuries of the Christian era.

There are many more good reasons to believe that Dionysius is not what he pretends to be. Unfortunately for his claims to authenticity he quotes Ignatius (*DN* 709B), whose works the disciple of Paul could

[7]H. C. Puech, "Libératus de Carthage et la date de l'apparition des écrits dionysiens," *Annuaire de l'Ecole Pratique des Hautes Etudes, Section des Sciences Religieuses* (1930–1), pp. 3–39. For further information on this supposed reference in Liberatus see Roques' article on Dionysius in the *Dictionnaire de Spiritualité*. Roques also disposes here of a supposed reference in Juvenal of Jerusalem (col. 247).

[8]E. Elorduy, "¿Es Ammonius Sakkas el Seudo-Areopagita?" *Estudios Eclesiasticos*, XVIII (1944), 501–57.

[9]For an account of our ignorance of Ammonius see E. R. Dodds, "Numenius and Ammonius," *Les Sources de Plotin, Entretiens Hardt*, V (1960), 24–32.

[10]C. Pera, "Denys le Mystique et la Theomachia," *Revue des Sciences Philosophiques et Théologiques*, XXV (1936), 5–75. For rebuttals of Pera see M. de Gandillac's edition of Dionysius [*Œuvres Complètes* (Paris, 1943), pp. 24–6] and Roques, in *Dictionnaire de Spiritualité*, col. 253.

not have known. It is astonishing that this slip did not betray him—and a salutary warning to us about the historical sense possessed by the ancients. On dogmatic grounds too it is now generally admitted that Dionysius must be late—so late in fact as to be after the *Henoticon* of the Emperor Zeno in 482. This decree—though itself leaning towards Monophysitism—was aimed at composing the feuds in the Church; it was hoped, vainly, that it might introduce a spirit of concord into the ecclesiastical brawlings. It is in such a spirit that Dionysius seems to be writing when in his seventh and eighth letters he urges his co-religionists to moderate the fury of their attacks upon heretical positions not by the sacrifice of truth but by the renunciation of polemic. Roques,[11] the greatest modern authority on Dionysius, holds that he generally wrote not according to the letter of the *Henoticon*, which, despite the intentions of its authors, proved to be the cause of further discord, but according to its spirit. Thus his own Christology, for example, has been, and is, interpreted both in a Monophysite and in an orthodox manner. His phraseology is, shall we say, pacific.

Let us briefly consider a famous dispute into which the Dionysian language led later theologians. It has already been mentioned that at the Conference of Constantinople in 533 the orthodox held the Dionysian writings to be Apollinarian. Doubtless the Dionysian phrase θεανδρικὴ ἐνέργεια (theandric operation) was one of those most open to dispute, as a controversy in the following century showed. The Emperor Heraclius, himself a Dyophysite, was apparently disturbed by the havoc wrought in his domains by the divisions between his Monophysite and Dyophysite subjects. Accordingly, in 631, Cyrus, the Patriarch of Alexandria, after negotiating with the Monophysites, composed nine anathematisms, acceptable, he supposed, both to the orthodox and to the Monophysites. In the seventh anathematism all those are condemned who do not confess that "this one and the same Christ and Son worked both the divine and the human by one theandric operation (θεανδρικὴ ἐνέργεια), as the holy Dionysius teaches." The phrase "ONE theandric operation" is significant. Another of the party aiming at the unification of Monophysite and Dyophysite Christianity, Sergius, Patriarch of Constantinople, justifies its use in a letter to Pope Honorius (*Mansi*, XI, 532E) with the remark that "often also the Holy Fathers, in order to gain a great number of souls, have shown a God-pleasing pliancy (οἰκονομία) towards certain expressions, without surrendering anything of their orthodoxy." But perhaps Sergius has

[11]R. Roques, in *Dictionnaire de Spiritualité*, col. 248.

made Dionysius' God-pleasing pliancy even more pliant. The original phrase of Dionysius is καινήν τινα τὴν θεανδρικὴν ἐνέργειαν, a new theandric operation. Sergius and Cyrus have substituted μίαν θεανδρικὴν ἐνέργειαν, one theandric operation. In other words they have credited Dionysius with the position which is now called Monenergism, a kind of Monophysitism. This may be a misinterpretation of the Areopagite; at any rate he has found defenders both today and in the seventh century, the most active of the latter being Sophronius, Patriarch of Jerusalem. Sophronius in a letter to the Pope observed, as Wolfson succinctly puts it,[12] that by changing the original Dionysian expression "a new theandric operation" to "one theandric operation," Sergius has changed its meaning from a belief in two operations that may be spoken of as "a new theandric operation" to a belief in "one" divine operation that may be spoken of as a "theandric operation." Maximus Confessor's commentary on Dionysius agrees with Sophronius; but it is certainly hard to maintain that Sergius and Cyrus deliberately distorted the Dionysian text. Dionysius' meaning is obscure, probably deliberately so, since, as we have seen, his intentions were pacific.

We must return to the question of dating. Something must be said about the phrase καθολικῆς ὑμνολογίας that occurs in chapter three of the *Ecclesiastical Hierarchy* (425C). Despite attempts to suggest that this refers to the singing of the Gloria at mass,[13] it is almost impossible to explain away the comment by Maximus Confessor (ad loc.) who presumably had the authority of John of Scythopolis behind him. Maximus thinks that the ὕμνος with which Dionysius is here concerned is the ὁμολογία or σύμβολον, that is, the Creed. Some manuscripts of the *Ecclesiastical Hierarchy* read ὁμολογίας for ὑμνολογίας. And we know that the singing of the Creed at mass was introduced by Peter the Fuller in 476. All in all Dionysius is not what he seems.

Nothing has been said so far about Dionysius' language. All that needs to be said is that much of it would have been unintelligible in the Apostolic Age. The technical terms of philosophy and theology, derived in many cases from post-Iamblichan Neoplatonism, must indicate by themselves a date no earlier than the fourth century A.D.

[12]H. A. Wolfson, *The Philosophy of the Church Fathers* (Cambridge, Mass., 1956), p. 475. Cf. *PG* 87[3] 3177B.

[13]For example by J. B. Thibaut, "Le Pseudo-Denys et la 'prière catholique' de l'Eglise primitive," *Echos d'Orient*, XX (1921), 283–94. *Contra*, R. Roques, *L'Univers dionysien* (Paris, 1954), pp. 264–5.

The old notion that Proclus copied Dionysius, and not the other way round, assumes the fact that the language of the fifth century was identical with that of the first, which it was not. Readers of the Apostolic Age could have understood neither Dionysius nor Proclus.

Let us for the moment, then, assume with Koch and Stiglmayr that the writings of Dionysius were composed some time after the *Henoticon* of 482 and some time before the Conference of Constantinople in 533. Later, perhaps, these limits may be narrowed; for the moment attention should be concentrated on the next stage of the problem: If the Dionysian writings were composed between 482 and 533, who wrote them? There are many contenders for the honour of having deceived thinkers of a thousand years, each put forward by a contending scholar or group of scholars. Since Stiglmayr was in the van of our new knowledge of the Dionysian writings, it is only reasonable that we briefly consider his candidate first. Let it be said at once that Stiglmayr did not reach his decision in haste. His first researches into the Dionysian writings appeared in 1895, but it was not until 1928[14] that he published the view that not only do the earliest references to Dionysius appear in the writings of Severus, Patriarch of Antioch, but that Severus himself composed the Dionysian corpus. Severus in fact was not only a Monophysite, but a man who was prepared to quote his own writings disguised as works of the apostolic age. Thanks to the earlier and just reputation of Stiglmayr as an expert on Dionysius, this claim was not answered with the severity that a lesser scholar might have earned, but when the onslaught on Stiglmayr's position came, it was decisive. Mgr. Lebon demonstrated beyond reasonable doubt[15] firstly that in the extant writings of Severus there is no trace of Platonism of any kind, a surprising fact if Severus were himself the author of the Dionysian writings; secondly that Severus' Christological attitudes were far more severely Monophysite than those of Dionysius. Severus was clearly in outright opposition to the orthodox positions of Pope Leo and the Council of Chalcedon, nor was he even a supporter of the *Henoticon.* The moderate attitude towards ecclesiastical infighting advocated in the writings of Dionysius would hardly have suited the Severan book. Although as far as I know Stiglmayr never

[14] J. Stiglmayr, "Der sogennante Dionysius und Severus von Antiochien," *Scholastik*, III (1928), 1–27, 161–89.

[15] J. Lebon, "Le Pseudo-Denys et Sévère d'Antioche," *Revue d'Histoire Ecclésiastique*, XXVI (1930), 880–915, and "Encore le Pseudo-Denys et Sévère d'Antioche," *ibid.*, XXVIII (1932), 296–313.

abandoned his belief that Severus, Patriarch of Antioch, was the author of the Dionysian writings, other scholars have unanimously found it unacceptable.

A claimant worth brief mention is the Syrian mystical writer Stephen Bar-Sudaili who lived at the turn of the fifth and sixth centuries. On chronological grounds his candidature is acceptable. It seems that the major point in favour of the claim that he is the author of the Dionysian corpus is that, like Dionysius, he refers to the writings and teachings of St. Hierotheus. We should recall at this stage that although Dionysius makes frequent references to St. Paul and to writers of the Apostolic Age, he admits far more doctrinal matter from this mysterious master Hierotheus, of whom we know nothing save what can be gleaned from the Dionysian writings themselves and from Bar-Sudaili. But despite the fact that both Dionysius and Bar-Sudaili acknowledge the authority of Hierotheus, their doctrines are far from identical; indeed great differences have frequently been pointed out.[16] Bar-Sudaili appears to have believed in the principle of emanation in the strict Neoplatonic fashion; Dionysius does not. Bar-Sudaili is greatly indebted to Origen and to the Origenist tradition for a number of his doctrines, particularly for his ideas on *apocatastasis* and the theory that identification with Christ is a stage in the mystic's journey to fusion with the Absolute. None of these Origenist ideas is present in Dionysius. Thus we can dismiss the claims of Stephen Bar-Sudaili.

Another possibility is Peter the Iberian, suggested by Honigmann[17] in 1952. Peter lived from 411 to 491 A.D.—a little early for the author of the Dionysian writings—but on chronological grounds he cannot be completely ruled out. Honigmann believes that the strong point in his identification is that by it he can not only account for Pseudo-Dionysius, but for Hierotheus as well. Peter himself is Dionysius and his friend and master John the Eunuch is Hierotheus. We know very little of either Peter or John—for what we do know we are largely indebted to Honigmann's own work—but this little tells against Honigmann's interpretation. John and Peter were Monophysites—most people now seem to brand the unfortunate divine Denis as a Monophysite—but they were even more extreme in their beliefs than Severus of

[16]E.g., by R. Roques in his article on Dionysius Areopagita in *Reallexikon für Antike und Christentum*, col. 1076.

[17]E. Honigmann, "Pierre l'Ibérien et les Ecrits du Pseudo-Denys l'Aréopagite," *Mémoires de l'Academie Royale de Belgique, Classe des Lettres et des Sciences morales et politiques*, XLVII (Brussels, 1952).

Antioch, the candidate of Stiglmayr. Almost without exception scholars have found it hard to believe that such convinced and militant Monophysites as the circle of Peter the Iberian could have had anything to do with such anti-polemical tracts as those of Dionysius. Furthermore, so far as we can tell, Peter the Iberian's dependence on John the Eunuch is not as comparable with the relation of Dionysius to Hierotheus as Honigmann believes. On doctrinal grounds again, Peter's Trinitarian attitudes do not appear to tally too well with those of Dionysius, nor does his doctrine of angels. Honigmann has made much of the fact that the deaths of Hierotheus and of John the Eunuch were celebrated on the same day of the year, but this—in the absence of more positive doctrinal or philosophical evidence—is hardly enough to prove his point.[18]

Perhaps this unsatisfactory situation is the most that inspired or less inspired guesses can achieve. It seems unnecessary to examine any further convinced opinions about the identity of the author of the Dionysian writings.[19] Various other solutions which are worthy of discussion have been put forward rather more tentatively. In these cases we are not invited to identify a particular individual with the author of the Dionysian writings so much as to consider a certain milieu from which that author might have arisen. This is a very much preferable method, but the milieux that have been suggested do not look the most attractive, except presumably to their advocates. It has already been mentioned that the writings of the supposed Areopagite were translated into Syriac by Sergius of Rešaina. Sergius died in 536 and his translation was published after his death. We are now invited to consider the possibility that Sergius himself was not only the translator of the Dionysian writings, but in fact the author.[20] As has been said, this theory is only put forward tentatively, and it is added that perhaps Sergius did not actually write the corpus, but that one of his friends did. At any rate it is in such a circle that the author of the

[18]In opposition to Honigmann's thesis, see I. Hausherr, "Le pseudo-Denys est-il Pierre l'Ibérien?" *Orientalia Christiana Periodica*, XIX (1953), 247–60 and R. Roques, "Pierre l'Ibérien et le 'Corpus' dionysien," *Revue de l'Histoire des Religions*, CXLV (1954), 69–98.

[19]The most recent attempt to identify Dionysius is that of U. Riedinger in an article entitled "Pseudo-Dionysius Areopagites, Pseudo-Kaisarios und die Akoimeten," *Byzantinische Zeitschrift*, LII (1959), 276–96. Riedinger proposes Peter the Fuller as author. This is open to most of the difficulties that preclude earlier suggestions.

[20]This is the suggestion of I. Hausherr, "Doutes au sujet du 'Divin Denys,'" 489, note 1.

Dionysian writings should be sought. Now I know nothing about Syriac and hence can only go on what I am told by the experts. The information they give me is that Sergius' translation is evidence that his command of Greek was perfect and that on that score he is a possible candidate for authorship. Furthermore it is certain that whoever wrote the Dionysian corpus and attempted to pass it off as a work of the Apostolic Age would not necessarily have been above putting out an alleged translation of that work as well. Yet grave doubts about Sergius still linger. One question in particular rises to the mind: Where did he learn his Platonism?

Perhaps this seems a ridiculous question. After all, one might reply, many of the Christian Fathers know something of Platonism: Clement of Alexandria, for example, or Origen, or Augustine, or Gregory of Nyssa. Dionysius could have learned something from them. Origen or Gregory in particular might have led him to the Platonic way of thinking. Yet in the case of Origen the difficulties are great. It is true that the doctrines of Origen and Dionysius are sometimes comparable; it is true that, when faced with similar problems, Origen and Dionysius sometimes offer similar solutions—both, for example, tend to speak of God's love as Ἔρως rather than as Ἀγάπη, though Dionysius is in fact more extreme on this point; it is true that they both interpret, or probably rather misinterpret, the famous text of Ignatius (*ad Rom.* 7: 2) ὁ ἐμὸς ἔρως ἐσταυρῶται (my love is crucified) in the same way, making ἔρως stand for Christ, rather than, as most modern scholars believe, for "my earthly passions";[21] it is true that, when Dionysius is looking for scriptural texts to support his view that God's love is more properly called Ἔρως than Ἀγάπη, he is driven to use the same two texts as Origen had previously employed. This may be because he is imitating Origen or expanding an Origenist idea, or it may, on the other hand, be because when he came to search in the Bible this was all he could find, just as it was all Origen could find when engaged upon a similar task. Yet despite certain similarities between Origen and Dionysius, there is none of the typical Origenist theology of Dionysius' own day in the Dionysian writings. This difficulty has already come up in the case of Stephen Bar-Sudaili, and there is no point in going over the same ground again.

[21]Cf. *DN* 709B and p. 297 of Vol. XIV of de la Rue's edition of Origen. The texts supporting Ἔρως cited by Origen and Dionysius are Wisdom 8:2 and Proverbs 4:6.

But Dionysius may, perhaps, have derived from Origen some kind of interest in Platonism which led him to the Neoplatonic writers. Origen of course was dead before Plotinus began to write and lived two hundred years before Proclus. Perhaps some will say, however, that after reading his voluminous works Dionysius turned to the Plotinian and Proclan philosophies. Yet if Origen had such a profound effect upon Dionysius' thinking, an effect which led him to devote many years of labour to the study of Neoplatonic philosophy, it is surprising that he had no more influence himself. As for such Fathers as Gregory of Nyssa, although it is true that their thought is affected, perhaps greatly affected, by Neoplatonism, it may be said firstly that a study of their writings would hardly arouse a devout desire to turn one's attention to Neoplatonism (Christianity rather would become of an increasingly all-embracing importance) and secondly that they themselves are not as deeply imbued with the refinements of Neoplatonic thinking as is Dionysius himself. In fact it seems probable that few Christians in the ancient world devoted much time to the study of Platonism or any other philosophy, after their conversion, except for the purposes of polemic. Augustine himself is an obvious case in point. It is true that he knows the *Enneads* of Plotinus through the Latin of Marius Victorinus; and he probably knows a good deal of Porphyry as well. But these he studied before his famous encounters with Ambrose and eventual arrival within the Christian fold. It does not seem likely therefore that Dionysius was inspired to undertake courses in the philosophy of Proclus because of the Neoplatonic tinges in any of the Christian writers with whom he may have been acquainted. It is far more likely that he studied his Neoplatonism *before* he became a Christian, and that his inspiration to do so came not from Christian but from pagan sources. And that brings us back to our original question: If Sergius of Rešaina, or one of his circle, or indeed anyone else, is Dionysius, where did he learn his Platonism? Did he come across the writings of Proclus by chance, or did he attend an institution where the works of Proclus were studied? It was not, we must realize, the custom to come across learned books by chance at this period. If one wished to become a philosopher, or to study philosophy, normal procedure was to betake oneself to a master who would pass on his lore to his pupils. It might well be that the searcher after truth would search for a long time and try many masters before he eventually found the one for whom he was seeking. This procedure was common from the Hellenistic age until the end of antiquity and after. At the opening of book seven of his *Lives of the Philosophers*, Diogenes Laertius writes about the Stoic Zeno as follows: "He was a pupil of Crates. Next they say that he attended the lectures of Stilpo and Xenocrates for ten years, as Timocrates says in his *Dion*, and those of Polemo as well." And five hundred years later Plotinus behaved in a similar way, as is related by Porphyry in chapter three of the life of his master. "At twenty-seven he was caught by the passion for philosophy: he was directed to the most highly reputed professors to be found at Alexandria; but he used to come away from their lectures saddened and discouraged. A friend to whom he opened his heart divined his temperamental craving and suggested Ammonius, whom he had not yet tried. Plotinus went, heard a lecture, and exclaimed to his comrade: 'This is the man I was looking for.' "

It is almost certain that this was the manner in which Dionysius, whoever he was, came across the Platonic writings. He went to a centre of learning and studied under various teachers until he found what suited him. If we return then to the question of Sergius of Rešaina, we can now supplement our original question, Where did he learn his Platonism? with the more precise problem, At which *centre* of Platonism did he study? And indeed we might ask, though this perhaps is not so difficult to answer: Was Sergius at any stage not a Christian? Do we know, or rather can we know, that he would ever have devoted his time to Platonic studies? It seems that until we can know, firstly that Sergius was, earlier in his life, a pagan, secondly that he knows a good deal of Platonism, thirdly that he studied Platonism at a particular university centre, if this phrase is permissible—that until we know all this, it is rather pointless to wonder whether he is in fact not only the translator but also the author of the Dionysian writings. He might be the author, if all these conditions were fulfilled, but until we can perceive clearly both the life of Sergius and the kind of person Dionysius must have been, we can only regard the suggestion that Sergius was in fact Dionysius as the merest conjecture. It might be true; proof, however, will not only be difficult, but impossible, to obtain.

Some suggest that we look for Dionysius among the friends of Sergius of Rešaina. Another suggestion, of a rather similar kind, has been put forward partly as a result of the work of Fr. von Balthasar,[22] who himself supports Sergius. Von Balthasar suggests in *Scholastik* that John of Scythopolis, who apparently wrote a commentary on

[22]U. von Balthasar, "Das Scholienwerk des Johannes von Scythopolis."

Dionysius sometime before 530, may have been aware that it was Sergius or one of Sergius' circle who was the author; J.-M. Hornus[23] in 1955 made the obvious next deduction that John of Scythopolis may have had something to do with the authorship himself, and promises to publish his further researches in this field in the near future. Perhaps therefore it is necessary to linger a while on John of Scythopolis also.

Our knowledge of John is shadowy. It has long been deduced that a commentary from his hand is the foundation of the extant commentary on the Dionysian corpus by Maximus Confessor–indeed von Balthasar seems to leave very little of the commentary to Maximus. This commentary of John of Scythopolis is conjured up principally from passages in Maximus which Maximus himself is unlikely to have written without an earlier work in front of him. In Photius (cod. 95) we can read that John of Scythopolis wrote twelve books against the deserters of the church, Eutyches and Dioscorus, and the sects which followed them, that he inveighed against the Monophysites of his day and in particular that he attacked a certain Nestorian named Basilius who died in 517. Now in our scholia to the Dionysian corpus there are references to two passages of Dionysius which are said to have been written against Basilians and Nestorians.[24] Putting these passages side by side with the fact that John of Scythopolis wrote against Basilius and that nowhere else are Nestorians called Basilians, scholars have long deduced that John of Scythopolis wrote the original note which has come down to us in the passage of Maximus. There is no need for further elaboration here. It is certain that John wrote some kind of commentary on the Dionysian corpus. The question is: Is there any connection between the commentator and the original author?

It seems no easier to believe that John of Scythopolis commented on his own text than to hold with Stiglmayr that Severus brought forward his own writings as documents of the Apostolic Age, or with Hausherr and von Balthasar that Sergius of Rešaina might have both composed the Dionysian writings in Greek and then translated them into Syriac. And again we may ask: Where did John of Scythopolis learn his

[23]J.-M. Hornus, "Les Recherches récentes sur le Pseudo-Denys l'Aréopagite," *Revue d'Histoire et de Philosophie Religeuse*, XXXV (1955), 404–38.

[24]See *Migne* 4, 71A (*Scholion on the Celestial Hierarchy*) and 181C (*on the Ecclesiastical Hierarchy*). Perhaps we should add here that in Codex 107 Basilius is said to have attacked John for being involved with Greek (pagan) rites. Though this may well be mere slander, it may slightly strengthen the case for identifying John with Dionysius.

Platonism? It is fortunate for us, it seems, that we do not know much about the views of John of Scythopolis, except for the comments on the Dionysian writings, if they are from his hand, for if we had more knowledge we might find that John knew no more Platonism than Severus.

Indeed it would seem that almost all the objections to Sergius of Rešaina as author would apply equally to the claims of John. Do we know that John studied Neoplatonism in any serious way while still a pagan? Do we know that he ever was a pagan? And if he was not, but was brought up in the Christian fold from his earliest years, why did he take up an elaborate investigation of the works of Plotinus and Proclus? And again *where* did he study his Platonism? Or was he that almost unknown freak in antiquity, the "do-it-yourself-philosopher," the masterless man? If he was, it is rather surprising that we do not know more about him, for he would have been a figure of quite exceptional originality. If however he had a master who taught him philosophy, who was that master? Was he Christian or pagan? And was the master himself in any kind of succession of philosophers? What relation did he have to the great schools of Athens and Alexandria?

Let us be clear on one point. All these questions and problems do not rule out the possibility that it is John of Scythopolis, or, as we said before, Sergius of Rešaina, who has earned the distinction of deceiving so many generations of savants and theologians. What must be explained, however, is that until such questions, or the majority of them, are answered, we can never be sure of very much about anybody's claims to authorship. The author might have been Sergius, or it might have been John. Sergius *may* have translated his own work into Syriac as a subtle refinement on his already elaborated deception of his contemporaries; John *may* have written a commentary on his own compositions and chuckled as he sat back to watch the fun, in perfect security that no one would see through this additional deception. But it is all so far away from good solid evidence.

Yet perhaps we should wait and see what M. Hornus can do, and suspend judgment about the claims of John of Scythopolis for the time being. I must admit, however, that his claims to authorship do not seem very strong—and, more important, that it is very hard to see how M. Hornus will be able to demonstrate them.

We must confess that up to now we have drawn a blank.[25] None of the candidates for authorship of the Dionysian writings has particu-

[25]The views of Riedinger (see note 19) do not afford us any further help.

larly good credentials. It begins to look, perhaps, as though the methods available to scholars are defective, or at least that they have not been employed with sufficient rigour. It would appear that up to now two methods have been employed, of which the second and better is a refinement on the first. The first method amounts to little more than picking a Christian of the right date and claiming that his brand of Christianity tallies with doctrines supposedly present in the Dionysian corpus. The second is to pick out not an individual but a milieu, from which a possible individual can later be selected as author. Unfortunately it appears that this latter method has suffered from the personal preoccupations of the scholars engaged in the search. Practically every modern researcher into the works of Dionysius has approached him from the Christian rather than from the Neoplatonic side. The method employed has very often amounted to an attempt to connect a supposed Monophysitism in Dionysius with a known Monophysitism elsewhere: hence Severus, Peter the Iberian, and even to some extent Sergius of Rešaina, who, according to one of his supporters,[26] passed through a complete range of christological positions, doubtless including that of the Monophysitism of Dionysius—that is, if Dionysius is a Monophysite. After the numerous failures to which this approach has led, it would seem to be time to review the method. I have already suggested the way I believe the problem should be approached when speaking of Sergius of Rešaina and John of Scythopolis. It should be approached through the undoubted Platonism of the Dionysian writings and by the aid of the question: Where did Dionysius learn all this Plotinus and Proclus? Severus, as has been shown by Lebon,[27] knows nothing about Platonism, or at least admits none into his writings as we have them. It is by no means unlikely that John of Scythopolis and Sergius were as ignorant of Platonism as Severus, and even if they were not, this does not preclude a new approach to the Dionysian problem. We shall revert to this new approach shortly, but before that it is necessary to pick up the threads of the problem of the *exact* date of the appearance of the Dionysian writings and to mention the most effective attempt—that of Roques[28]—to secure such an exact date, as far as it is possible to do so.

Before turning to claimants to the Dionysian writings, we showed that it is most likely that these writings appeared after the *Henoticon*

[26] I. Hausherr, "Doutes au sujet du 'Divin Denys,'" p. 489, note 1.
[27] J. Lebon, "Le Pseudo-Denys et Sévère d'Antioche," "Encore le Pseudo-Denys."
[28] In his article in the *Dictionnaire de Spiritualité*.

in 482 and before the Conference of Constantinople in 533. We can now look at the earliest references to them in more detail. First of all there is a letter of Severus to an abbot named John, which was probably written about 532, but possibly, as Stiglmayr believes, in 510.[29] This letter contains a reference to the famous phrase θεανδρικὴ ἐνέργεια. If it was written in 510, it is our earliest source of knowledge about the Dionysian corpus. There are further references in two treatises of Severus composed between 518 and 528[30] and it is likely that these are in fact our earliest material. We know that they were composed before 528, since in that year Paul of Kallinike translated them into Syriac. With Roques, therefore, we may say that if we allow a couple of years to elapse between the original compositions and the translation, the Dionysian writings must have been in existence in 525, or, if the letter to John is to be dated to 510, to some time earlier than that. Let us say that A.D. 525 will be satisfactory as an approximate date.

With this chronology clear we can revert to the question of Dionysius' Platonism. It is now almost universally admitted that many of Dionysius' ideas mark him out as a Christianized Proclus. What we must ask ourselves is: Where did Dionysius learn his Proclus? It seems likely that the answer to this question must involve the recognition that the author of the Dionysian writings studied at some centre where the works of Proclus were held in high esteem. This argument is of course important, as we have seen, against suggestions that particular Christian writers, known only for their theological opinions and in no way imbued with the spirit of ancient Greek philosophy, are responsible for the Dionysian material.

In the late fifth century A.D. there were two main centres for philosophical study: Athens and Alexandria.[31] Proclus himself studied at Alexandria before going to Athens and eventually becoming head of the Academy. His pupils were the leading thinkers of both the Athenian and the Alexandrian schools. Proclus died in 485. Marinus, who wrote his biography, succeeded him in his chair. Marinus was

[29]J. Stiglmayr, *Das Aufkommen der pseudo-dionysischen Schriften . . . ,"* pp. 47–8. Cf., F. Hipler, *Dionysius der Areopagite* (Regensburg, 1861), p. 103. For opposition to Stiglmayr see Roques' article in the *Dictionnaire de Spiritualité*, col. 249.

[30]For the dates of these treatises, the *Adversus Apologiam Juliani* and the *Contra Additiones*, cf. Honigmann, "Pierre l'Ibérien et les Ecrits du Pseudo-Denys l'Aréopagite," p. 5.

[31]Other centres existed, but the pre-eminence of Athens and Alexandria was so great that until these have been examined it would be premature to proceed further.

followed by Isidorus. After Isidorus' short reign came that of Damascius, who, arriving in Athens shortly after the death of Proclus, held his position of headship until the school was closed on the orders of Emperor Justinian in 529. At that time he appears to have been in his seventy-first year. After 529 there was no more philosophy at Athens. One of the reasons for the closing down of the school was that very few, if any, of the Athenian philosophers were acceptable to a Christian regime, in fact that very few of them were Christians or encouraged Christian pupils. This factor seems to be of some significance when we compare the fortunes of those at the Academy of Athens with those of their fellow philosophers at Alexandria. No doubt the traditional loyalty to paganism was stronger in the city of Plato and Aristotle.

But if the Athenian school in the time of Proclus and his successors was almost wholly pagan, the same was not true of the school of Alexandria, which, from about 490, was also under the direction of a pupil of Proclus. This pupil was Ammonius, who wrote a number of commentaries on Aristotle, some of which are extant, and on Porphyry's *Isagoge*. We know him too through the writings of his pupils, some of whom speak of him with the greatest respect. Perhaps the most important of them were Olympiodorus, the last significant pagan Platonist of antiquity, and Philoponus, who, it seems likely,[32] was a pagan when he entered the school and later a convert to Christianity. Olympiodorus too, though never converted to Christianity, almost certainly had Christian pupils. Beutler, the author of the article on him in Pauly-Wissowa,[33] believes that one of these pupils was Elias, who also commented on Aristotle. Certainly Elias acknowledges the authority of Olympiodorus. Whether he was actually a pupil is not absolutely certain, but it is likely enough. In other words, if we put all this evidence together, it looks as though the philosophical school at Alexandria, in contrast to that of Athens, was the scene of a peaceful changeover from pagan to Christian thinking.[34] What better milieu could be found for a Christian Platonist?

[32]Despite H. D. Saffrey, "Le Chrétien J. Philoponus et la survivance de l'Ecole d'Alexandrie au VIe siècle," *Revue des Etudes Grecques*, LXVII (1954), 402.

[33]*Real-Encyclopädie der Classischen Altertumswissenschaft* (*RE*), 18[1], cols. 207–227.

[34]According to Damascius (*Vita Isidori* 292) Ammonius came to an agreement with the Patriarch. This agreement presumably concerned the teaching of Christian pupils in the philosophical schools. Cf., Saffrey, "Le Chrétien J. Philoponus . . . ," pp. 400–1, and P. Courcelle, *Les Lettres Grecques en Occident* (Paris, 1948), p. 300.

Let us now consider briefly the career of John Philoponus. He appears to have been born at one of the two towns in Pontus named Caesarea somewhere about 470. He studied at Alexandria, as he tells us himself, under Ammonius. It seems likely that he was originally called Philoponus,[35] and that when he was converted to Christianity he took the name John. We know of course that at the time of the composition of the treatise on the eternity of the world against Proclus he was a Christian. He refers in this treatise to the 245th year of the era of Diocletian. Since this era was dated from A.D. 284, the reference Philoponus gives must be to the year 529, the year of the end of the Athenian schools. From similar internal evidence we can date his commentary on Aristotle's *Physics* to the year 517. This work gives no indication that its author is Christian. There are two references in Philoponus' commentary on the *Categories* which Busse took to concern the Christian doctrine of angels. If this were true, it would be probable that Philoponus was a Christian before 517, since a teacher could be expected to comment on the *Categories* before tackling the *Physics*. Yet it is unlikely that Busse is correct,[36] and if he is not, there is little reason to deny that Philoponus became a Christian between the years 517 and 529.

Philoponus' new Christianity did not wholly divert him from philosophical studies, and in particular his beliefs led him into polemical work against certain aspects of pagan philosophy. It is well known that he was a bitter foe of the pagan Aristotelian commentator Simplicius and that he wrote not only against Proclus on the eternity of the world, but against Aristotle also. His career in the Church was not smooth, however. It appears that he fell into heresy. We hear of a blast delivered by the hostile Severus against "John the Grammarian of Caesarea."[37] His doom was finally pronounced at the Third Ecumenical Council at Constantinople in 680/1, where all the works of John Lover of Toil (Philoponus) were found vain and useless. The Fathers concluded that *ματαιόπονος* (Vain Toil) would be a more appropriate name.[38]

[35]Saffrey, "Le Chrétien J. Philoponus . . . ," pp. 403–4 denies this. In opposition to Saffrey's views of Philoponus is the article in Pauly-Wissawa (*RE*, 9^2, cols. 1764–1793).

[36]The relevant passages are Philoponus, *In Categ.*, p. 49, 23–26 and p. 52, 10 (Busse). For the use of the word "angelic" by a pagan philosopher, see the discussion of the views of Marinus in Philoponus' *Commentary on the De Anima* (p. 535, 8, Hayduck).

[37]Cf. Saffrey, "Le Chrétien J. Philoponus . . . ," p. 401.

[38]*Mansi*, XI, 501A.

But it is not our business to decry or console the unfortunate Philoponus. Rather he was brought into the discussion as an instructive case. It would be pointless to guess that it was Philoponus himself who composed the Dionysian corpus. If he was not converted till about 520, this is probably a little too late for the man we are seeking, and in any case there is no compelling reason to push his claim. Yet the career of Philoponus is nevertheless instructive. Educated by a pupil of Proclus in a philosophical milieu, author of philosophical commentaries, most probably while still a pagan, author of works of Christian philosophy after his conversion, John Philoponus could very much resemble the author of the Dionysian corpus. Let us suppose that the so-called Dionysius entered the school of Ammonius, say, in 500, was converted in 505, and some time in the next twenty years began to write. He would know his Neoplatonism well; he would be a Christian; he could—if necessary—be a Monophysite. Perhaps his new-found Christian fervour, joining hands with the old Platonic enthusiasm, would provide the motive for his committing the pious fraud of claiming apostolic authenticity. It seems from the fact that the Dionysian works were known to Severus, that they were translated into Syriac by Sergius of Rešaina, and that they were commented by John of Scythopolis, that Syria-Palestine may have been the actual place of composition. The training of the author, however, should have taken place in Alexandria.

It has often been said in the past that the author of the Dionysian writings was probably not brought up as a Christian, but was converted to Christianity late in life, just as the historical Dionysius was converted late in life by St. Paul. Stiglmayr himself was, I believe, the first to advance this argument, as evidence for the authorship of Severus, for Severus was only baptized in 488—at the age of at least twenty-five. Although such an argument can hardly be much evidence for ascertaining the particular man who composed the Dionysian writings, it can perhaps be used to establish something about that man. It would fit our proposed pupil of the Alexandrian philosophers as well as it fits Severus.

We should look, then, for the future Dionysius the Areopagite in Alexandria, among the philosophers of the early sixth century. We should be careful, however, to look for someone who was by no means the uncritical pupil. Contrary to certain current authorities, Dionysius is not the blind follower of Proclus he has sometimes been painted. The most striking example of his independence, perhaps, is his recognition that Neoplatonic emanation theory is not Christian. Not everyone in positions like his realized this fundamental difference. Nor should we assume that his language is always a mere echo of the Neoplatonists. Proclus is fond of using the image of the chain of being, stretching down from the One to matter. This image is rooted in emanation theory. For example, Proclus speaks on two occasions in his *Commentary on the Alcibiades* of Plato of the ἐρωτικὴ σειρά, the chain of love (31.2, 9; p. 14, Westerink). Nygren, in the chapter on Dionysius in his book *Eros and Agape*, implies that the same imagery is frequent in Dionysius, when he writes: "The fundamental thought of Pseudo-Dionysius' theory is thus briefly as follows. It is the idea of the Chain of Love that joins heaven and earth, that leads the divine Eros-forces down to the lower world and that leads the whole desire of the lower world up toward the Divine again."[39] But the word σειρά (chain) only occurs once in Dionysius (at *DN* 680C), and although it is quite true that the pseudo-Areopagite sees the cosmos in terms of some kind of procession from and return to the One, we should not deduce that by means of the image of the chain of being he came to regard the universe as any kind of theophany. This would in fact clash with another aspect of his thought which cannot easily be explained away by the magic word "Proclus," namely his continual reference to the utter incomprehensibility of the One or God. The theme had already assumed importance in the writings of John Chrysostomos. Dionysius may be indebted there. At any rate the idea would repay further study. But there is a Neoplatonist too who so emphatically teaches the incomprehensibility of the First Principle that he has earned the title of irrationalist among those few moderns who have tried to follow his arguments. This is Damascius, who was teaching in Athens between about 490 and the closing of the schools in 529. His views on the One were perhaps used by Dionysius as a counterweight to those of Proclus—and perhaps were more acceptable to Dionysius' new-found Christianity.

I do not wish to propose dogmatically that Dionysius' writings bear the stamp of a student of Damascius as well as that of Proclus. I am well aware how difficult it is to distinguish the effects of various individuals within the later Neoplatonic school. The example of Creuzer is before anyone who pronounces on this point without an elaborate and careful weighing of the evidence, which I cannot claim

[39]A. Nygren, *Eros and Agape*, translated by P. S. Watson (London, 1953), p. 583; cf. 588.

to have made. Creuzer, in 1820, thought that he could detect the effects of the writings of the younger Olympiodorus in the Dionysian corpus. He was doubtless misled by the fact that Olympiodorus was then supposed to have composed at least a part of his writings before 529 A.D. Yet it now appears most probable that the Dionysian corpus was complete before Olympiodorus began to write, and that Creuzer merely read his presuppositions into the Dionysian text. It may still be the case, however, that a detailed comparison of Damascius and Dionysius will shed further light.

I am well aware that much of this paper deals with well-covered ground. Perhaps at times it has degenerated into a kind of peep-show of scholarly failures and incredulities. A number of most important questions about Dionysius have been left aside. In particular nothing has been said about a problem which arises in all whodunits, namely Why did he do it? *Cui bono?* Nor has the political aspect been sufficiently considered. But the search for the divine Denis is not yet over. I am very doubtful whether he will ever be discovered. My main concern here has been with the manner in which the search should be carried out. The least I can hope for on the positive side, however, is that the suggestion that he is to be found in Alexandria, among the pupils of Ammonius, in about the year 510 A.D., will provoke someone to prove this impossible.[40]

[40]This essay is in substance the same as that read to the Oriental Club of Toronto on December 4, 1962.

10. Mamluk Egypt at the Eleventh Hour: Some Eyewitness Observations

G. M. WICKENS

THE GROWTH OF INTEREST in Mamluk Egypt is significantly indicative of a fundamental shift of emphasis, over the last thirty years or so, in Oriental studies in general and Islamic studies in particular. Islamists of the late nineteenth and the early twentieth centuries—I am thinking primarily of such men as E. G. Browne and R. A. Nicholson, but the same is true in lesser measure of an Ignaz Goldziher or a Theodor Nöldeke—seem to have viewed their studies as a preserve of well-bred, often wealthy gentlemen with a taste for literature and scholarship; and their viewpoint was in consequence most often unrealistically academic, narrowly philological, and self-satisfiedly censorious. A period like that of the Mamluks hardly qualified for serious study, as being post-classical linguistically, unproductive of true literature, barbarous and brutal in public life. Above all it clearly demanded, for its proper appreciation, some knowledge of sociology and economics, military organization and training, the techniques of metalwork and architecture, Turkish and Persian administrative terminology, as well as of the essential features of the Egyptian-Arabic colloquial. Stanley Lane-Poole might be thought to belong to a different tradition, but listen to him assessing the Mamluks, amid the stability and worthiness of late Victorian England: "A band of lawless adventurers, slaves in origin, butchers by choice, turbulent, bloodthirsty, and too often treacherous, these slave kings had a keen appreciation for the arts which would have done credit to the most civilised ruler that ever sat on a constitutional throne."[1] This certainly puts them in their place! Here is Edward Sell, writing forty-three years later and under the considerable handicap of publication by the Anglican Church Missionary Society in Madras: "The history of the Mamluks in Egypt is not connected with any religious movement in Islam, but possesses considerable historical interest and throws some light on the condition of a country under uncontrolled Muslim rule. A body of men, originally

[1] *The Art of the Saracens in Egypt* (London, 1886), p. 39.

introduced into Egypt as purchased slaves, for about two hundred and fifty years formed an oligarchy which exercised supreme control, made and unmade Sulṭāns at pleasure, and used the Khalīfa of Islām to do their will in confirming their appointment of rulers. Divided into factions among themselves, they presented a united front to all opponents. As a rule they had no social or domestic relations with the people over whom they ruled, but maintained rigidly their own separate existence. Their leaders amassed great riches, and now and again some of them encouraged learning and erected magnificent buildings; but as a race they were cruel and treacherous."[2]

Now this evaluation, albeit tendentious, and coming though it does from a far lesser scholar than Lane-Poole, represents a considerable advance on the earlier position. Some attempt, at least, is made to view the Mamluks as an interesting social phenomenon manifested against a rich and varied backcloth of historical action and daily life. But in the 1920's we were still far from knowing, and in most cases from even wanting to know, how exactly the Mamluks were purchased, trained, and maintained, how their forces were organized, how the general political and economic machine of the Mamluk state functioned, what the average citizen felt and did under their rule. Nor was there much excuse for such an attitude: other comparable disciplines, for example, classics and mediaeval studies, had long since sought the answers to similar questions, and in the particular case of the Mamluks the raw materials were superabundant, however scanty they might often be in other periods of Islamic history. Fortunately, as I have indicated, a marked change has now come about, associated with such names as D. Ayalon, G. Wiet, J. Sauvaget, and W. Popper, to name only a few. Our only danger now, and it is a natural one at this stage, is that of becoming lost in minutiae: of thinking, for example, that there is an intrinsic importance in knowing the exact sum paid, on a certain pay-day, in a given month, in a specific year, to Sergeant X of the Fifth Regiment, while ignoring the larger fact that Vasco da Gama's circumnavigation of the Cape, and the consequent spread of Portuguese traders into the Indian Ocean, was the real reason why Sergeant X was being paid at all just then, for he was being sent to defend the shrinking Mamluk influence in Calicut.

My purpose in this article is to give you some immediate glimpses of life in Mamluk Egypt at the end of an era. (It may well make you think of what we know of life in Nazi Germany in 1943 and 1944, or

[2]*The ʿAyyub and Mamluk Sultans* (1929), p. 22.

indeed, at times, of present-day life in the west in the face of relentless Communist encroachment.) I want also to comment briefly on some of the passages I translate, in the hope of giving them a fuller meaning in the light of the modern scholarship to which I have alluded. But, before coming to the main part of the paper, let me say a few words on the general background to the events described, and the peculiar interest attaching to the work and person of the eyewitness to whom we are indebted, Ibn Iyās.

Outside late Mamluk Egypt, their destinies closely associated with hers, three powers were in the ascendant and two in decline. They were respectively Turkey, Persia, and Portugal on the one hand, and Venice and the Papal States on the other. The rise of Turkey was, of course, associated with the Ottomans, and was shortly to culminate in the reign of Sulaiman the Magnificent. Turkey, despite an outward show of benevolence, constituted the chief threat to Mamluk survival. Rivalling Turkey, and hence sometimes in loose and inefficient association with the Mamluks, stood Persia under the Safavid dynasty. Portugal's menace was chiefly economic in effect, albeit backed by strong military and naval power, inasmuch as she was appropriating to her Cape route the very last trickle of east-west trade still passing through Mamluk middlemen since the fall of Constantinople. Venice was, of course, Portugal's moribund rival, and hence again, like Persia, in an unavailing, spasmodic, and desperate collaboration with Mamluk Egypt, its former business partner. The Papal States come into the picture partly because of their interest in the Holy Places (still under Mamluk control) and partly because of the papal tendency at this date to support Portugal as against Venice. It may be mentioned that the Mamluks tried at one critical juncture to relieve the Portuguese pressure by threatening to close the Holy Places to Christian pilgrims: the Pope correctly judged, however, that *inter alia* the Mamluks needed this source of revenue too badly to cut off their noses in this way, however much inclined to face-spiting they otherwise were. One crucial military factor underlying this whole struggle, as D. Ayalon has so effectively and overwhelmingly confirmed,[3] is the almost total reluctance of the Mamluks to use gunpowder other than for siege purposes, at a time when the other powers were becoming skilled in the employment of field-pieces and hand-guns. Few late mediaeval "parfit gentle Knights" could have felt more strongly on this matter

[3] *Gunpowder and Firearms in the Mamluk Kingdom* (London, 1956); also elsewhere in Ayalon's several Mamluk monographs and articles.

than the Mamluks seem to have done. So much for the general picture in broad outline: there are other subtle, and in themselves important aspects, particularly the secondary permutations and combinations such as Turkey's relations with Venice, or Persia's with France, but they are not of immediate concern.

What of the internal situation in Egypt? It is as well to allow full weight to Sell's assessment of the Mamluks as aliens—non-Arab and fundamentally non-Muslim—riding, often literally, roughshod over a resentful but helpless population of peasants and merchants. This is amply borne out by our own author's immediate comments, as will become apparent; and nothing else could suffice alone to explain the great initial success and popularity of the Ottoman conquest.

A few words on the Mamluk organization may be desirable here. The Baḥrī Mamluks (A.D. 1250/60–1382/90), from Qalā'ūn onwards (that is 1279 to the end), were headed by a more or less hereditary dynasty, but in the case of the Burjīs (1382/90–1517) attempts by individual Sulṭāns to start a royal line came to nothing. The result is that the Burjīs are never shown as a genealogical tree, but simply as a list of names (about one to every five years on an average), with frequent repetitions and overlappings, particularly in the later years of their rule.

By the Burjī period there were three main classes in the Mamluk organization: first, the royal mamluks (*al-mamālīk al-sulṭānīya*), who were themselves divided into two broad classes, according as they were obtained by Sulṭāns at first hand or from other mamluk owners; the latter category were again subdivided as between those whose former owners had been Sulṭāns and those whose masters were executed or dismissed mamluk officials. The second general category was that of the *mamālīk al-umarā'*, the mamluks owned by the amīrs, that is, by the officer corps, so to speak, of the Mamluk army. The third general category was the *ḥalqa*, the Circle, who were not really mamluks at all, but free-born cavalrymen, though they were progressively dismounted. They included the sons of the amīrs and of the ordinary mamluks (*aulād al-nās*) and were regarded from the very first as an underprivileged group; they came to include in the course of time all sorts of hangers-on who wished to profit from the Mamluk organization but were debarred by the "misfortune" of free birth from doing so in the normal way. This society, it will be seen, was from our point of view utterly paradoxical: power lay in the hands of continuous streams of specially purchased slaves—often called Circassians, but in fact including representatives of all the white-skinned races of the Mediterranean, eastern Europe, and the Near East—and power could not be handed on to one's descendants, who would be born with the "stigma" of freedom. Slaves were often purchased in batches, and they were certainly trained and educated in groups or corps, always thereafter retaining strong ties with their classmates, so to speak, and with their purchaser.

This being so, it will be obvious, on a moment's reflection, that the key group in the whole state machine were the mamluks of the reigning Sulṭān. Their natural coherence was reinforced by their being garrisoned together in the citadel at Cairo, while the other groups—even those coming to a Sulṭān from his predecessors—would have normally no real common interest, nor, in their widely scattered garrisons, the opportunity to discover one. These purchased ones (*mushtarawāt*) or, as they were often called, *ajlāb* or *julbān* (from a root JLB connoting "importation"), would in due course appoint the next Sulṭān from among themselves, and so on. Thus there was some continuity, albeit of a very loose kind, and the potentialities for friction were enormous. In an age where privilege as an end in itself is sought as the highest good, it may come as something of a surprise to learn that these powerful persons were normally expected to serve as shock troops whenever serious danger threatened the state. Significantly, the task of dealing with the Portuguese was not thought worthy of them, being left to the almost lowest form of animal life in the Mamluk state, the Fifth Regiment of arquebusiers; even a number of black slaves were included on these expeditions, and the Mamluks, it must be remembered, had a colour prejudice, a fundamental contempt for the capacity of the Negro and the generally dark-skinned Egyptian, almost unequalled till our own time.

Now, a few words about our author. Ibn Iyās (or Ayās—the spelling, especially of proper names, was already a poor guide to pronunciation by this time) has written a work which, as usual, is little but a synopsis of preceding writings for the period up to his own lifetime: from then on, however, he regales us with a sort of private diary of public events, very rare of its kind in Arabic and certainly of unique value for the crucial years 1502–17. Though his brother was a master-at-arms in the Citadel, it is interesting to note that Ibn Iyās does not write as one having access to special information. His most frequent opening words for each entry are: "It is rumoured (divulged) that . . . ," *ushīʿa anna.* It is this that gives his diary its special value, at any rate to historians who are capable of seeing that what the mass of the people are said to have suspected, or hoped, or feared has a significance nearly as great as that of the events that official records describe as actually happening. As the late and great J. Sauvaget says, partly quoting from another source: "C'est un vrai journal d'un bourgeois du Caire sous les derniers Mamelouks."[4] We are indebted to Paul Kahle, Muhammed Mustafa, and Moritz Sobernheim for at last making the journal for these years accessible: it is a pity that their version[5] is so skimpy as regards *apparatus criticus*, so inaccurate and hurried as to have deterred others from following in their wake, though various translations have been promised for many years past.[6]

When our quotations open, Sulṭān Qānṣūh Ghaurī has been on the throne some fourteen years, an unusually long period. He is a tough old man, but well past his prime. His whole reign has been one of heavy taxation and spendthrift splendour, but only latterly has trouble become really apparent. Ibn Iyās' entry for New Year's Day, 921 (February 15, 1515) reads like a comprehensive, Shavian stage direction for the whole drama shortly to unfold. We may pass over the inevitable lengthy official lists (a sort of *dramatis personae*, albeit of minor characters for the most part) and set down verbatim a few of the author's terse paragraphs so classically indicative of decay. All the usual ingredients are immediately present: indecision in high places, the use of low-grade troops in forlorn causes, provocation on minor issues and studied insults by a superior but still cautious enemy, and denunciation of this enemy as a thoroughly bad man.

[435] The first of the year fell on a blessed Thursday, and the Caliph,[7] together with the Four Judges, went up to offer congratulations on the New

[4]*Introduction à l'histoire de l'Orient musulman* (Paris, 1946 and later), p. 160.

[5]*Die Chronik des Ibn Ijâs* (Leipzig-Istanbul, 1936) (Bibliotheca Islamica, V). Pagination shown in the present article refers to this text.

[6]When this paper was delivered (February 10, 1959), G. Wiet's French translation of the relevant part (under the title *Journal d'un bourgeois du Caire*, Paris, 1955–60) was apparently already three years old, but neither I nor the University of Toronto Library was able to obtain a copy prior to the appearance of the second part in 1960 (in fact, the library accession is dated October 19, 1961). The publication at this late date of the present paper was nevertheless urged by my colleagues, since Wiet's translation (fluent and scholarly for the most part) often fails to offer the full flavour of the original unliterary text, has no comments worth mentioning, and covers the whole work without pointed appeal of interest to a general audience. An English translation covering the year following the one selected by me appeared in 1921 (W. H. Salmon, *Oriental Translation Fund of the Royal Asiatic Society*, New Series, XXV).

[7]The last of the Egyptian Abbasid puppet figureheads, Mutawakkil ʿalà Allāh Muḥammad b. al-Mustamsik bi-Allāh Yaʿqūb. Wiet's translation associates him with "les quatre *autres* cadis" (I, 401), though Ibn Iyās does not say this exactly.

Year. The Sulṭān was in the Maidān,[8] having a few days previously proclaimed a parade for the members of the Fifth Regiment.[9] Rumour had it that he was sending an expeditionary force to India on account of the high-handed conduct of the Franks in the Indian Ocean. But when the troops had paraded for his inspection on that day, there was no written order or instruction concerning them, he merely saying to them: "Turn out again on Sunday!"

On the same day an envoy arrived from Salīm Shāh the Ottoman, King of Byzantium,[10] bearing correspondence from the latter to the Sulṭān, to the effect that a dispute had arisen between one of the sons of Shāh Suwār b. Dhālghādir (*sic*) on the one hand and his paternal uncle ʿAlī Daulāt on the other, the question at issue being the lands of the younger man's father. In his indignation, he had betaken himself to the Ottoman, whereupon Salīm Shāh espoused his cause; he had accordingly sent to request the Sulṭān to make over to Suwār's son the father's territory, held by ʿAlī Daulāt. The Sulṭān, however, would not comply and was extremely upset that day by such a report, consulting with the amīrs on the matter. It may be that this trouble between the Ottoman and the Sulṭān will spread: The issue is in the hands of Almighty God.

On the same day, another rumour was current to the effect that the Ottoman had lent military aid to Suwār's son, proceeding to a surprise attack on his uncle, ʿAlī Daulāt; a fearful battle between them ensued, in which ʿAlī Daulāt's son and grandson were killed, besides a large part of his army; ʿAlī Daulāt himself was said to have taken refuge in the fortress of Zamanṭū, but the Ottoman was pressing him hard. These reports distressed the Sulṭān. It was also rumoured that in the communication he had sent the Sulṭān [436] the Ottoman had shown extreme arrogance, referring in it to "Our Majesty"[11] in respect of himself, but, towards the Sulṭān, only to "Your Highness"[12]—this being a sort of manifestation of contempt for the Sulṭān; for this Salīm Shāh the Ottoman was excessively boorish, loving to stir up seditions; he was bloodthirsty too, and had killed his brothers and their children, some of them (to give an example of his ruthlessness) still being at the breast.

There follow passages, which I will not translate, indicating first, considerable hesitation, confusion, and conflicting orders as regards the disposition of the mamluks nearest to the Ottomans, that is, those at Aleppo; next we learn that the Sulṭān distributed the *nafaqa*, that is, the special war bonus, to those amīrs who had not been paid at all since the death of the last treasurer. There are several possible implications here: certainly, it was often a cheap way of buying

[8]The open area used for horse-racing, etc., as well as for parades.

[9]Cf. my remark about this unit at the end of my introductory observations on Mamluk organization.

[10]Malik al-Rūm, i.e., Selim I (1512–20).

[11]*maqām-nā al-sharīf.*

[12]*maqām-kum al-ʿālī.*

temporary loyalty and contentment (rather like saving on promotions while salary scales are being raised); again, it might have been a sign that war was seriously expected; or, yet again, it might have been intended merely to give the Ottomans the impression that this was the case, for pay parades were public matters not to be missed by Ottoman agents. Next, on Sunday as promised, the Fifth Regiment is again reviewed and told to get ready to move to India on a date some two months hence. They were promised, it is said, an extra one-third or more monthly pay if they did well in this campaign, and "voices were raised in benediction." The forces mistakenly or treacherously ordered back from Aleppo are publicly commanded to present themselves to the Sulṭān at the citadel, when no punitive action will be taken: as Ibn Iyās says: [437] "They had hidden in houses and not one appeared." Some days pass now with more messages coming in about the Ottomans' continued exploitation of the flimsy cause of the young man *versus* his uncle; there are frequent high level meetings between the Sulṭān and his commanders, but nothing is done. Indeed, there are several holidays with picnics and fêtes of all kinds, and there is much preoccupation with fitting receptions for the returning pilgrims after their long journey from Mecca. Honours and orders are conferred.

Here I quote Ibn Iyās' entry for Monday, the tenth of Ṣafar (March 26): [442] "It is rumoured that last night the Mint in the Citadel, within the Royal Enclosure, was robbed of 8,000 dinars and more of new gold which the Sulṭān had had minted for the payment of war bonus. It is all gone and no one has any idea who did the deed. When the news reached the Sulṭān he called the overseers in the mint to account for the sum stolen, but some time has passed and nothing much has come of it." How shall we judge this episode? Was it a way of getting out of paying the *nafaqa*, or of squeezing the doubtless corrupt mint officials, or both? Or was it literally true, and, as such, an indication of how far and fast things were slipping? Or, finally, was it just a rumour? We have no means of knowing more certainly, for such matters are not of course normally mentioned in official histories, and only occasionally in administrative records. However, we do learn further on that, on the insistence of the mamluks (or of some of them) that the *nafaqa* should be advanced, the Sulṭān was obliged to ransack his private treasury, particularly of all the possessions of his dead womenfolk (cloth, crystal, china, ambergris, precious stones, and splendid garments are all mentioned), and these were forcibly sold to somewhat unwilling merchants at high prices as a means of raising ready cash. (The phrase is frequently used: "he let loose a volley at them"[13]—but it is not clear whether this means anything more than, as we might say, "he blasted them" or "blew them up." At any rate, we in our age are easily able to conceive of the sort of mixture of brutality, threats, and persuasion that might in such circumstances have been brought to bear.) The pay parade duly took place on March 29, after rumblings of discontent among the mamluks and predatory incursions on their part against the civil population, but matters were only slightly alleviated by the fact that the really worthwhile payments were made to the royal mamluks, and to certain selected elements among the others. On Tuesday, April 10, appears the following entry: [445] "On this day the Sulṭān appointed a person belonging to the royal guard[14] named Jānim, to go to Salīm Shāh the Ottoman, King of Byzantium (Selim I), in order to discover what he was about, whether he was intending to march against the Sulṭān's territory or against that of the Ṣūfī (that is, the Safavid Shāh Ismāʿīl I), for rumours had been numerous to the effect that the Ottoman was about to do the former. So this Jānim went off for this purpose, and also, it was said, on account of certain relatives of the Sulṭān who, on their way from Circassia, had been captured by a Tatar ruler. Jānim was therefore being sent to buy them back from the Tatar for a considerable sum." "This Jānim" we shall meet again, giving an account of his mission which sounds like something from a farce on the British Foreign Office at its most inept.

On Thursday, April 12, an exemplary execution takes place: [446] "On that day, the Sulṭān decreed the throttling of one of the *aulād al-nās*, who was a ne'er-do-well and a criminal, with many murders to his credit. He was garrotted at the gateway of the street in the Seven Water-Tanks district." It may be noted that, though the preceding pages are full of brutalities committed by the mamluks in general, an example is made only of one of the rag, tag, and bobtail of the Mamluk forces, the *aulād al-nās*.

On April 25 we have an announcement all too common in these pages: [447] "Today died the Amīr Asanbay the Deaf, one of the drum-and-trumpet amīrs[15] and one of the prominent mamluks of

[13]*aṭlaqa fī-him al-nār.*
[14]*khāṣṣakīya.*
[15]*amīr al-ṭablkhānāh* (*sic*), i.e., he was of the second grade of high-ranking officers.

Al-Ashraf Qait-Bay.[16] He was well versed in lance-play; he had missed promotion, though there was nothing to his discredit. He died suddenly and without warning." This last formula, linking his blameless reputation with his lack of promotion and his sudden death is, as I say, frequent though not general: one is therefore tempted to assume that Ibn Iyās is using it deliberately.

We may pass now over a number of incidents which, taken together or separately, ought to be generally recognized in our day as the warning signs of impending decadence and disaster: I refer to such things as administrative blunders, particularly in the regulation of the armed forces, sudden and dramatic economic changes, lavish and frivolous expenditure on entertainment, a decline in public morality, and so on. Let us come instead to the one feature perhaps most characteristic of our own age and its troubles—actual or suspected treason; the entry is for Monday, May 7: [449] "It is rumoured that Khushqadam, Superintendent of the Granaries,[17] has fled, together with a band of royal mamluks, a boat with sixteen oars having been made ready for him in advance. It is said that he took about ten mamluks with him, leaving Cairo in a casual manner. The rumour runs that he has gone to join Salīm Shāh the Ottoman, Emperor of Byzantium (Selim I), in whose service as an officer he is said to have a brother. In any case, he has gone. By origin this Khushqadam is one of the purchased slaves of Sulṭān Qānṣūh (in other words, this is treachery at the very heart of the ruling Sulṭān's power), who had given him command of ten. . . ." Ibn Iyās then goes on to tell us how he had risen in the Mamluk hierarchy, but had been mulcted (doubtless "squeezed") of 5,000 dinars by the Sulṭān; subsequently he had had the misfortune to marry the daughter of a high Mamluk civil servant, who himself fell into disgrace, whereupon Khushquadam was again "squeezed" by the Sulṭān for his father-in-law's alleged defalcations and ordered (this adds insult to injury) to divorce the daughter. Of such stuff is treason born!

This defection must in many ways have been the Burgess-Maclean affair of the time. Certainly, four or five months later, in September of the year, Ibn Iyās is crediting him with a crucial role as Selim's expert adviser on Egypt: [471] he was, it seems, stressing to him such facts as the poor morale of the mamluks themselves, the dis-

[16]A long-ruling Mamluk, A.D. 1468–95. The dead man in fact belongs to a past age of glory.

[17]*shādd al-shuwan* (*sic*).

content of the people (particularly of the merchants) at mamluk extortion, the effect of debasement of the coinage and similar economic devices then being practised to avert the evil hour, the composition of the armed forces and their order of battle, and so on. Ibn Iyās winds up this catalogue thus: "He gave him complete accounts of all the judges in Egypt, telling him that they were accepting bribes to pervert the religious ordinances [restoration of the true faith is always a popular rallying cry in Islam]: he encouraged him to march against the Sulṭān's territory and minimized the difficulties involved. He explained to him how he should send warships against Alexandria and Damietta." And so on and so on; he even suggests that Khushqadam inspires the increasingly contemptuous wording of the Ottoman correspondence with the Sulṭān. It becomes, the more one reads this section, increasingly difficult not to believe that Ibn Iyās was taking his opportunity to air his own grievances, and those of his class, against the tyranny they had suffered so long; and also, of course, to suggest his satisfaction that the end could not be far delayed. Indeed, with suitable, face-saving *absit omens* he compares the whole situation to one at a period some 200 years earlier when a Baḥrī Mamluk ruler became embroiled, to his discomfort, with the Persian-Mongol Ghāzān Khān, the situation being similarly exacerbated by the activities of a renegade whom the Mamluk Sulṭān had himself expelled.

As so often at a time of crisis in a nation's affairs, nothing would go right. Here is the entry immediately following the long passage summarized above: [472] "On Wednesday, September 28, news came from Suez of the sinking of one of the craft the Sulṭān had fitted out for the Indian campaign. It had crashed into a reef and broken up, sinking with all its cargo; part of the forces in her were also lost. But the people took no augury thereby." This must surely be ironical?

Let us return once more, however, to another glimpse of the eternal pay disputes. Here is the entry for Thursday, May 17, ten days after Khushqadam's defection: [453] "On this day the Sulṭān made up the *nafaqa* (the war bonus) to certain of the *qarāniṣa* (that is, the mamluks he had inherited from former Sulṭāns). Previously he had resolved not to grant it to them at all, but when he did so he 'gave them poison in the fat,' posting some to the Eastern Zone, some to the Western Zone, some to Aqaba and Aznam, and others to Manfalūṭ. But he spoke to them openly, saying 'Anyone who wants the *nafaqa* must leave immediately, those who don't can stay at home and take it easy.' Most of the mamluks involved forbore to claim the *nafaqa*, those who did set off without delay." Two things at least are obvious here—how bad morale had become (though these were not, of course, the absolute *élite* of the corps), and secondly how poor a manager of men, how undiplomatic a plotter, Qanṣūh had grown in his old age.

As late as Monday, June 25 [457] the Sulṭān is still as much preoccupied with his Portuguese-Indian venture as with the real threat from Turkey: he now decides to stiffen his low-grade contingent for this former campaign with a leavening of his own mamluks, with some of those inherited from other sulṭāns, and also with some *aulād al-nās.* Ibn Iyās says that the more the Sulṭān hears of Frankish insolence on the high seas, the more determined he is to build ships. At Suez, whence they can hardly be brought to bear in a crisis against the fine Turkish fleet, he builds "some twenty ships, and fits them out with weapons, guns, and cannon,[18] and other implements of war. He made Salmān the Ottoman captain over these ships, and under him was a numerous company of Ottoman and Barbary sailors, about 2,000 men, some say more." We already know what happened to one of these ships before the campaign had yet got under way, but even had all gone well, it was obviously folly to pour wealth, material, and skill into such a project at this time and place, and then to put it in the hands of foreign mercenaries, not to say pirates.

I promised that we would see the return of Jānim, the royal guard sent to discover Selim's real intentions. The entry is for Thursday, June 28, two and one-half months after his departure: [459] "On being admitted he reported that the Ottoman had treated him with extreme generosity, giving him on his return a robe of honour made of crocodile skin trimmed with sable fur." As Ibn Iyās observes laconically: "Motion and rest are both in the hand of Almighty God." Incidentally, on this occasion, he refers to Jānim as a saifī, that is, as we now know, a mamluk taken over from a deceased or disgraced Mamluk official, the lowest grade of royal mamluk.[19] Clearly the intelligence services of the Mamluk state were not considered of top priority. (We do in fact know in general that their intelligence service was far inferior to that of the Turks.)

The following Tuesday sees this entry: [459] "The Sulṭān distributed the war bonus to the force destined for India, it taking the form of voyage-money of 50 dinars for every mamluk [this was quite a sum]. He also promised them that before they sailed he would advance

[18] *silāḥ, makāḥil, madāfiʿ.*
[19] Wiet converts this, without explanation, into "Saif al-Dīn."

them six months' regular pay. It is said, moreover, that he excused any of the *aulād al-nās* who complained of physical infirmity or who had a venereal disease. He went on to speak plainly to them, saying: 'Anyone incapable of making the journey by salt water shall let me know, and I will excuse him the voyage.' This (in the words of Ibn Iyās) was reckoned a kindly act on his part." Later there is an echo of these promises, when certain men try unavailingly to "go sick" after first spending their *nafaqa*. Further trouble also breaks out when the promised six months' advance of regular pay is reduced to one of four months [460].

It is interesting to see crime and punishment of the crudest and most melodramatic sort flourishing amid the general disorder:

[461] On Saturday, July 22, the Sulṭān ordered the garotting of four people, a white Byzantine slave-girl, an Abyssinian slave-girl, a young man of low origins and a *qauwās*.[20] The reason was that the two last corrupted the slave-girls, persuading them to kill their master, a retired and landed member of the *aulād al-nās*. They did so and threw his body in the sewer, taking all they could find in the house and making for Aṭfīḥ. Five months passed, and then the facts came out, a little slave-girl informing against them. They were seized by one of the elders of Aṭfīḥ and sent to the Sulṭān, who put pressure on them until they confessed to the killing and the disposal of the body in the sewer. The Sulṭān ordered the local magistrate to investigate the matter; he examined the sewer and found the body, the skin of which had become desiccated. When he reported the facts to the Sulṭān, he ordered a proper burial and the granting of the dead man's landed property to another mamluk. Finally he gave instructions for the strangulation of those who had done this thing: when they were being taken to execution all Cairo was in a stir over them on that day. They were taken to the site where they had killed their master, a place near the Gateway of Happiness, and there the four were executed and their affair terminated.

I can think of only a handful of instances elsewhere in older Islamic writings where such incidents are described, and nowhere at such length as this.

On Monday, August 7, an envoy of Selim's arrives bearing the head of ʿAlī Daulāt, the uncle whose cause the Sulṭān had half-heartedly espoused, and also the heads of ʿAlī's son and right-hand man. The Sulṭān just does not believe it, though all Cairo had apparently been seething with rumours of ʿAlī Daulāt's defeat for some weeks past. Ibn Iyās actually makes the Sulṭān say: [462] "They are the heads of

[20] *ṣabīy ibn nās laffāf wa-shakhṣ qauwās*. Cf. Wiet (I, 425): "un jeune garçon, fils de mamlouk *Laffâf* (?) et un fabricant d'arcs."

Frankish princes which he has laid hands on simply in order to be able to send them to me." Clearly, the pace is accelerating, both in respect of Selim's arrogance and show of naked force, and also as regards the deterioration of Mamluk morale and judgment at the highest level. The entry for next day reads as follows:

[463] The Sulṭān did not emerge from the Duhaisha Palace to come down to the race-course, and it was rumoured that he had taken a drug, having become exhausted in body and assailed by a trembling in consequence of the Ottoman envoy's arriving with ʿAlī Daulāt's head. On the same day sharp words passed between the Sulṭān and the amīrs and they upbraided him in their speeches. They said (for example): "Our Lord Sulṭān, the greater part of the territory of Aleppo has passed from our grasp into that of the Ottoman. The Friday sermon there is now delivered in his name, and coins are struck likewise [the two classic signs in Islam of a fundamental change of allegiance]. He has begun the construction of a fortress at the Baghras Pass and another at Bāb al-Malik. Meanwhile the Sulṭān's hand lies in cold water [a common figure of speech at the time for apathy], and the affairs of the realm are in decay. Most of the population of Aleppo and elsewhere, on account of the tyranny and cruelty of our governors, incline to the Ottoman for the sake of his justice to the mass of the people. This is no right state of affairs." (Ibn Iyās goes on) These words of the amīrs offended him, but he kept control of his anger. However, on that day, he did not go down to the race-course to sit in judgment among the people.

The next entries show other and larger bodies of mamluks asserting their will against the Sulṭān to the extent that he is obliged to surrender a hated favourite to them to be ignominiously done to death; also they extract from him a decree that in effect gives them free rein to loot shops and warehouses: an undated entry, for about mid-August, reads: [465] "The Sulṭān has issued a proclamation throughout Cairo to the effect that no market-man or merchant may slight the Sulṭān's mamluks or grasp the bridle of any of their horses. Any who do so shall have their hand severed, if their life be not forfeit! This proclamation has been a great cause of ruin to the people, for the mamluks have begun to force their way into the markets, seizing precious stuffs from off the very stalls, with none able to prevent them." Ibn Iyās goes on to say in general how wretched the lot of the people has become, but then he puts his finger shrewdly on the particular crux involved here: "The mamluks, in consideration of the murder of Sunbul the favourite referred to above and also of this proclamation, have been pacified in their demands for the *nafaqa*."

On August 14 confirmation comes [465] from Syria of all the points made by the amīrs in their speeches of reproach to the Sulṭān for his dilatoriness. The Syrian delegation suggest that prompt action can still save something from the wreck. The Sulṭān first becomes violently upset (one is reminded of Hitler's alleged rug-chewing) and then calls yet another in a long series of ineffective war councils. Two days later on his way through Cairo to the citadel, the Sulṭān is halted by a deputation of merchants: [466] "They complained to him of their molestation by the mamluks, and of their snatching of precious stuffs from off the stalls. He, however, gave no attention to the matter, and it seems that the merchants began to use coarse speech to the Sulṭān, who went up to the citadel in an extremely black mood at the behaviour of the common people."

On Monday, August 21, that is, five days later, the Sulṭān has recovered sufficiently to review the forces leaving for India [466]. We learn that they paraded in full dress and were each called forth by name; Salmān the Ottoman, the leader of the expedition, is given various presents and honours and is confirmed as commander-in-chief of the new fleet. Ibn Iyās' own words are worth quoting in respect of the second and the third in command, for they contain a good measure of quiet contempt: "He confirmed as second captain[21] a person named Yashbak, a commander of ten [that is, an amīr of the lowest rank]. As third captain[22] he appointed a person called Demirdash the Cretan. In fact, his origin was Frankish, but he used to sell Cretan wine, and so became known by this nickname. The Sulṭān showed him favour by giving him a command of ten, and making him chief of the military contingent. Such things (says Ibn Iyās) belong to the blunders of the age." The Sulṭān makes a speech and prays for victory and the force sets off with a brave show of drums, trumpets, banners, and—as I indicated already—even some cannon and hand-guns, albeit too few, too late, and in the wrong place. Ibn Iyās must surely be indebted for once to his master-at-arms brother for his exact knowledge of the composition of this force: [467] "Fifty members of the royal guard; 150 members of the *jamdārīya* [a closely associated body]; 450 of the Fifth Regiment of arquebusiers, including the *aulād al-nās* and others; and 5,344 sailors and mercenaries, Turkomans and men from the Barbary Coast."

On the same day Selim's envoy, after a fortnight's stay in Cairo, is given audience on his return home, carrying as Ibn Iyās puts it (doubtless with a touch of meiosis, bearing in mind the severed heads)

[21] *al-bāsh al-thānī.*
[22] *al-bāsh al-thālith.*

"an answer to the information delivered by his hand." Almost immediately after his departure the Sulṭān, it seems, wrote a further message to Selim, but could find none of his followers willing to deliver it, they saying: "He is a coarse, bloodthirsty man, who will kill anyone bringing him such an answer." It seems likely, from the phraseology employed on both occasions, that the Sulṭān must have veered from a mood of appeasement to one of provocation in a matter of a few hours. Clearly there is material here for psychological speculation. (This is, incidentally, a good example of how Wiet's smooth translation, combining both occasions, obscures the subtleties of the situation.)

Gradually the Sulṭān seems to face the fact that war with Turkey cannot be avoided and must indeed be prepared for. There are still picnics and parties, but occasionally entries like the following appear: [473] "On Monday, October 3, the Sulṭān, in his private enclosure, proclaimed to the army that they should look to their weapons and be alert, for he was about to distribute the *nafaqa* and intended to march on Friday. This announcement was made at every pay parade thereafter in the Royal Enclosure. It was rumoured that the Sulṭān would himself lead the army against the Ottoman, and such rumours persisted for a time, but then died away."

On the following Thursday [474] the last of the pay parades is completed, and, a similar general proclamation being made, it was confirmed that a detachment [no more!] was leaving for Aleppo. Ibn Iyās goes on: "When the Mamluks heard this, they came down from the citadel, firing at the people [there is little doubt as to what is meant this time by the expression "letting loose a volley"] and stealing the mules of judges, scholars, and merchants. They attacked their streets and dwellings. They pulled lawyers off their mules in the middle of the markets and took the beasts from under them. Among other things, they stole the mule of Shaikh Burhān al-Dīn b. al-Karakī, who was lecturing at the time in the Ashrafīya College, and he was forced to hand over a considerable sum to get it back." Ibn Iyās goes on to mention further instances of this outrageous behaviour against the learned and quasi-sacred professions. In some cases, it seems, the beasts were worth hardly anything intrinsically (he calls them *akādish*, "jades" or "hacks"), and it is clearly his intention not only to bemoan the lot of the virtuous in these troublous times, but also to indicate the sorry state of the Mamluk army's equipment.

The Sulṭān did not march with his small force to Aleppo, but went instead, without any warning, to inspect the coastal defences at

Alexandria and Rosetta [474]. Unfortunately he chose the month of Ramaḍān for this tour of inspection, and though he himself seems to have had a renewed access of nervous (not to say neurotic) energy, his followers complained and fell by the wayside in consequence of the arduous fasting exercises. He himself fell ill in Alexandria, but was back by mid-Ramaḍān.

Architecture and the arts continued to flourish. In mid-Ramaḍān, that is, late October in that year, Ibn Iyās tells us: [477] "The mosque-college of the Amīr Baibars [founded nearly two and one-half centuries earlier by this greatest of the Mamluk Sulṭāns, and still one of the monuments of Cairo] was completed. . . . It has turned out most beautiful and elegant. The Friday sermon was delivered in it during this month." But as against this symbol of business as usual, the Nile rose and remained at an unprecedented height, spoiling the crops and preventing the annual occupation of the centre island. As Ibn Iyās puts it [478], "in this year no house or shop on the island has been rented." Ibn Iyās notes, moreover, that even the robes of honour bestowed at the end of Ramaḍān are this year made of coarse material.

On Tuesday, November 15 [479] the Sulṭān decides to repeat an earlier mistake by dispersing some of his more reliable mamluks to various provincial stations. Most of them do not want to leave, in any case, but after considerable altercation they are persuaded to do so (no stronger word is needed, apparently) by the Sulṭān. It is interesting to see that, at this time, the preferred stations, if one *had* to leave Cairo, were Damietta and Rosetta; Aqaba, Aznam, and Alexandria were the "punishment" stations.

Money, however, remains the main preoccupation, both of the Sulṭān and his subjects. The following extraordinary entry [481] is dated Tuesday, November 29,[23] just a few months before the final desperate battle was joined:

On this day there befell an extraordinary occurrence. The Sulṭān went down to the race-course, and, having seated himself, had brought before him a Jewish person named Joseph Shinshowa, a merchant in the Frankish trade, a fluent Turkish speaker (this achievement is often mentioned as something still quite rare), who had at one time been an overseer in the Mint. The rumour was that he had fallen behind in the handing over of fines and old dues to the extent of 12,000 dinars. The Sulṭān had first sent him to the treadmill, where he remained several days without producing any of the

[23]The original, followed by Wiet, erroneously gives the date as 18 Shauwāl, identical with the date of the previous Saturday. The dating becomes irregular here, and I have made necessary amendments.

money owing, so he brought him up before him, and there, in his presence on the race-course, had his ankle-joints pressed with screws. As the pain grew too great to bear, he turned Muslim, shouting: "I confess that there is no god but God, and I bear witness that Muhammad is his apostle. I cut myself off from every faith that is not Islam." The bystanders, both military and civil, recited the formula *Allāhu Akbar*, but the Sulṭān paid no attention to his conversion, leaving him wearing the yellow turban and ordering Yaḥyà b. Nukār, Acting Governor's Secretary,[24] to take charge of him and to continue punishing him until all the money was extracted from him. Indeed, he said: "There are plenty of Muslims, and Islam has no need of this one."[25] So Ibn Nukār clapped him in irons again and took him away to be punished until the money should be extracted. In the words of the old proverb (says Ibn Iyās), "When you get rough with a Jew he turns Muslim."

For the first time in many years the bedouin now begin to cut the main north-south arteries of the Mamluk empire, attacking small groups of soldiers, pilgrims, and mail-carriers. There is a graphic description [482], in the best pony-express manner, of a mail-carrier trudging on foot for several days in one ragged garment, after losing his pouch, his mount, and his clothes.

On Saturday, December 10, eleven days after the torture of the Jew, comes the following grotesque item. All the leading mamluks had gone in a body to the Sulṭān and, more or less respectfully, suggested action: [485] "The Sulṭān tore up his cloak and began weeping and eventually fainted. They threw water on his face, and as he recovered he said: 'I no longer wish to be Sulṭān, send me where you will, and appoint the Amīr Kabīr in my place.' The Amīr Kabīr was terrified and horror-stricken at these words." How much of this was an act, how much a genuine mental breakdown, we cannot tell. Certainly, several times thereafter Qanṣūh goes through a ritual of deposing himself and being re-appointed by the council of mamluks and the Caliph.[7] Yet, while he was doubtless by now not altogether accountable for his actions, it is difficult to understand why these unprincipled, strong-minded, and sometimes capable men put up with him for so long. It may well be the old story of factions cancelling each other out, of personal interests coming before all else. It was certainly not merely loyalty to him or a lingering respect for what he once had been. There is at least a parallel of sorts here with Hitler and his henchmen, or Stalin and the Politburo. The Amīr Kabīr's terror at thus being singled out as having the ambition to step into his master's shoes, is easily intelligible. This was having the finger put on one with a

[24] *dawādār al-wālī*.

[25] Wiet (I, 445) mistranslates this ironical passage completely.

vengeance! Moreover, it needed no great seer to foretell that Qanṣūh's successor, however he came to power, would not last long. Tuman Bay, who did eventually succeed, played out a strange (but again, to us not unfamiliar) dual role of quisling and rallying force, but his performance was not a record run. It lasted less than four months.

I am uneasily aware, though not sorry, that I have in this paper attempted too many things. Let me admit that I have (as what I conceive to be a prime duty on such an occasion) attempted to entertain, or (if you prefer it) to present a difficult technical subject in a way interesting to an audience composed not only of non-specialists, but mostly of non-Islamists. To the Islamists, and to those whose interests border on or look towards Islam, on the other hand, I have tried to make an appeal—an appeal to leave occasionally the stony beach of Arabic philology and the shallow muddy waters of early Arab history and literature, and to plunge into the rich and moving depths of the main, the high seas of Islamic studies—that ocean that links us to other humanistic disciplines, or gives us some reflection of them.

11. Avicenna's Theory of Prophecy in the Light of Ash'arite Theology

M. E. MARMURA

I

THE QUESTION "What is prophecy?," for which we still seek answers, was asked in mediaeval Islam. It was asked, that is, in a culture that regarded the mission of Muhammad as the central fact of its history, his prophethood as the basis of its conception of the state. It confronted the theologian in his role as the intellectual defender of the faith, as it did the philosopher in his political thinking. Indeed, the latter, in formulating his theory of the state, gave us in effect a theory of prophecy. This theory is Platonic: the prophet is identified with the philosopher-king or made akin to him; Muslim law and institutions are interpreted within a framework that derives from the *Republic* and the *Laws*.

That the Islamic philosophers gave an account of prophecy in Platonic terms, no one disputes. But in so doing, did they not stray from the path of true belief? Were they still good Muslims? This question was raised in eleventh-century Islam and is still being discussed. Some modern scholars argue that the philosophers were actually offering an intellectual defence of prophecy against current scepticism.[1] Other scholars defend the philosophers by pointing out that in this theory "their starting-point" was their "faith in God and His revelation through His apostle Muhammad."[2] And it is true that in Avicenna's theory, the oneness of God and the prophethood of Muhammad[3] form a necessary premise. In other words, the basic tenet

[1]F. Rahman, *Prophecy in Islam* (London, 1958), pp. 63–4.

[2]E. I. J. Rosenthal, *Political Thought in Medieval Islam* (Cambridge, 1958), p. 150.

[3]Strictly speaking, the oneness of God and the existence of a law-giving prophet. Muhammad is not usually referred to directly. In Avicenna's section on prophecy in the metaphysics of *al-Shifā'*, there is the allusion to Muhammad as "the greatest of legislators." A more direct reference is given in the treatise *Fī Ithbāt al-Nubuwwāt* (*On the Proof of Prophecies*), where Avicenna speaks of "the validity of the prophethood of Muhammad" as "obvious to the reasonable man once he

of the Muslim religion is affirmed. Indeed, the philosophers' severest critic, al-Ghazālī, attests that they believe in God and prophecy; yet he condemns them as utterly irreligious for their very views on prophecy.[4] Al-Ghazālī, that is, does not consider the philosophers' affirmation of the Islamic tenet a sufficient requirement for Islamic belief.[5] In what sense did he hold this insufficient?[6] In this paper we shall investigate this sense and attempt to articulate the issues the mediaeval Muslims deemed at stake. Since in his criticism of the philosophers' theory al-Ghazālī voiced the Ashʿarite position, we must first say something about the views on prophecy held by this dominant school of theology in Islam.

II

Although the theological discussion of prophecy is not without philosophical significance, it has particular interest for the Islamist. For

---

compares him with other prophets." Ibn Sīnā, *al-Shifāʾ: al-Ilāhiyyāt (2)*, edition supervised by I. Madkur (Cairo, 1960), p. 450, l. 7; Ibn Sīnā, *Tisʿ Rasāʾil* (Cairo, 1908), p. 124. The first of these references will be abbreviated: *"Ilāhiyyāt."*

[4]Al-Ghazālī, *al-Iqtiṣād fi-l-Iʿtiqād* (Cairo, no date), p. 111.

[5]The problem here is perhaps best characterized as that of "Islamic belief." In what does this consist? The exegetical aspect of the debates on this question, the attempt to differentiate and relate the terms *islām* and *īmān*, "faith" or "belief," whose use in the *Qurʿān* is not always synonymous, tended to blur the issues. Al-Ghazālī complains of the confusion wrought by some of the discussions of these terms. He attempts to clarify the ambiguities by analysing these terms on the lexical, exegetical, and theological levels. He reaffirms what some of his Ashʿarite predecessors have held: that *īmān* is an aspect of *islām*. All *īmān* is *islām*, but the converse is not true. Al-Ghazālī, *Iḥyāʾ ʿUlūm al-Dīn* (4 vols., Cairo, 1957), I, 115 ff. See also A. J. Wensinck, *The Muslim Creed* (Cambridge, 1932), pp. 22–4, 34, 37; B. D. MacDonald, article "Imān" in the *Encyclopædia of Islam.*

[6]In the controversy over the problem of Islamic belief, it was not so much the necessity of affirming the Islamic tenet as a requirement for belief that was at issue, as it was the sufficiency of such an affirmation. Does the mere verbal affirmation (*al-iqrār bi-l-lisān*) without acknowledgement in the heart (*al-maʿrifa bi-l-janān*) suffice? What about the requirement of obedience (*al-ṭāʿa*) and works (*al-ʿamal bi-l-arkān*)? See, for example, al-Juwaynī, *al-Irshād* (Cairo, 1950), pp. 369–99; al-Ghazālī, *Iḥyaʾ*, I, 115–24; al-Shahrastānī, *Nihāyat al-Iqdām Fī ʿIlm al-Kalām*, edited by A. Guillaume (London, 1934), pp. 470–7. The answers the various schools gave to such and related questions regarding sins and divine punishment and forgiveness reflected certain views about the nature of God, his attributes, his creation. The conception of the deity, whose existence and oneness were being affirmed, was at the heart of the problem. Al-Ghazālī does not attack the philosophers because they did not believe in God and prophecy, but because of their conception of the deity and prophethood.

prior to al-Ghazālī's attack on the philosophers' theory of prophecy,[7] it was closer to the main stream of Islamic intellectual opinion than were the theories of the philosophers. It tells us something about the questions that were foremost in the mind of the mediaeval Muslim whose education centred, in the main, around the Islamic sciences which included theology, *kalām*. And it is in terms of some of these questions that we propose to discuss Avicenna's theory. Three of these questions that recur in Ashʿarite writings seem most relevant: What is prophecy? Is prophecy possible? What is the criterion for differentiating the genuine prophet from the fake?

In answering the question "What is prophecy?" al-Juwaynī[8] begins by rejecting some previous theological answers. Prophecy, he maintains, cannot be explained by reference to the prophet's body or any accident of his. Nor could one define it in terms of the prophet's knowledge of his Lord, since such knowledge can be supposed in people who are not prophets. Nor, he continues, can it be defined as consisting in the fact that the prophet knows himself to be a prophet; for we still would have to know what this prophetic quality is which the prophet discerns in himself. In the final analysis, he then states, "prophecy derives from the saying of God, the Exalted, to whomsoever he chooses, 'be my messenger.'" This, al-Juwaynī continues, is of the same order as the divine ordinances. The acts decreed by God have no intrinsic qualities that make them necessary. They derive their necessity from the speech of God.

Hence, al-Juwaynī does not define prophecy in terms of any characteristic of the prophet himself, but in terms of God's command. The answer might strike the modern ear as that of the scriptural literalist. Actually, it is al-Juwaynī the legal theorist and Ashʿarite metaphysician who is speaking. Underlying this answer is an elaborate occasionalism, constructed, to be sure, by the Ashʿarites to allow as literal an interpretation of the scripture as possible, but a metaphysics none the less. More than three centuries of theological debate and theorizing are behind this answer. It presupposes a view of the world that denies intrinsic values and natural causes. There is no objective good: the

[7]Al-Juwaynī's short but incisive attack on the philosophers' metaphysics (*al-Irshād*, pp. 234–7), does not include their theory of prophecy. It is with al-Ghazālī's comprehensive critique of the philosophers' metaphysics and their theory of prophecy that we begin to witness the theologians discussing the philosophers' theories directly and at length.

[8]Al-Juwaynī, *al-Irshād*, p. 355.

good is whatever God commands. All natural change in the world is caused by God without the interaction of natural causes. The world, which for the Ashʿarites consists of atoms and accidents, is a series of creations *ex nihilo*, annihilations, and recreations by the omnipotent God. What appears as causal uniformity is nothing but the custom (*sunna*) of God, which he can change at will. Ultimately, all explanations must terminate in God's acts beyond the ken of human knowledge. So with prophecy. It cannot be explained in terms of its own inherent nature. There is no necessity that makes certain people prophets, apart from the fact that God chooses them. There is nothing inherent in man that determines this choice.[9] In fact, the sending forth of prophets is not necessary, because God could create all men virtuous without the need of revelation. Why he has not done so, is again an aspect of divine wisdom which we cannot understand. This idea that prophecy is not necessary brings us to the second question: Is prophecy possible?

The Ashʿarite writers report arguments, which they attribute to the Brahmans, that deny the possibility of prophecy. Whether this attribution is accurate is not relevant for our purpose here.[10] What is relevant is that there were arguments known in Islam that denied the possibility of prophecy, and which the Ashʿarites had to answer. Several arguments are reported, but two of these are of particular relevance to the discussion of Avicenna's theory. Both arguments attempt to show that the supposition of prophecy as a genuine revelation of God to man would contradict some divine attribute. In the first argument one must differentiate two aspects, an ethical one and an epistemological one.[11] In its ethical form the argument maintains that since all men are of the same genus, it would be a contradiction of divine justice if God were to favour one individual rather than another with his revelation.

[9]The question of whether prophethood is divinely bestowed on an individual as a reward for his righteous living, or whether it is pre-election (the Arabic term used is *ibtidāʾ*), was discussed by certain of the Muʿtazilites. Al-Ashʿari, *Maqālāt al-Islāmiyyīn* (2 vols, Cairo, 1954), II, 122, 162. To regard it as a reward implies that something outside divine Providence determines God's acts. This is unacceptable to the Ashʿarites and is denied by al-Juwaynī (*al-Irshād*, pp. 269, 273). The suggestion of the Ashʿarite al-Bāqillānī that prophethood might be a divine reward is an argument *ad hominem* and does not represent what he actually holds. Al-Bāqillānī, *Kitāb al-Tamhīd*, edited by R. McCarthy (Beirut, 1957), p. 106.

[10]For example, the argument from specification (see below) attributed to the Brahmans is also associated with Abu Bakr al-Rāzī. See P. Kraus, "Raziana II," *Orientalia*, N.S., V (1936), 38 ff.

[11]Both aspects are to be found in al-Bāqillānī's account, but they are not clearly differentiated (*al-Tamhīd*, pp. 104–5).

The epistemological form introduces the issue of specification (*al-takhṣīṣ*): If all men are of the same genus, there can be no specifying principle that can set aside one man from the rest, to be endowed with the prophetic gift. To the argument in its ethical form, the Ashʿarites reply that justice is defined in terms of God's acts. An act is just because God commands it. Hence, to speak of an act of God as being unjust is a contradiction. As for the argument in its epistemological form, again the Ashʿarites reply that no specification can be required to determine God's setting aside one individual from the rest for the prophetic task. Otherwise God's acts would have been determined. We would have denied God free choice. Free choice is defined as the ability to choose between similars when there is no determinant to specify any of the individuals to be chosen.[12]

The second argument attributed to the Brahmans relates to the divine attribute of wisdom.[13] God, it maintains, creates men with reason which enables them to arrive at the good. To reveal to them the good through prophets becomes a superfluous act. A superfluous act is an unwise act. Hence, the existence of prophecy is impossible because such an existence would contradict the attribute of divine wisdom. The Ashʿarites answer this argument by rejecting outright the premise that reason, unaided by revelation, can arrive at the good. Once again, the good is what God commands and the commands of God are revealed to men through prophets. In answering the Brahmans, however, the Ashʿarites were careful to tread a middle course.[14] Prophecy is possible; that is, the sending forth of prophets does not contradict any of the divine attributes. But prophecy is not necessary, and in two senses: God could have created man without the need for prophets, and there is nothing in the divine nature that impels God to send forth prophets. This latter theory was implied in the doctrine

[12]The doctrine that the eternal divine will is by definition an attribute that differentiates and chooses between similars is given by al-Juwaynī and al-Ghazālī, though not always in connection with prophecy. It plays an important role in al-Ghazālī's argument that the world has a finite beginning in time. Al-Juwaynī, *al-Irshād*, p. 115; al-Ghazālī, *Tahāfut al-Falāsifa*, edited by M. Bouyges (Beirut, 1927), pp. 37–8.

[13]Al-Bāqillānī, *al-Tamhīd*, p. 121; al-Juwaynī, *al-Irshād*, p. 303; al-Ghazālī, *al-Iqtiṣād*, p. 88. See also F. Rahman, "Brahmans," *Encyclopædia of Islam* (2nd edition). This argument is closely related to the Muʿtazilite view that reason can arrive at the good. Unless the good can be arrived at independently of revelation, they maintain, one cannot know that what the prophet reveals is good, and hence a genuine revelation.

[14]Al-Ghazālī, *al-Iqtiṣād*, p. 88.

held by certain of the Muʿtazilites, to the effect that God must act in accordance to that which is best for his servants,[15] a doctrine diametrically opposed to the Ashʿarite view that equates all values with God's commands. For the Muʿtazilite doctrine implies that the good is objective, that God must act according to it; this, from the Ashʿarite point of view, imposed a limitation on God's omnipotence.

As for the last question concerning the criterion by which the genuine prophet is differentiated from the fake, it again involved Ashʿarite occasionalism. The criterion is the miracle. It is the miracle which verifies for us the genuine prophet's claim to prophecy. It is done by God on the prophet's behalf, and through him so that men will believe him. The magician can perform some uncommon acts. But these acts, though unusual, are within the realm of human possibility.[16] The true miracle is that which is beyond such a realm, as, for example, the changing of the staff into a snake by Moses. For the philosophers, such miracles are impossible because they contradict the essential nature of things and the necessary causal laws. Hence, the language in which these miracles are conveyed in the scriptures must be interpreted metaphorically. The Ashʿarites, on the other hand, denied necessary causal connection. Everything is utterly contingent and the direct creation of God. The uniform pattern of nature to which we are accustomed is not in itself necessary, and can be changed by God at will. Miracles are instances of such changes meant to verify the genuine prophet's claim to prophecy.

With the Ashʿarite position on such questions in mind, we can now proceed to discuss the Islamic philosopher's theory of prophecy; in particular, that of Avicenna.

III

The answer the philosophers of Islam gave to the question "What is prophecy?" was, as one would expect, a philosophical explanation. The traditional definition of the prophet as the man who receives revelation

[15]This is the doctrine of *riʿāyāt al-aṣlaḥ li-l-ʿibād.*

[16]Al-Juwaynī, *al-Irshād*, pp. 308–9; al-Ghazālī, *al-Iqtiṣād*, p. 89. For al-Juwaynī, the miracle by definition is the unusual event that supports the genuine prophet's claim to prophecy. An unusual happening associated with someone who makes no such claim is not a miracle. In such works as *al-Iqtiṣād* and *al-Mustaẓhiri,* al-Ghazālī lays great stress on the miracle as the sole criterion for establishing the genuineness of a prophetic claim. There is less emphasis on the miracle in his later work, *al-Munqidh.* Al-Ghazālī, *al-Munqidh min-al-Ḍalāl,* Arabic text and French translation by F. Jabr (Beirut, 1959), pp. 43–4 (Arabic text).

through the intermediacy of God's angel would not suffice. For what is this angel, and what is revelation? What faculty of the human psyche is capable of receiving revelation, and in what form does it receive it? Not only did the philosophers attempt to answer these questions; in a sense, they had to do so. For they were born to a culture that might well be described as Qurʿāno-centric. They were reared no less on the Islamic sciences than they were on the body of science and philosophy transmitted to them from the Greeks. As metaphysicians whose task was to explain all phenomena in terms of their system, they could not very well ignore such central facts of their culture as the *Qurʿān* and Muhammad. Moreover, it was through their formulation of a theory of prophecy that they were able to pursue their philosophical activity without leaving themselves entirely vulnerable to charges of irreligion and heresy. For in this theory, they not only affirmed the validity of prophecy, but they expounded their doctrine of scriptural interpretation. Revelation, they held, is expressed in language which the masses can understand. The masses must accept it literally and must not ask questions about its inner meanings. Scripture is full of symbols and suggestive language meant to stimulate the philosophically apt for theoretical speculation. Hence, there is a higher level on which scripture can be understood, but it must only be thus interpreted by those capable of so doing. This is a very small class in the community, the demonstrative class. It consists of individuals who have the native ability and the actual philosophical training. It is these people who can perceive that the symbolic inner meaning of scripture tallies with the demonstrative knowledge which Aristotle's method yields.

This is not to say that the philosophers were insincere, that they merely fabricated the doctrine of interpretation as a measure of self-defence. Nor does this necessarily invalidate the view of F. Rahman that the philosophers were actually giving a philosophical defence of prophecy against the religious scepticism of thinkers in the tradition of the physician al-Rāzi.[17] This is simply to point out that, sincere or not, the philosophers could not have pursued their philosophizing in the way they did without some such doctrine of interpretation.

It is to Alfarabi (al-Fārābī) that the philosophical theory of prophecy in Islam owes its formulation. The basic concepts of Avicenna's theory are those of Alfarabi. There are, however, some differences. For Alfarabi, the legislator must be both philosopher and prophet. He achieves philosophical wisdom when his rational soul is

[17]Rahman, *Prophecy in Islam*, p. 63.

actualized and is united in some manner with the active intellect. His prophetic revelation is attained through the imaginative faculty. Thus, although both philosophical wisdom and prophetic revelation must be present in the legislator, these involve different operations of the soul. Avicenna, on the other hand, as we shall see, allows two types of prophetic revelation, intellectual and imaginative. Moreover, the psychological account of how the soul attains intellectual knowledge differs in the two philosophers.[18] There also appears to be a difference in emphasis in their theories as a whole. Alfarabi seems to be the more theoretical; his primary concern seems to be with the nature of political patterns as such. For even though it was he who first identified the meanings of "philosopher," "legislator," and "*imām*" and used such Arabic cultural terms as *jāhiliyya* to describe certain types of regimes,[19] it was Avicenna who made the more deliberate and detailed effort to explain Muslim institutions within the framework of the theory, and to interpret scriptural passages in philosophical terms.

For Avicenna, the prophet is a man who dwells in the world of generation and corruption, a world which is the last of a series of emanations, each proceeding from a higher one, the highest an emanation proceeding directly from God. In the celestial realm, the emanations consist of the spheres, each with its soul and intellect. The celestial soul of each sphere is analogous to the practical soul in man.[20] It moves the sphere by way of desire. It desires the celestial intellect of the sphere which acts as the teleological cause. The celestial intellect of each sphere contains the eternal universal ideas. The celestial

[18]For Alfarabi's distinction between philosophical wisdom and prophetic revelation, see al-Fārābī, *Kitāb Arā' Ahl al-Madīna al-Fāḍila,* edited by A. Nader (Beirut, 1959), pp. 94, 104. The difference between the accounts of Alfarabi and Avicenna with regard to the reception of intellectual knowledge from the active intellect may be summed up as follows: In Alfarabi, the material images acquired through the senses are transformed by the illuminary action of the active intellect and rendered abstract. Once the rational soul is thus actualized, it attains an immaterial status and as such can become the object of its own conceiving. In this it resembles the active intelligence and the other celestial intellects. This resemblance enables some human intellects to conceive an aspect of the active intellect. In Avicenna, the material images themselves are not transformed into abstract concepts. They merely prepare the soul to receive the intelligibles from the active intellect. In the case of the prophet, this preparatory stage with the learning processes that are associated with it is not necessary. The reception is direct. See Rahman, *Prophecy in Islam,* chapters I and II.

[19]Al-Fārābī, *Taḥṣīl al-Saʿāda* (Hyderabad, 1345 A.H.), p. 42; *al-Siyāsa al-Madaniyya* (Hyderabad, 1345 A.H.), pp. 57 ff.; *Kitāb Arā' Ahl al-Madīna al-Fāḍila,* pp. 109 ff.

[20]*Ilāhiyyāt,* p. 387, ll, 4–6.

intellects are pure intelligences and hence, for Avicenna, cannot know the particulars in the world of generation and corruption, since such knowledge requires a bodily organ of apprehension. The celestial souls, on the other hand, are not pure intelligences and have a material aspect which enables them to know the particulars in the world of generation and corruption.[21] Their knowledge of such particulars, however, is superior to human knowledge, for they are instrumental in causing particular events, and hence they can predict future particular occurrences.[22] Both the celestial intellects and the souls are identified by Avicenna with the angels. The intellects he calls "cherubim" (*al-karrubiyūn*);[23] the souls, "active angels" (*al-malāʾika al-ʿamala*).[24] Revelation is the reception of knowledge from these angels. From the celestial intellects the prophet receives universal knowledge. This includes the ethical norms which he translates into particular prescriptions of law for governing society in the best possible way. From the celestial souls he receives particular knowledge, foreknowledge of particular events. There are, therefore, two kinds of prophetic revelation, and they involve different psychical faculties of the prophet. The reception of particular images from the celestial souls involves the imaginative faculty.[25] While such images can be received by all men in their dreams, nevertheless, when received in dreams by the ordinary man, they are often confused with other somatic images caused by the animal or other desires of man. Hence, prediction on the basis of dream interpretation is hazardous and difficult because it is not always possible to separate the somatic from the celestial image. The prophet, however, receives the celestial images in his waking hours, where the problem of confusing them with other somatic images, as in the dream, does not arise. He can then translate the celestial symbols and prophesy the future with certainty.

It should be pointed out that Avicenna in his major psychological writings does not attempt to prove that prophets receive such celestial images. He seems to accept this as a fact. He merely endeavours to explain this fact in terms of his psychology. The same holds true regarding his discussion of the second type of revelation, the intellectual. Again, it is an explanation, not a proof. Now, Avicenna's

[21]*Ibid.*, pp. 386, ll 4–8; 436, ll. 14–15; 437, l. 10.
[22]*Ibid.*, pp. 437–48.
[23]Ibn Sīnā, *Tisʿ Rasāʾil* pp. 113, 114.
[24]*Ilāhiyyāt*, p. 435, l. 8.
[25]For Avicenna's discussion of this type of prophetic reception, see *Avicenna's De Anima*, edited by F. Rahman (London, 1959), pp. 173 ff.

emanative epistemology is well suited to account for this intellectual revelation. All intelligibles are emanations received from the active intellect. Of these, the primary intelligibles, that is, the self-evident logical truths, are received directly by all men. The more complex universals, the secondary intelligibles, are received by the class of men capable of abstract thought. The majority of this class, however, cannot receive them directly. The reception, in their case, must be preceded by the acquisition of the primary intelligibles and by certain operations of the soul on the material and particular level: sensation, imagination, estimation, and cogitation or imaged thinking. These operations are the necessary preparation that enables the soul to acquire the secondary intelligibles. Moreover, the majority of this class of men receive the intelligibles in stages; their knowledge is always partial. The prophets, however, are men who receive the secondary intelligibles without the preparatory operations of the soul and learning processes associated with them. They receive both the primary and the secondary intelligibles directly. Their knowledge is intuitive. Moreover, prophets receive all or most of the intelligibles present in the active intellect instantaneously (*dafʿatan*).[26]

How is this direct reception possible? Avicenna gives us in his *De anima* a standard argument which he repeats elsewhere in his psychological writings for the possibility of prophecy.[27] This is the argument from intuition. Men, he argues, vary in their intuitive capabilities. Thus, for example, some men arrive at the middle term of a syllogism intuitively, while others cannot do so at all. Moreover, there is variation in the intuitive capacities of those who can. Thus, with some men it is only after a long and arduous process of cogitation that they intuit the middle terms. Others need less time and effort. Some can arrive at more than one middle term at any one time, while others cannot. This variation in intuitive capabilities represents a progression which must be finite in scope. For it is limited in the direction of weakness since there are men who cannot intuit at all. If limited in the direction of weakness, it must be limited in the direction of strength. It finds this limit in the ability to intuit all the middle terms sought without any preparatory cogitative process. From this Avicenna

[26] *Ibid.*, pp. 249–50. This instantaneous reception does not mean, Avicenna explains, that this type of prophetic knowledge is not ordered. Its order is logical, not temporal.

[27] *Ibid.*, p. 249. Ibn Sīnā, *Kitāb al-Najāt* (Cairo, 1939), pp. 166–7; *Aḥwāl al-Nāfs*, edited by F. Ahwani (Cairo, 1952), pp. 123–4; *Kitāb al-Ishārāt wa-t-Tanbīhāt*, edited by J. Forget (Leiden, 1892), p. 127.

concludes, not that men with such intuitive capacities must exist, but that "it is possible" (*fa yumkin idhan*) that they exist. These are the prophets.

We are not concerned here with the form of this argument and the theory of infinity it presupposes. What is of significance here is that it is an argument for the possibility of prophecy which must be contrasted with the Ashʿarite argument. Unlike the latter, it is not concerned with the question of whether the supposition of prophecy would contradict some divine attribute. The possibility of prophecy is sought in the prophet himself.

But if in most of his psychological writings Avicenna is content to argue for the possibility of prophecy,[28] elsewhere he argues for its necessity. The existence of prophecy is necessitated by the efficient, material, and teleological causes. To begin with, all existents, other than God, are necessitated by their efficient causes, and prophets are no exception. Moreover, all corporeal existents or those associated with the corporeal are conditioned, in part, by their material circumstances. The bodily composition of a human being at birth determines the kind of soul that is created with him.[29] This is very true of the prophetic soul. Indeed, the reason why the prophet is an individual whose appearance on the historical scene is not very frequent is that "the matter receptive of a perfection like his occurs in few bodily compositions."[30]

The most pointed sense, however, in which necessity enters the theory is the teleological. It has to do with Avicenna's conception of God as a being who must act for the best, a theory not unlike that of some of the Muʿtazila, and very much opposed to Ashʿarite doctrine. This teleological necessity forms the basic premise on which Avicenna's proof of prophecy rests. Avicenna argues as follows:

It is known that man differs from the other animals in that he cannot lead a proper life when isolated as a single individual, managing his affairs with no associate to help him satisfy his basic wants. For one man needs to be complemented by another of his species, the other, in turn, by him and one like him. Thus, for example, one man would provide another with vege-

[28]There seems to be one psychological argument for the necessity of prophecy. This is in the first part of his treatise *Fī Ithbāt al-Nubuwwāt* (*On the Proof of Prophecies*). The proof is problematical and requires independent treatment, see my article, "Avicenna's Psychological Proof of Prophecy," *JNES*, XXII (1), Jan., 1963, 49–56.

[29]Ibn Sīnā, *Risālā Aḍḥawiyya Fī Amr al-Maʿād*, edited by S. Dunya (Cairo, 1949), p. 90.

[30]*Ilāhiyyāt*, p. 443, l. 16.

tables while the other would bake for him; one man would sew for another while the other would provide him with needles. Associated in this way, they become self-sufficient. For this reason men have found it necessary to live in cities and form associations. . . .

If this is obvious, then man's existence and survival require partnership. Partnership is only achieved through reciprocal transactions, as well as by the various trades practised by men. Reciprocal transactions demand law and justice; law and justice, a lawgiver and a dispenser of justice. This lawgiver must be of a nature that enables him to address men and make them adhere to the law. He must, then, be a human being. . . .

Thus with respect to the survival and actual existence of the human species, the need for this person is far greater than the need of such benefits as the growing of the hair on the eyebrow, the shaping of the arches in the feet and many others that are not necessary for survival but which at best are useful for it. Now the existence of the righteous man to legislate and to dispense justice is a possibility, as we have previously remarked. It becomes impossible, therefore, that Divine Providence should ordain the existence of those former benefits and not the latter which are at their basis. Nor is it possible that the First Principle and the angels after him should know the former and not the latter. Nor yet is it possible that that which he knows to be in itself within the realm of possibility but whose realization is necessary for introducing the good order, should not exist. And how can it not exist, when that which depends and is constructed upon its existence, exists? A prophet, therefore, must exist and he must be a human.[31]

In this proof, there are actually two senses in which prophecy is necessary, both opposed to Ashʿarite doctrine. Prophets are necessary for introducing the good order. The implication in this first sense is that the majority of men are created incapable of arriving at the good life unaided by divine law. To this the Ashʿarites would agree in part. But in Avicenna's deterministic system, this implies more. It implies that the existing state of affairs could not have been otherwise. God could not have created all men virtuous. To this the Ashʿarites, as we have pointed out, would vehemently disagree. The second sense in which prophecy is necessary in the proof is that the good order which requires prophets must be ordained by God, because God by his very nature must act for the best. This, again, is diametrically opposed to Ashʿarism.

The Platonism of this theory manifests itself in the nature and function of the prophet, as well as in the framework of the city-state the prophet organizes. The law-giving prophet is very similar to the

[31]Avicenna, *Healing: Metaphysics X*, translated by Michael E. Marmura in Ralph Lerner and Muhsin Mahdi, eds., *Medieval Political Philosophy* (New York, 1963), pp. 99–100 (*Ilāhiyyāt*, pp. 441–3). By kind permission of the Free Press of Glencoe. Hereafter cited as *MPP*.

philosopher-king. In his *Aqsām al-ʿUlūm*, where Avicenna seems to be defending himself against the accusation (to be later levelled again at him by al-Ghazālī) that he regarded the law as trickery, he speaks of the law (*al-nāmūs*) as revealed and as the standing permanent pattern or exemplar (*al-mithāl al-qāʾim al-thābit*).[32] Although the term *mithāl* is probably not used here in the strict Platonic sense of exemplar or form, the statement has Platonic overtones and it is tempting to interpret Avicenna as giving some Platonic version of the Ashʿarite doctrine of an eternal *Qurʿān*. This, however, is dangerous. Scripture, as a source of law, cannot be for Avicenna the very eternal word, or rather, "thought," of God as the Ashʿarites held.[33] We must remember that he emphasizes the fact that the prophet in setting down the law exercises his practical political judgment. What Avicenna seems to hold is something as follows:

The prophet receives from the celestial intellects, through the mediation of the active intellect, eternal universal knowledge which in his system must include moral norms. At the same time, he is fully cognizant of the limitations of the human material he has to deal with in this world of changing particulars. He thus makes individual prescriptions of the law on the basis of his intuition of eternal verities and his knowledge of men in their particular surroundings; prescriptions designed to produce the greatest practical good in this world which, in turn, is conducive to the good life on the intellectual level and which prepares men for the after-life. Inasmuch as these prescriptions are conditioned, in part, by the eternal truths which the prophet receives as emanations, they are in this sense revealed. Moreover, although these prescriptions are individual and conditioned by the particularity of the world of generation and corruption, they do stand as the pattern to be followed.

Of the knowledge the prophet receives from the celestial world, Avicenna maintains, he must not divulge any to the public save the bare minimum, and even there he must couch it in language which the masses can understand, but which contains symbols and signs

[32]Ibn Sīnā, *Tisʿ Rasāʾil*, p. 108.

[33]For the Ashʿarites the *Qurʿān* was the word of God, but not in the sense that this consisted of the actual sounds, letters, and syllables, as some held. Thinking, for the Ashʿarites, was not necessarily verbal. Verbal thinking takes place in time and cannot be eternal. Most of the Muʿtazilites, on the other hand, denied the possibility of non-verbal thinking and this was one of their arguments that the *Qurʿān* is created by God and is not his eternal word. For a summary of the issues involved and an articulation of the Ashʿarite position see al-Juwaynī, *al-Irshād*, pp. 99–118.

meant to guide those who are intellectually capable and trained for theoretical speculation. He must tell the masses

> that they have a Maker, One and Omnipotent, . . . that He has prepared for those who obey Him an after-life of bliss, but for those who disobey Him an after-life of misery. This will induce the masses to obey the decrees put in the prophet's mouth by God and the angels. But he ought not to involve them with doctrines pertaining to the knowledge of God beyond the fact that He is one, the truth, and has none like Him. To go beyond this and demand that they believe in His existence as being not referred to in place, as being not subject to verbal classifications, as being neither inside nor outside the world or anything of this kind, is to ask too much. This will simply confuse the faith they have and involve them in something from which deliverance is only possible for one who receives guidance and is fortunate, whose existence is most rare.

The prophet, Avicenna continues, must let the masses "know of God's majesty and greatness through symbols and similitudes derived from things that for them are majestic and great, adding this much—that he has neither equal, nor companion, nor similar. Likewise, he must instill in them belief in the resurrection in a manner they can understand and their souls find rest therein. He must tell them about eternal bliss and misery in parables they can understand and imagine. Of the true nature of the after-life, he should only indicate to them something in general: that it is something which 'no eye has seen and no ear heard,' and that there are pleasures (which) are great possessions, and miseries that are perpetual torture."[34]

The basic framework of Avicenna's political state is likewise Platonic: "The legislator's first objective in laying down the laws and organizing the city must be to divide it into three groups: administrators, artisans and guardians. He must place at the head of each kind a leader, under whom he will place other leaders, under these yet others, and so forth until he arrives at the common run of men. Thus none in the city will remain without a proper function and specific place: each will have his use in the city. Idleness and unemployment must be prohibited. . . ."[35]

Although the basic framework of the state is Platonic, the institutions placed within this framework are Islamic. The family is a Muslim family.[36] The laws of marriage and divorce, of the status of the woman and the child, are Islamic. Prohibitions of gambling and usury are Qurʿanic. In effect, Avicenna uses the broad Platonic framework to

[34] *MPP*, pp. 100–1 (*Ilāhiyyāt*, pp. 441–3).
[35] *Ibid.*, p. 104 (*Ilāhiyyāt*, p. 447). [36] *Ilāhiyyāt*, pp. 448 ff.

explain and justify Islamic ways. The masses must be governed by the religious law. Since the prophets do not appear in every generation, their legislation and teaching must be remembered.[37] Hence the duties of prayer, fasting, and pilgrimage must be imposed, for these are the reminders of the legislation and the teaching of the prophet. To see to it that the city continues to be governed by the prophetic law, successors are needed to administer the state. Hence, Avicenna discusses the institution of the caliphate, the requirements a man should fulfil to be entitled to this position of leadership, the problems of succession, and the function of the caliph.[38] Nothing basically contrary to Sunnism is advocated. The caliph is a learned and politically able man, but he is not a prophet nor an *imām* either in the moderate Shiʿite sense of having to belong to a particular lineage, or in the more extreme Shiʿite views that endow him with supernatural powers. Perhaps there is no better example that illustrates how Avicenna justified Islamic attitudes within this theory than his discussion of holy war (*jihād*). After stating that cities opposing the laws of the prophet must be fought, he goes on to consider cities that have praiseworthy laws of their own, though not laws identical with the state he is describing. Perhaps the long history of Islam's relation to Christian states was in the mind of Avicenna when he wrote:

> If a city other than his has praiseworthy laws, the legislator must not interfere with it unless the times require the declaration that no law is valid save the revealed law. For when nations and cities go astray and laws are prescribed for them, adherence to the law must be assured. If the adherence to the law becomes incumbent, it might very well be the case that to ensure this adherence requires the acceptance of the law by the whole world.
>
> If the people of that other city which has a good way of life find that this new law, too, is good and praiseworthy and that the adoption of the new law means restoring the conditions of corrupted cities to virtue, and yet proceed to proclaim that this law ought not to be accepted and reject as false the legislator's claim that this law has come to all cities, then a great weakness will afflict the law. Those opposing it could then use as argument for their rejecting it that the people of that city have rejected it. In this case these latter must also be punished and holy war waged on them. But this holy war must not be pursued with the same severity as against the people utterly in error. Or else an indemnity must be imposed on them in lieu of their preference.[39]

His discussion of prophecy in the *al-Shifāʾ* ends with words that pay the highest tribute to prophets: "If one combines with justice, specu-

[37] *Ibid.*, pp. 443 ff.
[38] *Ibid.*, pp. 451 ff.
[39] *MPP*, pp. 108–9 (*Ilāhiyyāt*, p. 453).

lative wisdom, he is indeed the happy man. And whoever, in addition to this, wins the prophetic qualities, becomes almost a human god. Worship of him, after the worship of God, becomes almost allowed. He is indeed the world's earthly master and God's deputy in it."[40]

There is much in Avicenna's theory of prophecy that should gladden the hearts of the devout and of those who walk in more traditional paths. And yet, to see why the Ashʿarite spokesman, al-Ghazālī, condemned it, we must return to the three questions the Ashʿarites were concerned with: "What is prophecy?" "Is prophecy possible?" "What is the criterion for distinguishing the true prophet from the fake?"

In the course of our discussion of Avicenna's theory, we have said something about the first two questions. Avicenna, in effect, defines prophecy within a metaphysical framework of necessary emanation unacceptable to the Ashʿarites. The psychological aspect of his account of prophecy is in reality a naturalistic explanation that defines prophecy in terms of the prophet, and not directly in terms of God's commands. Moreover, Avicenna is not content to argue for the possibility of prophecy. He argues for its necessity. This again is contrary to the Ashʿarites' theistic voluntarism and occasionalism. It is, however, the last question regarding the criterion of true prophecy, the question of miracles, which, more than anything else, was to evoke the wrath of the Ashʿarite al-Ghazālī. Not that Avicenna denies miracles or rejects their need: "The prophet must also possess characteristics not present in others so that men could recognize in him something they do not have which differentiates him from them. Thus to him must belong the miracles about which we have spoken."[41]

The reception of revelation by the prophet, whether through his imaginative faculty or his rational soul, is for Avicenna of the miraculous order. Moreover, the prophet is capable of other miracles. Just as in the ordinary man the psychological states have physical effects, in some men this influence can transcend their own bodies.[42] They can influence the outside world. Prophets are such men. They can summon such occurrences as storms and rain. However, in all these miracles, the order of nature has not been contradicted. These miracles are explicable causally. Miracles reported in the scriptures and traditions that violate the essential nature of things are, for the philosophers, impossibles. The language reporting them must be taken metaphori-

[40]*Ibid.*, p. 110 (*Ilāhiyyāt*, p. 455). [41]*Ibid.*, p. 100 (*Ilāhiyyāt*, p. 442).

[42]Rahman, ed., *Avicenna's De Anima*, pp. 200–1; Ibn Sīnā, *Kitāb al-Ishārāt*, p. 220.

cally by those capable of correct interpretation. In other words, Avicenna accepts certain kinds of miracles, but not all that are reported in the *Qurʿān*. The Ashʿarites, on the other hand, argue for the possibility of the miracles rejected by Avicenna by denying causal necessity in nature. This denial allowed the literal acceptance of much of the scriptures. We find that in al-Ghazālī's criticism of the philosophers' theory of prophecy, it is these two issues, miracles and scriptural interpretation, that are the most important. For the political struggle between Sunnism and Shiʿism rendered these issues vital in the doctrinal conflict that was part of the political struggle.

IV

The second half of the eleventh century witnessed the political revival of Sunnism when, in 1055, the Seljuke sultanate replaced the Buyid Shīʿites as the dominant power in the Eastern caliphate. But this also meant an accentuation of the struggle between Sunnism and Shīʿism, particularly in its extreme Ismāʿīlī forms. Although the Seljukes were able to curb militarily the power of the Ismāʿīlī Fatimid caliphate of Cairo in Syria, the Ismāʿīlī underground in the Seljuke realm intensified its rebellious activity and campaigns of doctrinal propaganda. The Sunni powers had to ward off both the physical and doctrinal attacks of the Ismāʿīlīs. The task of combating the Ismāʿīlīs doctrinally was undertaken by the theologian. It is in this context that the career of al-Ghazālī has to be partly understood.

From 484–488 A.H. (1091/2–1095), al-Ghazālī taught at the Niẓāmiyya in Baghdad. This was one of the network of religious colleges established in important cities of the Seljuke realm by the great wazir of the Seljukes, Niẓām al-Mulk. The prime purpose of these colleges seems to have been the teaching of Shāfiʿī law, and al-Ghazālī was a teacher of law.[43] But to this period belong some of his most important theological works, in particular his *Tahāfut al-Falāsifa* and *al-Mustaẓhirī*.[44] In the first work he undertook to refute the

[43]For a critical discussion of the Niẓāmiyyas and the policies of Niẓām al-Mulk see the article of G. Makdisi, "Muslim Institutions of Learning in Eleventh Century Baghdad," *Bulletin of the School of Oriental and African Studies* (*BSOAS*), XXIV/I (1961), 1–56. See also A. L. Tibawi, "Origins and Character of al-Madrasah," *BSOAS*, XXV/II (1962), 225–38.

[44]*Al-Mustaẓhirī* is both a theological and legal work. It undertakes to refute Ismāʿīlī doctrine and it also gives legal opinions regarding relations between Sunnis and Ismāʿīlīs.

metaphysical systems of Alfarabi and Avicenna. In the second work, written in 1095 at the request of the Abbasid caliph al-Mustaẓhir, he undertook to refute the Ismāʿīlī *bātiniyya*. Although the primary aim of these works differs, a connection can be detected between them. *Al-Mustaẓhirī* reveals a secondary motive for al-Ghazālī's attack on the philosophers.

To begin with, the philosophers' metaphysical and psychological account of prophecy gave the Ismāʿīlīs the model for explaining their views of the reception of esoteric knowledge by their infallible *imām*. Now, al-Ghazālī tells us that in his *al-Mustaẓhirī* he will refute only those doctrines of the Ismāʿīlīs which are not shared by any other group. The doctrine of the reception of esoteric knowledge, he tells us, is taken from the philosophers' theory of prophecy. Since he had already refuted this theory in his attack on the philosophers, he will not repeat himself.[45] And indeed, the philosophers' theory of prophecy was attacked in the sixteenth discussion of his *Tahāfut*.[46] There al-Ghazālī maintains that the philosophers' theory that the spheres have souls, that these souls have knowledge of particular events, and that such knowledge is transmitted to the prophet is arbitrary. Nothing has been given to prove it or even show its plausibility. It might even lead to contradictory consequences that would render it false. The theory must allow the possibility that the prophet, a mere human being, can know the infinite future events in the eternal world the philosophers subscribe to.

In the second place, there is a similarity between the philosophers and the Ismāʿīlīs with respect to their attitude towards scriptural interpretation. Both upheld the idea that scripture contains hidden truth that is only known to the select few. Indeed, the name *bāṭinī*, "inner" which describes Ismāʿīlī doctrine refers to their theory of esoteric knowledge. It is true that what the philosophers and the Ismāʿīlīs hold to be the hidden truth is not always identical. But the philosophers' theory gave an intellectual sanction to this trend in viewing scripture. More important is the Aristotelianism that underlies the philosophers' theory of scriptural interpretation that denied many of the Qurʿanic miracles and statements referring to the after-life. The issue of miracles becomes of particular importance in the Sunni-Ismāʿīlī conflict. The Ismāʿīlīs claimed for their *imām*, the then Fatimid caliph

[45]Al-Ghazālī, *Al-Mustaẓhirī*, edited by I. Goldziher (*Streitschrift des Gazālī Gegen die Batinijja-Sect*; Leiden, 1916), pp. 9–10.
[46]Al-Ghazālī, *Tahāfut*, pp. 261–7.

al-Mustanṣir of Cairo, supernatural knowledge that made him infallible. His position was not dissimilar to that of the prophet. But such a claim must somehow be verified. Where is this verification? In *al-Mustaẓhirī*, al-Ghazālī repeatedly points out that the claims of the true prophets to prophethood have been verified through their miracles, whereas the Ismāʿīlī *imāms* have produced nothing to verify their claims to infallible knowledge.[47] The miracle, then, is the decisive criterion; and it has to be something other than the unusual event of the philosophers, causally explicable.

Al-Ghazālī devotes the seventeenth discussion of his *Tahāfut* to the issue of miracles.[48] Not that he rejects the possibility of what the philosophers deem the miracles of the prophet; but, for al-Ghazālī, these do not go far enough. The philosophers deny the literal truth of many a miracle and assertion in the *Qurʿān*. They do so because their philosophy is grounded on the premise that necessary causal connection obtains in nature. Hence al-Ghazālī's critique of natural causation. Neither observation nor reason, he tries to show, can prove necessary causal connection in nature. If one is to deny the literal truth of a scriptural assertion and give it a metaphorical interpretation, he must first give demonstrative proof that such an assertion taken literally is impossible. Only then is such an interpretation legitimate. In their attempt to prove such assertions impossible in their literal sense, the philosophers assume their causal principle. But this principle has not and cannot be proven. As such, the impossibility of the literal truth of these scriptural assertions has not been proven.

Further, if much of the *Qurʿān* has been given in language which is not literally true, meant for the masses incapable of understanding demonstrative knowledge, then the prophet becomes a man who utters falsehoods. In several of his writings, al-Ghazālī repeats the charge that, for the philosophers, the individual prescriptions of the law are man-made utilitarian devices meant to control the masses.[49] This, to begin with, is contrary to the concept of divine law where some of its obligations are the very eternal words of God to be followed to the letter. The duties imposed by the law are not utilitarian devices. They are as necessary for the salvation of the soul as are the remedies of the physician for the healing of the body.[50] Moreover, if the prophet gives

[47]Al-Ghazālī, *al-Mustaẓhirī*, pp. 26, 27, 30, 33, 34, 35.

[48]Al-Ghazālī, *Tahāfut*, pp. 277–96.

[49]See, for example, al-Ghazālī, *Tahāfut*, pp. 5, 376; *al-Munqidh*, pp. 24, 47; *al-Iqtiṣād*, p. 111.

[50]Al-Ghazālī, *al-Munqidh*, pp. 45–6, 50, 52–3.

utterances for public consumption that are not literally true, then he cannot be trusted. If in some instances the prophet does not speak the truth, then there is no guarantee that in all other instances he does.[51]

It is the theory of metaphorical interpretation that has allowed the philosophers to uphold three doctrines which, for al-Ghazālī, are utterly irreligious. These are the doctrines of an eternal world, of God's knowledge of particulars in a universal way, and of non-bodily resurrection. Such doctrines are irreligious because they deny God will, knowledge, and omnipotence. They are not sanctioned by the language of the *Qurʿān*. Indeed, the language pertaining to the last two doctrines is explicitly contrary to them. If such doctrines are, as the philosophers believe, true, and if the prophet has for pragmatic purposes concealed them and given expression to their contrary, then he would have uttered falsehoods. Thus these doctrines, for al-Ghazālī, are irreligious not only because they deny God the attributes of power, will, and knowledge, but because they further make of his prophet a liar.[52]

We have indicated, I believe, the sense in which al-Ghazālī considered the mere affirmation of the oneness of God and the prophethood of Muhammad on the part of Avicenna insufficient as a requirement for true belief. Here the question is not of sincerity.[53] Avicenna is not accused by al-Ghazālī of giving merely lip service to this fundamental tenet of Islam. Rather, what is at stake is the conception of the deity and prophethood. Is Avicenna's God the God of the *Qurʿān*? Al-Ghazālī's answer is an emphatic denial. And if Avicenna's God is not the God of the *Qurʿān*, neither can his prophet be the messenger who revealed the *Qurʿān*.

[51]Al-Ghazālī, *al-Iqtiṣād*, p. 111.
[52]*Ibid.*
[53]See *supra*, note 6.

12. A Study of Ancestor Worship in Ancient China

C. C. SHIH

ANCESTOR WORSHIP is a religious practice in China that has come down from the remote ages to the present. It is one of the most distinctive features of Chinese culture. To understand it and its influence on the various stages of Chinese culture, one must study its origins carefully.

Since the archaeological discovery of the inscribed oracle bones at the site of the Shang royal tombs in 1899, these inscriptions have become invaluable material for research. For the first time, the actual records and the actual objects used by the Shang royal house have made it possible to base a study of the culture of ancient China on actual evidence rather than on conjecture. It has been estimated recently that among Chinese scholars alone, more than three hundred have used this new material in re-examining a wide range of subjects. Recent studies of the oracle inscriptions have in some cases corroborated traditional history, but they also have enabled us to rectify some errors in classical literature, some false interpretations of governmental documents and historical material, and to re-evaluate some traditional sources and beliefs.[1]

The main sources for this study are the oracle bone and bronze inscriptions and other excavated cultural remains. Myths, legends, and traditions are eliminated unless they are supported by the archaeological evidence. A study of the ancestor worship of ancient China must begin with that of the Shang because the oracle inscriptions and cultural remains of the Shang provide the earliest and first reliable and sufficient material for such a study. Furthermore, the Shang people were originally one of the Neolithic tribes of prehistoric China, the stock who laid the foundation of Chinese civilization by introducing the bronze culture,[2] and developing a written language, advanced arts,[3] and an efficient political organization.[4] With

[1]Wang Kuo-wei, *Ku Shih Hsin Chêng* (Peking, 1935).

[2]Ch'en Chung-mien, *Hsi Chou Shê Hui Chih Tu Wên T'i* (Shanghai, 1956), pp. 93–6.

[3]Li Ya-nung, *Yin Tai Shê Hui Shêng Huo* (Shanghai, Jên Min Publishing Co., 1955), p. 102.

[4]*Ibid.*, p. 88.

the rise of the Shang, China definitely entered her historic period. It is the earliest dynastic period to be fully supported by archaeology.

Of all the known oracle bones dating before 1400 B.C., only two bear inscriptions.[5] Those of the late Shang bearing inscriptions are fragmentary. However, they are sufficient to give a fairly clear picture of the religious life of the ancient Chinese. The available 100,000 pieces of oracle records[6] reveal that the central religious activity of the Shang people was ancestor worship, although many other deities were worshipped at the same time. The other deities recorded on the bone inscriptions are the gods of the rain, wind, sun, moon, stars, clouds, rivers, mountains, earth, the four directions, and the Mother of the East and the Mother of the West. But above all, the Shang people believed that there was one supreme god, the highest of all deities, called "Ti." He was the omnipotent one who, according to the oracle records, was often asked through divination about the events which would affect the fate of the people and the nation. The majority of the inquiries were concerned with rain, famine, crops, war, good and bad luck.

Though the Shang supreme god was omnipotent and omniscient, strangely enough none of the oracle inscriptions make mention of his worship or of sacrifice to him.[7] On the contrary, the records and objects discovered in the excavations reveal endless elaborate and complicated ceremonies of worship and sacrifice to ancestors. In other words, all the evidence shows that ancestor worship played the most important role in the religious life of the Shang people. Based upon statistics from all the oracle records available, it can be stated that the Shang nobles called upon their ancestors for aid and offered sacrifices to them more frequently than to all the other deities combined. One is quite justified, then, in saying that ancestor worship was the national religion of the Shang people. It has been generally thought that worship and war were the two most important affairs of a state in ancient China, but worship of the ancestors was regarded as even more important than war in Shang times. The Shang people believed that ancestors possessed sufficient power to exert influence for both good and ill upon the affairs of men and the fate of the

[5]*Wên Wu Ts'an K'ao Tzŭ Liao* (Peking, 1954), p. 6.

[6]Tung Tso-pin, "Some Statistics of the Oracle Records," *Ta Lu Tsa Chih* (Formosa), VI(12) (1953), 5–11.

[7]Hu Hou-hsüan, *Chia Ku Hsüeh Shang Shih Lun Ts'ung* (Chengtu, 1944), Series 1, Bk. 2, p. 6. Tung Tso-pin, "Chung Kuo ku tai wên hua ti jên shih," *Ta Lu Tsa Chih*, III(12) (1951), 27.

nation, and that ancestors kept the strictest watch over their descendants, protecting, rewarding, or punishing according to deeds committed. And since their favour had to be gained and their anger propitiated, ancestors were reverently worshipped and sacrifices were regularly offered. It was assumed that the needs of the dead were essentially the same as those of the living. Thus, in the form of sacrifices, the Shang people provided their ancestors in the other world with the things they had enjoyed while alive.

The Shang rulers occupied themselves extensively with sacrifices to the ancestors. They were offered at different times, in various places, and in diverse fashions. Some were offered on fixed days, others on special occasions, and others at regular intervals. During the last years of the dynasty it took a ruler a whole year to complete the cycle of five different rites of worship and sacrifice for all the ancestors concerned, not including all the other special sacrifices. Consequently the term *ssŭ*, originally meaning sacrifice, came to be used as the term for "year."

Sacrificial objects were of various kinds. They included wine, cattle, sheep, dogs, pigs, fowl, millet, wheat,[8] and even human beings. Wine was offered at every sacrifice. Animals were regularly offered and ordinarily in small numbers although there were a few exceptions in regard to the sacrifices of cattle and sheep. One of the sacrifices offered consisted of three hundred cattle, one hundred sheep, and one hundred cups of wine.[9] Human sacrifices were offered fairly often. The highest number of human victims involved in any one sacrifice was three hundred. According to sources available to the writer, such a large sacrifice was offered twice.[10] The rest of the time the number varied from two to thirty.

Since the dead ancestors were served as if they were living, the Shang kings, besides regularly offering sacrifices, made lavish expenditures for the erection of tombs and temples. Every departed king had his own tomb and temple. The tombs were considered to play the same role in the after life as the ancestors' palaces had in this life, and the temples were meant to be their courts where worship was performed, sacrifices offered, troubles told, and guidance sought. The tombs were erected under the ground while the temples were

[8]Hu Hou-hsüan, *Chia Ku Hsüeh Shang Shih Lun Ts'ung*, II, Bk. 1, 130.

[9]Lo Chên-yü, *Yin Hsü Shu Ch'i Hou Pien* (1916), I, 28.

[10]Lo Chên-yü, *Yin Hsü Shu Ch'i Hsü Pien* (1933) II, 16. Jung Kêng, *Yin Ch'i Pu Tz'ŭ* (Peiping, 1933), p. 26, no. 245.

above the ground on a platform. The pit of the largest known tomb for a king was no less than twelve hundred square meters.[11] In the excavated tombs we have found the precious belongings and valuable possessions that were buried with the dead ancestors. They included: ornaments of all kinds made of jade, stone, marble, mother of pearl, turquoise, ivory, bone, or horn; weapons of all kinds made of bronze or stone; sacrificial utensils and complete sets of eating and drinking vessels made of bronze or pottery; cowries in great quantity. In addition, the remains of a surprisingly large number of humans and horses with carriages were discovered in many of the small tombs which surrounded the big royal tombs.

Nor was the structure of the temples any less lavish than that of the royal tombs. In the thirteenth, fourteenth, and fifteenth excavations made in 1936 and 1937, the location of the foundations of ancestral temples was discovered. Some of the temples were close to thirty feet wide and one hundred feet long. Surrounding each temple a good many victims had been buried in pits or tombs, which also contained utensils and weapons of all sorts, horses, cattle, sheep, dogs, and carriages; the human victims served as guards, soldiers, and servants of both sexes. In one instance, a total of about eight hundred and fifty human victims was buried.[12] Judging from the oracle records, these burials must have been part of an elaborate religious service held upon the completion of each of the four different stages of construction of the ancestral temple.[13] The temples and tombs unearthed from the last three excavations alone were sufficient to show what an important role ancestor worship played in Shang times.

Why was ancestor worship carried to such extremes in Shang times while the Ti, the acknowledged highest deity of all, appears to have been neglected? Why have we no record of any ceremony of worship or sacrifice to him? This is quite a puzzle. Professors Tung Tso-pin and Hu Hou-hsüan, authorities on oracle bones, have suggested that the divine and omnipotent Ti was too high and holy to accept the sacrifice of the earthly ruler, that the Ti could not be sacrificed to in the same manner as the ancestors.[14] Another theory which might shed

[11]Hu Hou-hsüan, *Yin Hsü Fa Chüeh* (Shanghai, 1955), p. 80.

[12]Shih Chang-jü, "Hsiao T'un c ch'ü ti mu tsang ch'ün," *Li Shih Yü Yen Yen Chiu So Chi K'an* (Taiwan, 1952), No. 23, p. 487.

[13]*Ibid.*, pp. 476–87.

[14]Hu Hou-hsüan, "Yin pu tz'ǔ chung ti Shang-ti hê wang-ti," *Lishi Yanjiu* (Peking), Nos. 9 & 10, 1959.

light on the question is provided by the scholar Kuo Mo-jo who, on the basis of the *Shan Hai Ching* (the Mountain and Sea Classic), a rich collection of mythology, asserts that the first ancestor of the Shang royal family, Ku, was at the same time the Supreme God Ti;[15] hence to offer sacrifice and worship to the first ancestor Ku was equivalent to offering to the Ti.

It is hard to say which of these theories is closer to the truth. One thing, however, is clear. Although no source is available to prove that any ceremonies of sacrifice or worship were performed in honour of the Supreme Ti in Shang times, there is evidence that ancestral worship was practised long before the Shang period. The discovery of the Upper Cave at Chou K'ou Tien in 1933 gave us sufficient evidence that the inhabitants of the latter part of the Palaeolithic Age buried their dead with their belongings and adornments. Around the corpse was sprinkled hematitic powder.[16] Judging from the findings in Anyang, the Shang capital, this funeral custom seems to have had a religious significance similar to that of the Shang ancestor burial. Also, the burials in the lower cave were close to the living kindred so that the spirits of the departed could easily watch over and protect them. The Shang people observed the same practice, having the tombs of their ancestors and the palaces of the living kings built side by side. Moreover, the excavated late Neolithic site of Lung Shan reveals that the pre-Shang people also buried their dead in the midst of their settlements. And at this same site, oracle bones, though all uninscribed, were found.[17] To judge from their use during late Shang times, these oracle bones must also have been the medium for communication with the spirits during the pre-Shang period. Therefore, whether or not the Shang people were the descendants of the Upper Cave men, an unbroken tradition of ancestor worship had possibly persisted in north China. Ancestor worship originated, most probably, in the family organization of the matriarchal as well as the patriarchal societies. The family was believed to continue to function in the other world and the ancestors, being endowed with supernatural power, were to continue to rule and protect it. Ancestor worship, in its origins, re-

[15]Kuo Mo-jo, "Hsien Ch'in t'ien tao kuan chih chin chan," *Ch'ing T'ung Shih Tai* (Chungking, 1946), pp. 21–3.

[16]P'ei Wên-chung, *Chung Kuo Shih Ch'ien Shih Ch'i Chih Yen Chiu* (Shanghai, 1948), p. 75.

[17]Liang Ssŭ-yung, "Hsiao-t'un, Lung-shan yü Yang-shao," *Studies presented to Ts'ai Yüan-p'ei on his 65th Birthday*, Pt. II, 1935, pp. 555–65. *Ch'eng-Tzŭ-Yai*, Archaeologia Sinica, No. 1 (Nanking, 1934), pp. 85–9.

flected the earliest spiritual life of the prehistoric Chinese but was basically a family matter.

From the evidence of ancestor worship in prehistoric times one can perhaps deduce how the idea of the Supreme God, Ti, gradually developed. In primitive times the basic needs of the human race were food and shelter. In securing food and shelter people were constantly exposed to wild animals and neighbouring enemies. Since they believed that their departed ancestors were endowed with supernatural power and were interested in their welfare, they turned to their ancestors for protection and guidance. Worship and sacrifice were therefore offered. By sacrifice the son was supposed to gain the favour of the gratified ancestors, who were to repay him by supporting him in his need and conferring upon him all sorts of blessings. While improving ways and means of conquering the hardships of life, the primitives gradually also increased the source of their food supply by stock-raising and agriculture. By this time they had begun to realize that the timely rain, the sunshine, the fertile land were all important factors affecting their living, and they therefore began to worship and sacrifice to the spirits of the rain, wind, sun, moon, earth, rivers, mountains, and so forth. As agriculture became more developed and life became comparatively settled, they became aware, more than ever, of the sunrise, the sunset, the light, and especially the regular cycle of the seasons. They then began to realize the existence of a supreme god, who governed both nature and the inferior deities. This might be the sequence of events by which the concept of a supreme god developed in China. This theory is supported by some archaeological evidence. The discovery of the Upper Cave remains reveals the fact that the proto-Chinese of the late Paleolithic age, who maintained their life by fishing and hunting, resorted to their ancestors for protection. During the Neolithic age, when they first began to increase their food supply by agriculture and domestic animal-raising, they probably started to worship and sacrifice to the deities of nature, since droughts, floods, stormy weather, and other natural disasters were all calamities caused by deities who could be propitiated by worship and sacrifice. The importance of these deities, especially the god of rain, is well supported by numerous oracle records which often ask, for example: "Will there be rain enough for the millet crop?" "Will the wind cause any calamity?" These nature deities were at first independent. The idea of a supreme deity, Ti, probably was not conceived until the time when the ancient Chinese had their first ruler. In other words, after the ancient Chinese had their first ruler on earth they then perceived that likewise there must be a ruler above, supervising and controlling all the nature deities. According to legend and tradition, Chinese history started with the Hsia as the first dynasty. However, only the succeeding dynasty, the Shang, has been fully substantiated by archaeology. But the Hsia should not be regarded as wholly fictitious although the history of the Hsia still lacks archaeological evidence. It is well known by tradition that the Hsia dynasty was overthrown by Ch'eng-t'ang, the first ruler of the Shang people. And the descendants of the Hsia continued to live under the Shang and Chou dynasties. Therefore, the idea of a supreme god ruling the lesser deities was probably conceived at least by the time that the Shang ruler established the first dynasty of historical China. But most likely it was first conceived during the pre-Shang period when the Hsia ruling house was in power. The supreme god was first considered to have direct dominion over the natural forces, but not over human affairs; the ancient Chinese therefore continued the practice of asking blessing and assistance of all kinds from their ancestors who were believed to sit beside the heavenly ruler and to be able to intercede for them. They continued their worship and sacrifice to ancestors and, in a lesser degree, to the other deities. They did not offer worship and sacrifice to the Supreme God Ti for a considerable time after they began to acknowledge his existence.

Although the Ti was recognized as the most powerful being, ancestors were regarded as having so much power over the affairs of men and nations that in late Shang times the title of the supreme deity, Ti, was added to the names of departed fathers and grandfathers to show the holiness and power of the god-like ancestors. For instance, Tsu Chia was called Ti Chia and Wen Wu Ting, Wen Wu Ti. Soon the last two kings of Shang were called Ti I (1209–1175 B.C.) and Ti Hsin (1174–1111 B.C.) in their lifetime,[18] indicating that they were the most powerful rulers on earth under the Supreme Ruler. These indicated that a closer relationship between the Ti and the people was developing. The tendency to have a closer feeling toward the Ti and recognize him as a source of blessings, assistance, and guidance evidently appeared at the beginning of Chou times.

[18]Hu Hou-hsüan, *Chia Ku Hsüeh Shang Shih Lun Ts'ung*, Series 1, Bk. 2, pp. 10–11.

ANCESTOR WORSHIP IN CHOU TIMES

By the last part of the twelfth and the beginning of the eleventh centuries B.C. the rule of the Chou dynasty was firmly established in China. Ancestor worship and sacrifice were carried on as in the Shang period with some modifications and developments, which will be discussed very briefly below.

At the beginning of the dynasty a new milfoil method of divination was introduced and became very popular. However, according to the evidence from the *Book of History* and the *Book of Odes*, the oracle bone was still used, though with decreasing frequency, and did not die out even at the end of the dynasty. This fact is disclosed by the 1954 excavations in Shensi[19] and Shansi[20] where oracle bones were unearthed. Of those found at Shansi, one had an inscription. After careful study, it was concluded that these bones from these two excavations had been used for divination during the Ch'un Ch'iu and Warring States periods, respectively.

One characteristic of Chou ancestor worship is the gradual growth of emphasis on ethics and humanitarianism with regard to sacrifice. During the early Chou dynasty an increasingly strong feeling developed against human sacrifice and, in time, the practice became less and less common. Great sacrifice in Shang times was the only means of gaining the ancestors' favour, but in Chou times virtue came to be considered more important than sacrifice. A wicked and oppressive ruler could not expect any favour or blessing from the ancestors no matter how elaborate his sacrifice was. Beginning with the time of Confucius, worship and sacrifice as a means to obtain favours gradually fell into disuse, especially among the intellectuals. The rites were considered the duty of a virtuous and devoted son.

Ancestor worship in Chou times was marked by a significant change in the concept of the Ti, the Supreme God. As a result the important role formerly played by the ancestors was gradually given to the Supreme God Ti, or "T'ien" (Heaven) as the Chou people called him. This change is shown clearly on the bronze inscriptions. Besides bronze inscriptions we have sufficient genuine classical literature to support the facts. Through these sources we learn of the following important developments.

[19] *Wên Wu Ts'an K'ao Tzŭ Liao* (Peking, 1956) No. 2, pp. 38–40.
[20] *Ibid.*, No. 7, p. 27.

THE TI WAS PERSONIFIED. In Shang times the concept of the Ti was that of a supreme god, high above, remote and impersonal, exercising direct dominion over natural forces only. But in Chou times the Ti or T'ien was personified and is supposed to have spoken to King Wên in person.[21] He was interested in the welfare of the people and the affairs of the nation, and definitely exercised direct dominion over human affairs. Consequently the Chou people began to turn directly to the Ti for guidance, aid, and protection. On one of the bronze inscriptions, for example, the Ti was asked to protect the king and the empire, and was considered to have given the land and people to the ruler.[22]

THE TI WAS WORSHIPPED WITH SACRIFICE. On the inscription of the Ta Fêng Kuei, a bronze vessel of the reign of King Wu, first ruler of Chou, it is recorded: "Shih hsi Shang Ti," which means to serve the Supreme Ti with "hsi," sacrifice.[23] Other bronze inscriptions and the classical literature also provide evidence that the Ti was worshipped with sacrifice during the Chou dynasty.

THE MANDATE OF HEAVEN. The Chou ruler was considered to have been appointed by the heavenly ruler, T'ien. He took over the empire by the order of the Supreme God, who chose only the virtuous and righteous to rule. If the ruler turned out to be oppressive and did not rule in the interest of his subjects, T'ien would choose another to displace him. Such a concept was first recorded in early Chou documents[24] and the *Book of Odes*[25] under King Ch'eng, the second ruler of Chou. In the bronze inscriptions we find the same concept in the Ta Yü tripod[26] of the reign of the third ruler, King K'ang.

THE SON OF HEAVEN. Since the ruler on earth was considered to have been appointed by the T'ien, ruler in heaven, the idea of a father and son relationship soon developed. This relationship was first recorded on the early bronzes, the Chou Kung Kuei[27] and the Hsien I[28] of the

[21]J. Legge, *Chinese Classics*, IV. *Shih Ching* (London, 1871), Pt. 2, "Ta ya; Huang I," pp. 448–55.

[22]Kuo Mo-jo, "Ta yü tripod," *Liang Chou Chin Wên Tz'ŭ Ta Hsi* (Tokyo, 1932), pp. 32–4.

[23]*Ibid.*, p. 1.

[24]J. Legge, *Chinese Classics*. III. *Shu Ching* (London, 1865), Pt. 2, "Ta kao," pp. 363–74; "K'ang kao," pp. 381–9; "Chiu kao," pp. 399–412.

[25]Legge, *Shih Ching*, Pt. 2, "Ta ya; Wên Wang," pp. 428–31; "Hsia wu," pp. 458–60; "Wên, Wang yu shêng," pp. 460–4.

[26]Kuo Mo-jo, *Liang Chou Chin Wen Tz'ŭ Ta Hsi*, pp. 32–3.

[27]Kuo Mo-jo, *Chin Wên Ts'ung K'ao* (Peking, 1952), pp. 303–9.

[28]*Ibid.*, pp. 374–5.

King Ch'eng period, second reign of the dynasty. The son of heaven was accordingly called "Hsia Ti," the ruler below. As the son of heaven and the most powerful ruler on earth, he was supposed to exercise righteousness and execute justice and thus secure the well-being of the people and the peace of the world under the supervision of the Supreme God or Father in heaven. By this indirect method God cared for the people universally.

THE ASSESSOR FOR THE HEAVENLY RULER. According to the evidence from classical literature and the bronze records, the son of heaven, after his death, would be assessor for the heavenly ruler.[29] In sacrifice, the ancestors, as assessors, would sit beside the heavenly ruler, T'ien, to receive offerings.

THE CHILD-GIVER. Right up to the end of the Shang dynasty childbirth was believed to be under the care of the three powerful ancestresses Pi King, Pi Ping, and Pi Chi.[30] At the beginning of the Chou dynasty even this power was transferred to the Ti, to whom sacrifice and prayer for such blessing were offered.[31]

The change of concept illustrated in the preceding six examples clearly indicates the increasing priority of the worship of the Supreme God over the worship of the ancestors. If the same trend had steadily continued, the worship of the Ti might finally have developed as the state religion. But about two centuries later, or by the middle of the ninth century B.C., civil war and frequent famine, caused by unprecedented drought, occurred. Because of the long period of suffering, faith in both the Ti and the ancestors began to be shattered, especially among the low-ranking nobles, called *shih*. Doubts and condemnation of both the Ti and the ancestors were vividly expressed in the *Book of Odes*.[32] In 624 B.C., in his speech, Ch'in Shih (the last chapter of the *Book of History*), Duke Mu of Ch'in, an enlightened statesman, asked no blessing or assistance from either T'ien or his ancestors, although in all the earlier chapters of this book such a blessing was regularly implored. Instead, he asked his ministers to preserve his descendants and people. Without doubt, he was influenced by the thought of his time. Half a century later, another statesman, Tzu Ch'an, a forerunner of Confucius, said, "The way of heaven is distant while the way of

[29]Kuo Mo-jo, *Liang Chou Chin Wên Tz'ŭ Ta Hsi*, pp. 46–7.
[30]Tung Tso-pin, "Chung Kuo ku tai wên hua ti jên shih," p. 27.
[31]Legge, *Shih Ching*, Pt. 2, "Ta ya; Shêng min," p. 465.
[32]Legge, *Chinese Classics*: *Odes*. "Ta ya: Tang," pp. 505–10; "Sang jou," pp. 519–27; "Pan," pp. 499–503.

man is near."[33] This means that in time of crisis one can depend only upon oneself and not on a deity, not even the T'ien, to solve one's problem. The contrast between the realistic and practical outlook expressed by these two statesmen and the blind belief in the divine power of the Ti revealed in the early Chou literature is clear. By the time of Confucius, in the second half of the sixth century B.C., a rational or philosophical interpretation of the deity, T'ien, and the ancestors was being developed. The personified T'ien soon became "Tao," or Principle, or the Way of Life, and ancestor worship became a filial expression by dutiful sons.

In the teaching of Confucius, the traditional ancestor worship developed into an enlightened ethos. From his time on the worship and sacrifice offered to ancestors were not for the purpose of pleasing the departed spirits in order to seek personal gain or private advantage. They were conducted purely in a spirit of filial piety, which was considered the fountain of all the other virtues. Hsün Tzu, the Confucianist of the third century B.C., said: "They (sacrifices) represent the height of piety and faithfulness, of love and respect. . . . Superior men consider them to be activities of man while ordinary people consider them something that has to do with spirits and ghosts."[34] Tseng Tzu, a disciple of Confucius and a leading figure in the idealization of filial piety, pointed out: "There are three degrees of filial piety: the highest is the honouring of our parents; the second is not disgracing them; and the lowest is being able to support them."[35] A man who lives an upright life and practises the doctrine of humanity is considered a dutiful son. The motivation for self-control and a righteous life is not to be found in allegiance to God (T'ien) but in allegiance to one's parents or ancestors. This is where the religious significance of ancestor worship comes in. A man conducts himself with uprightness and does good deeds for his fellow men, not because he ought to, but because he is a dutiful son, whether the parents are living or not. Such a man will be trusted to carry out the standard family and social relationships. In government he will be loyal to his superiors and show brotherly love to those below him. In society he will be truthful with his friends and respectful to his elders. In battle he will fight bravely.

[33]Legge, *Chinese Classics.* V. *Tso Chuan* (London, 1872), Pt. 2, p. 671.

[34]H. H. Dubs, *The Works of Hsün Tze* (London, 1928), chap. 19, pp. 244–5.

[35]J. Legge, *Sacred Books of the East.* XXVIII. *Li Ki* (Oxford, 1895), chap. "Ki 1," p. 226.

In other words, filial piety embodies all the ethical virtues.[36] The doctrine of filial piety has perpetuated the worship of ancestors. It has been a guiding force in moulding the Chinese culture and life, and a living and unifying force in Chinese society from the time of Confucius to the present, and remains the chief of Chinese virtues. Even now, in the twentieth century, it is not uncommon to find many Chinese who, after becoming ardent Christians or Buddhists or Taoists, still continue to practise ancestor worship. This characteristic of the religious life of the Chinese may seem strange to occidentals, but it is a special feature of Chinese culture derived from filial piety, the essence of ancestor worship in modern China.

[36]J. Legge, *The Chinese Classics.* I. *Confucian Analects* (London, 1893), Bk. 1, chap. 2.

Selected Writings of Theophile J. Meek

Compiled by RONALD J. WILLIAMS

Abbreviations: *AASOR* = *Annual of the American Schools of Oriental Research*; *AJSL* = *American Journal of Semitic Languages and Literatures*; *BASOR* = *Bulletin of the American Schools of Oriental Research*; *CJRT* = *Canadian Journal of Religious Thought*; *HUCA* = *Hebrew Union College Annual*; *JAOS* = *Journal of the American Oriental Society*; *JBL* = *Journal of Biblical Literature*; *JNES* = *Journal of Near Eastern Studies*; *JQR* = *Jewish Quarterly Review*; *JR* = *Journal of Religion*; *RA* = *Revue d'assyriologie et d'archéologie orientale*; *UTQ* = *University of Toronto Quarterly*; *VT* = *Vetus Testamentum*.

1910

"A Hymn to Ishtar, K. 1286," *AJSL*, XXVI (1909/10), 156–61.

1913

Cuneiform Bilingual Hymns, Prayers and Penitential Psalms. Autographed, transliterated and translated with notes from the original tablets in the British Museum (*Beiträge zur Assyriologie*, Bd. X, Heft 1), Leipzig, 1913.

1914

"The Sabbath in the Old Testament (Its Origin and Development)," *JBL*, XXXIII (1914), 201–12.

1915

"Critical Notes," *AJSL*, XXXI (1914/5), 286–7.

1917

"Old Babylonian Business and Legal Documents," *AJSL*, XXXIII (1916/7), 203–44.

1918

"A Votive Inscription of Ashurbanipal," *JAOS*, XXXVIII (1918), 167–75.

1919

"Some Bilingual Religious Texts," *AJSL*, XXXV (1918/9), 134–44.

1920

"Explanatory List, Rm. 2, 588," *AJSL*, XXXVI (1919/20), 154–60.

"Some Explanatory Lists and Grammatical Texts," *RA*, XVII (1920), 117–206.

"A Proposed Reconstruction of Early Hebrew History," *American Journal of Theology*, XXIV (1920), 209–16.

1921

"Some Religious Origins of the Hebrews," *AJSL*, XXXVII (1920/1), 101–31.

1922

"Canticles and the Tammuz Cult," *AJSL*, XXXIX (1922/3), 1–14.

1923

"Was Jeremiah a Priest?" *The Expositor*, 8th Series, XXV (1923), 215–22.

"Babyloniaca," *JAOS*, XLIII (1923), 353–7.

1924

"The Poetry of Jeremiah," *JQR*, XIV (1923/4), 281–91.

"Babylonian Parallels to the Song of Songs," *JBL*, XLIII (1924), 245–52.

"The Song of Songs and the Fertility Cult," in *The Song of Songs: A Symposium*, edited by W. H. Schoff (Philadelphia, 1924), 48–69.

1925

"Light from the Old Testament on Primitive Religion," *CJRT*, II (1925), 32–6.

1927

The Old Testament: An American Translation, with J. M. P. Smith, L. Waterman, and A. R. Gordon, Chicago, 1927.
"The Interpenetration of Cultures as Illustrated by the Character of the Old Testament Literature," *JR*, VII (1927), 244–62.
"The Trials of an Old Testament Translator," *CJRT*, IV (1927), 290–304.

1929

"Aaronites and Zadokites," *AJSL*, XLV (1928/9), 149–66.
"The Co-ordinate Adverbial Clause in Hebrew," *JAOS*, XLIX (1929), 156–9.
"Some Emendations in the Old Testament," *JBL*, XLVIII (1929), 162–8.
"The Structure of Hebrew Poetry," *JR*, IX (1929), 523–50.
"Some Old Testament Problems in the Light of Recent Archaeological Discoveries," *CJRT*, VI (1929), 374–81.

1930

"The Co-ordinate Adverbial Clause in Hebrew," *AJSL*, XLVII (1930/1), 51–2.
"The Translation of *Gêr* in the Hexateuch and its Bearing on the Documentary Hypothesis," *JBL*, XLIX (1930), 172–80.

1932

"The Akkadian and Cappadocian Texts from Nuzi," *BASOR*, No. 48 (1932), 2–5.

1933

"Some Gleanings from the Last Excavations at Nuzi," *AASOR*, XIII (1933), 1–12.
"A Visit to Satan," *Canadian Geographical Journal*, VII (1933), 116–26.

1934

"Translation Difficulties in the Old Testament," *Religion in Life*, III (1934), 491–506.

1935

Old Akkadian, Sumerian, and Cappadocian Texts from Nuzi, Cambridge, Mass., 1935.

"The Iterative Names in the Old Akkadian Texts from Nuzi," *RA*, XXXII (1935), 51–5.

"Primitive Religion in the Old Testament," in *From the Pyramids to Paul*, edited by L. G. Leary (New York and London, 1935), 139–49.

The Old Testament: An American Translation, revised by T. J. Meek. Chicago, 1935.

"Ali's Holy Shrines," *Asia*, XXXV (1935), 349–51.

1936

"The Israelite Conquest of Ephraim," *BASOR*, No. 61 (1936), 17–19.

"'Bowsprit' in the Oxford Dictionary," *Words*, III (1936), 8–10.

"The Orientation of Babylonian Maps," *Antiquity*, X (1936), 223–6.

Hebrew Origins (The Haskell Lectures for 1933–34), New York and London, 1936.

1937

"Notes on the Early Texts from Nuzi," *RA*, XXXIV (1937), 59–66.

1938

"Magic Spades in Mesopotamia," *UTQ*, VII (1937/8), 228–48.

"The Present State of Mesopotamian Studies," in *The Haverford Symposium on Archaeology and the Bible*, edited by E. Grant (New Haven, 1938), 158–87.

"Lapses of Old Testament Translators," *JAOS*, LVIII (1938), 122–9.

1939

"Moses and the Levites," *AJSL*, LVI (1939), 113–20.

"Bronze Swords from Luristan," *BASOR*, No. 74 (1939), 7–11.

1940

"Hebrew Poetic Structure as a Translation Guide," *JBL*, LIX (1940), 1–9.

"Primitive Monotheism and the Religion of Moses," *Review of Religion*, IV (1939/40), 286–303.

"The Hebrew Accusative of Time and Place," *JAOS*, LX (1940), 224–33.

1941

"The Accusative of Time in Amos 1:1," *JAOS*, LXI (1941), 63–4.
"Again the Accusative of Time in Amos 1:1," *JAOS*, LXI (1941), 190–1.
"The Metrical Structure of II Kings 19:20–28," *Crozer Quarterly*, XVIII (1941), 126–31.
"The Beginnings of Writing," *UTQ*, XI (1941/2), 15–24.
"The Next Task in Old Testament Studies," *JR*, XXI (1941), 398–411.

1942

"Monotheism and the Religion of Israel," *JBL*, LXI (1942), 21–43.

1943

"Four Syrian Cylinder Seals," *BASOR*, No. 90 (1943), 24–7.
"Ancient Oriental Seals in the Royal Ontario Museum," *Berytus*, VIII (1943), 1–16.
"The Challenge of Oriental Studies to American Scholarship," *JAOS*, LXIII (1943), 83–93.

1944

"Ancient Oriental Seals in the Redpath Library," *BASOR*, No. 93 (1944), 2–13. Reprinted as McGill University Publications, Series VII, Library, No. 28.

1945

"The Syntax of the Sentence in Hebrew," *JBL*, LXIV (1945), 1–13.

1946

"The Asyndeton Clause in the Code of Hammurabi," *JNES*, V (1946), 64–72.
"Recent Trends in Old Testament Scholarship," *Religious Education*, XLI (1946), 70–6.

1948

"A New Interpretation of Code of Hammurabi §§117–19," *JNES*, VII (1948), 180–3.
"Old Testament Notes," *JBL*, LXVII (1948), 233–9.

1950

Hebrew Origins, 2nd edition, New York, 1950.

"The Code of Hammurabi; The Middle Assyrian Laws; The Neo-Babylonian Laws; Mesopotamian Legal Documents," in *Ancient Near Eastern Texts Relating to the Old Testament*, edited by J. B. Pritchard (Princeton, 1950), 163–88, 197–8, 217–22.

"The Explicative Pronoun *šu/ša* in the Code of Hammurabi," *Archiv Orientální*, XVIII, Pt. I (1950), 78–81.

1951

"Archaeology and a Point in Hebrew Syntax," *BASOR*, No. 122 (1951), 31–3.

"Some Passages Bearing on the Date of Second Isaiah," *HUCA*, XXIII (1950/1), 173–84.

1954

"The Revised Standard Version of the Old Testament: An Appraisal," *Religion in Life*, XXIII (1953/4), 70–82.

1955

"The Code of Hammurabi; The Middle Assyrian Laws; The Neo-Babylonian Laws; Mesopotamian Legal Documents," in *Ancient Near Eastern Texts Relating to the Old Testament*, edited by J. B. Pritchard, 2nd edition (Princeton, 1955).

"Result and Purpose Clauses in Hebrew," *JQR*, XLVI (1955/6), 40–3.

1956

"Job xix 25–27," *VT*, VI (1956), 100–3.

"The Song of Songs: Introduction and Exegesis," in *The Interpreter's Bible*, edited by G. A. Buttrick, Vol. V (New York and Nashville, 1956), 89–148.

"The Book of Lamentations: Introduction and Exegesis," in *The Interpreter's Bible*, edited by G. A. Buttrick, Vol. VI (New York and Nashville, 1956), 1–38.

1958

"The Code of Hammurabi; Mesopotamian Legal Documents," in *The Ancient Near East: An Anthology of Texts and Pictures*, edited by J. B. Pritchard (Princeton, 1958), 138–70.

1959

"I Kings 20:1–10," *JBL*, LXXVIII (1959), 73–5.
"Translation Problems in the Old Testament," *JQR*, L (1959/60), 45–54.

1960

"Translating the Hebrew Bible," *JBL*, LXXIX (1960), 328–35.
Hebrew Origins, 3rd edition (Harper Torchbooks), New York, 1960.

1962

"Old Testament Translation Principles," *JBL*, LXXXI (1962), 143–54.

1963

"A New Bible Translation," *JBL*, LXXXII (1963), 265–71.

Index